THE AUTHOR

THIS IS THE FIRST BOOK by a remarkable student of Southwestern history. Dr. B. Sacks is a retired physician who has given many years to penetrating, scholarly research and study of the Anglo-American settlement with major focus upon Arizona. Historical articles of his authorship have appeared in THE AMERICAN WEST and ARIZONA AND THE WEST.

As an introduction to the first of two articles on "The Creation of the Territory of Arizona," the then editor of the latter publication, Dr. John Alexander Carroll, commented:

"Dr. Sacks, the leading authority on the early American period of Arizona history, is Historical Consultant of the Arizona Historical Foundation. He has in preparation monographs on Herman Ehrenberg, Sylvester Mowry, the Sonora Exploring and Mining Company, Samuel Colt's connection with Arizona, and the founding of Colorado City (Yuma). He also is annotating the journal of Samuel P. Heintzelman and preparing a history of Fort Buchanan in collaboration with Ray Brandes."

BE IT ENACTED:
The Creation of the Territory of Arizona

BE IT ENACTED:

The Creation of the Territory of Arizona

by B. Sacks, M.D.

ORIGINALLY PUBLISHED IN TWO PARTS IN
ARIZONA and the WEST

ARIZONA HISTORICAL FOUNDATION
PHOENIX 1964

Library of Congress Catalog Card Number: 64-17758

PRINTED IN ARIZONA

DEDICATED IN GRATEFUL MEMORY
TO THE LATE

FREDERICK WEBB HODGE

distinguished anthropologist and scholar, wise mentor and friend, who generously held the lamp which illuminated my first steps into the beguiling domain of Arizona history.

The Tale Behind the Book

An Introduction

Whatever sacred statistic it may reveal regarding the literacy of the American public, the boom in the book trade since World War II demonstrates abundantly that flush times are good for scholarship. For fifteen years there have been good times in the world of scholarly publishing. "Definitive" works pour from the presses like honey from the horn. Yet competent reviewers know, though often they will not acknowledge, that some learned books are not worth the infinite trouble it takes to get them into print. In this day of rapid research, instant exposition, and imperative publication in quest of what is called "authority" – but often is only a weapon in the personal war for academic preferment – few learned books are quite as "authoritative" and "distinguished" as advertised. Few combine in fullest measure the ingredients of scholarly craftsmanship, thoughtful synthesis, and stylistic excellence. This book is one which does.

How *Be It Enacted* came to be written and published is a little story which I should like to tell. The tale behind the book begins in that most unlikely cradle, the committee meeting. The sterility and essential futility of such meetings would scarcely be denied by those veterans of committee service who gathered at the Arizona Pioneers' Historical Society on a warm afternoon in September, 1962, for the purpose of planning an historical convention to be held in Tucson six months thereafter. Most of these committee members had suffered through similar ordeals in previous years. While the first Arizona Historical Convention in the spring of 1960 had been plotted in its entirety by one University of Arizona professor and a curator of the Historical Society, arrangements for the fourth convention now required the projecting power of no less than ten. Parkinson's Law (not to be confused with the shaking disease of the same name) was clearly at work in the cause of history in Arizona.

This committee meeting opened inauspiciously with familiar rituals. Paper cups were passed around, cigarettes came out, pipes were fired up, and the minutes of the last meeting were drearily rehearsed. Some stronger features of previous conventions were mentioned obtusely by those immodest enough to claim credit for them. A few innovations were proposed, declared impractical or impossible in nebulous rulings, and discarded; others of equal inconsequence were adopted without enthusiasm and without formality of vote. One optimistic member predicted that the fourth convention would draw a thousand registrants; two pessimists trimmed the estimate to five hundred and three hundred respectively. Within 30 minutes most of the people at the table were doodling, fumbling for more tobacco, consulting watches, and obliquely urging postponement of further questions until the next meeting of the committee.

At this moment a good idea was suddenly in the air, and the meeting came alive. Someone had pointed out that the 1963 convention would fall on the

100th anniversary of the organization of the Territory of Arizona. The cubists laid down their pencils, called for hot coffee, and took to alert listening. A member now suggested that the territorial centennial might be made the theme of the forthcoming affair. A few grumbles were heard to the effect that the national commemoration of the Civil War already had spawned too many jubilees, costume balls, and military re-enactments in which the casualties from slipping saddles and sunstroke had exceeded the battlefield casualties of the original. There was no sustained protest on this point, however, and quickly it was agreed that one session of the two-day convention be devoted to learned discussion of the territorial movement that culminated in the organic act of 1863. The names of several distinguished southwestern historians were mentioned as possible participants for such a session, but objection was voiced to each on grounds of probable fallibility. Who knew enough about Arizona in that remote period to speak authoritatively? Then came the suggestion that salvaged the afternoon, making this meeting memorable. "Mr. Chairman, why don't we invite Doctor Sacks to come out from Baltimore and give us a big paper on the creation of the territory?"

The committee members knew something of the work of Doctor Sacks, Historical Consultant of the Arizona Historical Foundation, through laudatory comments by Barry Goldwater, President and principal sponsor of the recently activated research facility in Phoenix. Senator Goldwater long had been keenly interested in Arizona history and especially in the formative years. Into events and personalities of this period the researches of Doctor Sacks were the deepest ever undertaken. It was the hope of the Senator that results of such investigations would be published by the Foundation. Still, despite the fact that he had been in Arizona many times on missions of historical research, Doctor Sacks was not well known to devotees of its history. Few realized that he had spent years in searching at the Southwest Museum in Los Angeles, where his curiosity was first kindled by the late Frederick Webb Hodge, or that subsequently he had become a familiar and respected figure at the Library of Congress and the National Archives. It was indeed fortunate, then, that reports on his erudition, and on the immensity of collected materials in his study at Baltimore, had been carried back to the Southwest by persons whom he had aided in problems of research in Washington. One of these, a University of Arizona graduate student and recipient of a grant from the Arizona Historical Foundation for work at the National Archives in the summer of 1962, returned greatly inspired by what he had learned from Doctor Sacks. If anything new could be said about Arizona in the formative period, Doctor Sacks seemed the man to say it. It was moved, therefore, that he be asked to prepare a paper for presentation as the principal address at the Fourth Annual Arizona Historical Convention.

Doctor Sacks was not in good health, but he came to Tucson and spoke for one hour on the morning of March 16, 1963, to a large and appreciative audience on the University of Arizona campus. His address was plainly entitled "The Creation of the Territory of Arizona." Otherwise it was spectacular in every respect. So profound in its scholarship and startling in its disclosures, so splendid in synthesis and eloquent in presentation was the paper of Doctor Sacks that it will be long remembered in Arizona as a masterpiece of historical investigation and exposition. Its superior in content and literary quality one listener, the editor of ARIZONA AND THE WEST, had neither heard nor seen in the span of his professional experience. Since he was soon to give up the management of this historical quarterly of the University of Arizona and no longer would be selecting articles for its pages after the year 1963 had passed the half mark, the editor's first thought that morning was to obtain "The Creation of the Territory of Arizona" for immediate publication. To say that the editor was anxious is perhaps to understate the situation. In his fifth and last year in the editorial chair he finally had found a paper which, if published, might serve as an exemplar in his graduate seminars in regional history at the University of Arizona. The copy barrel of the quarterly was brimming with accepted materials and the makeup of forthcoming numbers was already scheduled, but such extraordinary circumstances called for editorial elasticity. If the editor could secure this paper, he would rearrange his schedules and publish it at once.

While pleased to be asked, Doctor Sacks protested that his paper had been prepared specifically for oral presentation. All the Irish inducements of the editor were employed to persuade the author that this paper could be put quickly into publishable form. Doctor Sacks explained that his paper was the preliminary draft of an expanded work planned for publication in book form by the Arizona Historical Foundation. He would consent to appearance of the paper in the journal if his associates were agreeable. This approval was extended without hesitation. A perfectionist in large things and small, Doctor Sacks wanted his article in the best possible form; the editor, long a victim of the same idiosyncrasy, wanted it not less so. The author remained in Tucson for three months, meeting often with the editor in day-long consultation on myriad matters of historical interpretation and emphasis.

Because "The Creation of the Territory of Arizona" was more than twice the length of the average article in the journal, it was published in two parts. The first part, covering the territorial movement between 1856 and the outbreak of the Civil War, appeared in thirty-four pages of the Spring 1963 number (Vol. 5, No. 1, pp. 29–62) of ARIZONA AND THE WEST; the second part, treating the crucial events of the years 1861–1863, took forty pages of the Summer number (Vol. 5, No. 2, pp. 109–48). Illustrative matter for both parts — mapwork by the Tucson cartographer Don Bufkin and reproductions of documents and portraits from the files of the author — filled fourteen additional unnumbered pages.

An article of such excellence is rare in the most meticulously edited of learned journals. By all the editor's standards this article was generally the finest to appear in the journal during his five-year proprietorship. By the historian's measurement of "new light" it was certainly the most significant. Here, in lucid text and deep supporting notes, Doctor Sacks related for the first time the full and complex history of Arizona's long, arduous, and uniquely interesting struggle for territorial status. Here the national, sectional, and local issues were presented in subtle blend, the principal and lesser personalities drawn in sharp relief, and every small and large advance toward territorial recognition adroitly explained in proportion and in perspective. It is, in short, the kind of study to which a professor of history may direct his graduate students with the challenge: "Go and do likewise!"

The new evidence marshaled by Doctor Sacks is indeed surprising. Most remarkable among his findings is the revelation that Charles Debrille Poston, a princely pioneer long revered as "Father of Arizona," was not the solitary champion of the territorial triumph of 1863 – as implied in his colorful versions of the "oyster supper" and the "lame duck" Congressmen. On the contrary, Arizona had many advocates a century ago, some familiar in American annals and some unknown until now. Both Jefferson Davis and Abraham Lincoln were enlisted in the cause of Arizona – for reasons different and yet quite similar – and Doctor Sacks has shown how Lincoln's birth in Kentucky may have influenced the destiny of the Southwest. Other towering figures, men of the prominence of Stephen A. Douglas of Illinois and "Bluff Ben" Wade of Ohio, played their distinctive roles, as did the powerful California politician William McKendree Gwin and the Texas patriot Thomas Jefferson Rusk. Forgotten for a hundred years, but now retrieved by the researches of Doctor Sacks, are the names of dozens of Arizona's earliest pioneers and bravest boosters, conspicuous among whom in the territorial movement were the brilliant but eccentric Sylvester Mowry, the veteran soldier Samuel P. Heintzelman, and the enthusiastic William Wrightson of Cincinnati. Every person who took an interest in Arizona affairs between 1856 and 1863 was motivated in some degree by the potential of the country in mineral wealth, but through these years every step toward territorial recognition was hampered or accelerated by the high winds of sectional strife nearly three thousand miles away. Thus this account of the organization of the Territory of Arizona is an integrated story of westward extension in the most critical period of American history.

Here ends the little tale behind *Be It Enacted: The Creation of the Territory of Arizona,* a notable book in many particulars. As now republished and enlarged, Doctor Sacks' centennial article is richly embellished with valuable appendices and a large array of illustrations. The author has included more than forty facsimiles of documents relating to the territorial issue, more than twenty portraits of the *dramatis personae,* and two rare maps suitable for framing. This publication of Doctor Sacks' findings in fullest form seems singularly appropriate in the year 1964, the 100th anniversary of the actual establishment of territorial government at Prescott. The book itself illuminates a point of some importance. It is sure proof that, even in our age of quantitative considerations and superficial measurements of almost everything, true scholarship is still possible. And in Arizona, where precious metals were once abundant, the gold and silver of fine historical research and writing may become more plentiful by power of example, more quickly recognized and encouraged, and better appreciated on the counting tables where quality is judged. Such at least is the hope of the erstwhile editor who has made a parable out of this introduction.

JOHN ALEXANDER CARROLL
Professor of History
The University of Arizona

March 1964

ACKNOWLEDGMENTS

Many libraries and archival collections contributed research materials for this study. The largest body of primary sources was found in the National Archives. Here were deposited the profusion of manuscript and printed Congressional bills relating to Arizona, the original petitions and memorials from the Gadsden Purchase, the Rio Grande Valley, and elsewhere, and the resolutions of territorial legislatures of New Mexico, one set being in the handwriting of Sylvester Mowry. The Journal of Samuel Peter Heintzelman, founder of Fort Yuma and Civil War general – so vital to this study – is preserved in the Library of Congress, and I am obligated to Dr. C. Percy Powell and his able staff in the reading room of the Manuscript Division for facilitating the examination of these volumes and other manuscript records.

I owe a special debt of appreciation to Mr. Buford Rowland, Chief of the Legislative Branch of the National Archives; Dr. W. Neil Franklin, Chief of the Diplomatic, Legal and Fiscal Branch; Captain Victor Gondos, Jr., Chief of the Army and Air Corps Branch; Miss Jane F. Smith, Chief of the Social and Economic Branch; Miss May E. Fawcett, Chief of the Audio-Visual Branch, and to the members of their competent staffs for unstinting and resourceful co-operation, which reached beyond the formal demands of duty. I wish to thank Hon. Ralph R. Roberts, Clerk of the House of Representatives, for generous permission to examine and reproduce manuscript House records now deposited in the National Archives.

For numerous manuscript records, illustrations, and the newspapers of the period under consideration, I am indebted to the facilities of the Arizona Pioneers' Historical Society in Tucson, the Department of Library and Archives in Phoenix, the Library of the University of Arizona at Tucson, the Sharlot Hall Historical Society at Prescott, the Huntington Library at San Marino, California, the California State Library at Sacramento, the Bancroft Library at the University of California in Berkeley, and various divisions in the Library of Congress.

It is a pleasure to acknowledge the gracious co-operation of Mrs. Yndia S. Moore, the Director of the Arizona Pioneers' Historical Society, and of Mr. Ray Brandes, Assistant Director and Historian, along with others of a most genial and helpful staff; Mrs. Marguerite B. Cooley, Director of the Department of Library and Archives at Phoenix, and to Mr. Joseph Miller of her staff; to Mr. Robert O. Dougan, Librarian of the Huntington Library, for permission to reproduce Abraham Lincoln's letter to Samuel Haycraft, and to Miss Mary Isabel Fry, Reference Librarian, and Miss Haydée Noya of the Department of Manuscripts; and to Mr. Allan R. Ottley, Librarian of the California Section of the California State Library.

I wish also to extend my thanks to Dr. Rex W. Strickland of Texas Western College at El Paso for generous permission to reproduce Kelley's rare 1860 map of the Territory of Arizona and the portrait of Governor Lewis S.

Owings; to Mr. Don Bufkin of Tucson for the fine diagrammatic maps of the various faces of the proposed Territory of Arizona; to Dr. Myra Ellen Jenkins, Senior Archivist of the State Records Center and Archives, Santa Fe, New Mexico, for a translation from the Journal of the Territorial Legislature of New Mexico and for a portrait of Delegate Miguel A. Otero; to Dr. Harwood P. Hinton, the present editor of ARIZONA AND THE WEST for editorial help; and Mr. George W. Baylor, Jr., of Tucson for permission to reproduce the portrait of his grandfather, Lieutenant Colonel John R. Baylor.

The sources of the various portraits and other exhibits used to illustrate the text are individually acknowledged elsewhere, and I wish to thank the photoduplication departments of the National Archives, the Library of Congress and other libraries for exercising great care and skill in preparing needed reproductions.

I have a very deep sense of obligation to Dr. John Alexander Carroll for his creative and talented editorship of the original article for publication in ARIZONA AND THE WEST of which he was then the editor, and for writing the sprightly and flattering Introduction to this book, and to Mr. Bert M. Fireman, Executive Vice President of the Arizona Historical Foundation, for his arduous and meticulous labors in preparing the text and illustrations for publication as a book, the format of which was devised by him. To both Dr. Carroll and Mr. Fireman I am indebted for a host of valuable and constructive suggestions. Senator Barry Goldwater, Chairman and President of the Foundation, has as always my grateful appreciation for his cordial and unfailing encouragement of my studies in Arizona history.

B. SACKS

CONTENTS

Introduction vii
Acknowledgments xi
Illustrations xv

PART ONE 1
Sectional Strife in the Fitful Fifties 3
The Actors and Their Motives 5
Delegates and Petitions 10
In the Halls of Congress 12
The Indefatigable Lieutenant 17
Burnside Rifles at Forty Paces 32
Arizona Defies Congress 35
Not Arizona but Arizuma 42
But Why Not Arizona? 45
NOTES for PART ONE 46

PART TWO 55
Rebellion in The Southwest 57
Arizona Turns Confederate 62
Ashley Reports A Bill 69
"Bluff Ben" Takes Charge 76
Behind the Scenes With Poston 82
The Oyster Supper and The Lame Ducks 87
Another Father of Arizona? 89
In Brief Review 95
NOTES for PART TWO 97

APPENDIX A 111
APPENDIX B 130
APPENDIX C 155
APPENDIX D 166
APPENDIX E 177
APPENDIX F 183
NOTES on CONTENTS of POCKET 188

INDEX 191

ILLUSTRATIONS

Sylvester Mowry 7
Charles D. Poston 8
Thomas J. Rusk 13
Stephen A. Douglas 14
Sonora Exploring and Mining Company Report 18–19
William M. Gwin 21
Title Page of Mowry's *Memoir* 22
Maps of Proposed Boundaries of Arizona 24–30
Richard S. Ewell 37
Granville H. Oury 38
Oury's Certificate of Appointment 39
Dr. Lewis S. Owings 41
Jefferson Davis 43
Facsimile of *Mesilla Times* 60
Baylor's Proclamation 64
John R. Baylor 65
James H. Carleton 67
Carleton's Proclamation 68
James M. Ashley 70
John A. Gurley 74
Benjamin F. Wade 79
Abraham Lincoln 81
Lincoln's Letter to Samuel Haycraft 84–85
Poston's Inkstand Gift to President Lincoln 86
Pages from Heintzelman's Journal 92–93
Samuel P. Heintzelman 94
Jones Memorial from Rio Grande Valley 113–117
Tucson Memorial of 1856 118–119
Kippen Memorial of 1857 120–121
Bradley Memorial of 1857 122–124
Petition of Residents of St. Louis 125
Petition from Citizens of New York 126
Rejection of Isham's Petition 127

Resolutions of New Mexico Legislature 128–129
Constitution and Schedule of Provisional Government 131–153
Governor Owing's Letter to Confederate Delegate 154
Senator Rusk's Manuscript S. 176 157
Gwin's Bill to Organize Arizona 158
Endorsement on S. 8 159
Senator Green's Bill 160
Confederate Bill to Organize Arizona 161
Working Copy of H. R. 357 in Senate 162–165
Recommendation of John A. Gurley for Governor 168
Letter to President from Three Senators 169
Undated Letter Recommending Gurley 170
Haycraft's Letter Recommending Poston 171
Endorsement of Poston from Kentucky 172
Recommendation of Poston for Indian Superintendent 173
Nominations of Gurley and Poston 174
Letter to Lincoln Concerning Gurley 175
Goodwin Recommended for Governor 176
Proclamations Establishing Territorial Government 178–179
McCormick's Letter from Navajo Springs 180–181
Lyman Trumbull 184
William A. Wheeler 184
Alexander H. Stephens 185
Galusha A. Grow 185
Miguel A. Otero 186
John N. Goodwin 186
Arizona Territorial Officials 187
Mowry's Map of Proposed Territory In Pocket
Robert P. Kelley's Map of Arizona In Pocket
Act Creating Territory of Arizona In Pocket

PART ONE

Originally published in *ARIZONA and the WEST*

VOLUME 5 NUMBER I SPRING 1963

Sectional Strife in the Fitful Fifties

In 1855 a correspondent wrote in a California newspaper that the Gadsden Purchase — those millions of acres of land south of the Gila River which the Republic of Mexico recently had ceded to the United States — was essentially "a barren, deserted, dreary waste — a desert — useful only as a dwelling place for the coyote, the owl, the rattle-snake, and the prairie dog." Further, he said, all the fabled mineral wealth of Sonora and Chihuahua lay south of the newly-established boundary.[1] There were important members of Congress who held similar views,[2] and mapmakers of the period labelled the country north of the Gila as wild and unexplored. These opinions have a strange ring today, applying as they do to lands which comprise the rapidly growing state of Arizona. Yet in the eight-year struggle which preceded enactment of the law in 1863 to separate what is now Arizona from the parent Territory of New Mexico and confer an independent administration, public ignorance of the region and lack of vision as to its potential development were not the most serious impediments to favorable action by Congress. The efforts of Arizonans to achieve territorial status did not constitute an isolated phenomenon, but rather one which has interrelationships with the entire territorial question beginning with the Northwest Ordinance of 1787[3] and more especially with the fateful events which foretold the Civil War.[4] As will be shown subsequently, the one great obstacle to territorial organization for Arizona — the chief factor which delayed it for so long — was the prevailing sectional strife of that decade which historians have called "the fitful fifties."

With the end of the Mexican War in 1848 a vast body of valuable land was ceded to the United States by the Treaty of Guadalupe Hidalgo, but its acquisition had the unfortunate effect of complicating the sectional question already in ferment. At mid-century Northern leaders were determined to admit California, populated overnight as a result of the discovery of gold, as a free state; and the Southern "slavocracy" was equally insistent that its "peculiar institution" should not be prohibited in new states and territories even if their geographical location was above the 1820 Missouri Compromise line of 36° 30′. At the same time Utah was clamoring for recognition as a territory, and the claim of New Mexico to the same privilege was being challenged by the state of Texas, which threatened to take action if her boundary dispute with the latter were not settled. The debate in Congress in the spring of 1850 was so acrimonious that disruption of the Union became a menacing possibility, and in the end the belief grew that a new compromise was imperative. After an omnibus bill had been considered and dismissed as impractical, a series of individual measures were finally agreed upon. The organization of the Territory of New Mexico (figure b)* on September 9, 1850, was tied to a settlement of the boundary question by which Texas was paid an indemnity of ten million dollars to relinquish her claims. Both Utah and New Mexico were established as territories without restriction on slave ownership, and California was admitted as a free state. Other vital features of the Compromise of 1850 provided for the abolition of the slave trade in the District of Columbia, so ardently sought by the North, and the adoption of a stronger fugitive slave law, which the South had long demanded.

Sweeping as it was, the Compromise of 1850 merely led to an uneasy truce which collapsed with the Kansas-Nebraska Act and the complete abrogation of the Missouri Compromise of 1820. Kansas and Nebraska were organized as territories without a slavery provision and under the principle of popular sovereignty as championed by Senator Stephen A. Douglas, the "Little Giant," of Illinois. Few legislative measures have attracted more attention from scholars than the highly controversial act of 1854, the historiography of which has been admirably assessed in a recent article.[5] Suffice it to say here that this most significant law profoundly influenced the territorial movement in the next few years. Indignation and reaction to the Kansas-Nebraska Act united discordant Northern elements into a more powerful antislavery coalition, and a similar consequence was the unification of Southerners into a more militant force. The strengthened antagonists were thus enabled to support their opposing views with greater determination and aggressiveness, and in Congress territorial questions were no longer subject to compromise. It was hardly an accident, therefore, that after Kansas and Nebraska were organized in 1854 no new territories were created until the final days of President Buchanan's administration in 1861, when other conditions prevailed and slavery as a political issue had lost its power to block territorial legislation. Attempts to organize Ari-

* Figures refer to a series of diagrammatic maps on pages 24 to 30.

zona, which began as early as 1856, were to be frustrated for the same reasons as those which interfered with the aspirations of other candidates for territorial recognition. By a strange quirk of history Arizona lost its only chance — admittedly not a large one — to be organized during the decade preceding the Civil War when a future governor of Arizona, John C. Frémont, failed in 1856 to be elected as the first Republican president.

The Actors and Their Motives

The factors which influenced the most ardent advocates of territorial organization in the 1850s were by no means uniform, though there were often individual motivations in common. Among the more obvious arguments for independent government were the pressure of populations, the discovery and working of mines, the opening of public lands to settlement, and Indian depredations and other Indian problems. In some instances a powerful stimulus was the fact that a projected transcontinental railway required organization of the region through which the road was to be run so that land could be acquired, surveyed, and sold. Without adequate military and legal protection an area would have no settlers, and without settlers the land could not serve as a source of income for the railroad. A major reason for the acquisition of the thirty thousand square miles embraced in the Gadsden Purchase was to obtain a strip of land for the passage of a transcontinental railroad along the southern route, and the first Arizona bill in Congress was doubtless strongly motivated by the proposed establishment of such a railroad. Advocates of the Overland Mail knew that protection of persons and property through Indian-infested country could best be achieved by territorial organization, and consequently a number of petitions emanating from various sections of the country were presented to Congress to organize the Gadsden Purchase, which the mail coaches would traverse.[6] Advocates of homesteads could reasonably expect the beneficiaries to vote for the party which made the acquisition of these acres possible, and there was the ever-present need for the administration to be in a position to award patronage in one form or another. Finally, there were individuals who desired political appointments in new territories, contractors who sought commitments to supply military posts and Indian reservations, and the inevitable land speculators and founders of townsites. Certain of these factors, of course, were more important than others in the instance of Arizona.

The signing of the statute in February, 1863, by which Arizona became a federal territory was the culmination of a series of events which began soon after the Gadsden Treaty was proclaimed into law in 1854. The Arizona movement was activated in the Southwest, in Washington, and in other parts of the country by individuals and groups. In New Mexico there were conventions and memorials urging action in Congress, annual elections to choose a delegate to carry the petitions of the residents to the national capital and to represent them in the House, and resolutions drafted by legislative assemblies in Santa Fé for presentation to Congress.[7] In Washington a number of bills were introduced into the House and Senate, debated in these chambers, and passed, rejected, or ignored. There were presidents,[8] high officials, and even a governor of California[9] who took an interest in the Arizona movement; and along the way there were such developments as the establishment of an extralegal provisional government, territorial organization under the Confederacy, and the erection of a military government under the auspices of a Union general.[10]

In the Southwest, in Washington, and elsewhere, there were individuals whose services in behalf of Arizona must be singled out for particular notice. Pre-eminent among those who worked assiduously to separate Arizona from New Mexico were two men early identified with the Gadsden Purchase. One was Sylvester Mowry, a native of Providence, Rhode Island, and a descendant of Roger Mowry who came to America in 1631.[11] A graduate of the United States Military Academy in the class of 1852,[12] he was sent to Utah where, as a dashing young officer under Lieutenant Colonel Edward J. Steptoe, he aroused the ire of the Mormons by showing an amorous interest in the local belles.[13] In 1855 Mowry led a march from Salt Lake City to Fort Tejon, California, which he carefully documented and mapped.[14] While stationed at Fort Yuma from 1855 to 1857 he became impressed with the mineral wealth and potential importance of the area and avidly sought to learn its Spanish history, to gather data on its various Indian tribes, and to investigate its resources. From 1857 to 1860 Mowry was to be Arizona's most active champion of territorial organization.

The other, Charles Debrille Poston, a versatile and persuasive man of mercurial temperament who became Arizona's first Superintendent of Indian Affairs and first delegate to Congress, was indeed one of its most remarkable pioneers. Poston was born on April 20, 1825, on a farm in the same section of Kentucky as Abraham Lincoln's birthplace. When his mother died in 1837 the twelve year old boy was

[*California State Library*]

SYLVESTER MOWRY
(c. 1832–1871)

This photograph of Mowry — Westpointer, politician, mine owner and popular clubman — was taken in San Francisco about 1863. Impressive in his soldierly bearing and fastidious in dress, this perennial bachelor held great attraction for the opposite sex. Prior to the Civil War, Mowry was Arizona's most zealous advocate of territorial organization.

[*National Archives*]

CHARLES D. POSTON
(1825–1902)

Photograph of "Father of Arizona," from the Brady Collection, taken in Washington about 1867. Poston spent most of the next ten years abroad, and returned to Arizona in 1877 as Register of the United States Land Office at Florence.

apprenticed to the clerk of Hardin County, Samuel Haycraft, a well-known personality in Elizabethtown, Kentucky. Later he was appointed deputy clerk, studied law, and married Haycraft's daughter.[15] In February, 1851, he became chief clerk in the surveyor's office of the Custom House in San Francisco, and his demotion in 1853 caused him to protest that the political appointee who succeeded him was a professional gambler.[16] The termination of Poston's services at the end of that year was no disaster, however, for a prosaic clerkship was not calculated to remain long compatible with his restless nature.

With financial help he now recruited a band of explorers which included as surveyor and interpreter the intrepid Herman Ehrenberg,[17] whose adventurous spirit was seasoned by his experiences in Texas, Mexico, California, and the Pacific Islands, but whose enthusiasm was no less ebullient than Poston's own. Together with some twenty-five tough and daring companions, Poston sailed from San Francisco for Guaymas, Sonora, on the British brig *Zoraida* on February 19, 1854.[18] This memorable voyage – which was interrupted by shipwreck in the Gulf of California – and the overland journey through Sinaloa and Sonora were to be graphically chronicled in reminiscences from the gifted pen of the leader of the expedition.[19] On their way back to California the explorers crossed the Mexican boundary just about the time that President Pierce proclaimed the Gadsden Treaty into law. Arriving at Fort Yuma in July, 1854, they were hospitably received by the commanding officer, Major Samuel Peter Heintzelman, who would play a significant role in Poston's career. After they were refreshed, they proceeded to locate a town on the strip of land which lay opposite the fort. Thus Poston and Surveyor Ehrenberg founded Colorado City, the precursor of present-day Yuma.[20]

Poston's journey left him deeply impressed with the potentials of development in the Gadsden Purchase and eager to exploit the area. Subsequently he visited New York, Philadelphia, and other eastern cities in search of investors, and in March of 1856 his efforts were finally rewarded by the formation of the Sonora Exploring and Mining Company at Cincinnati. It was arranged for Poston as manager, with the rank of colonel and commandant, to conduct a small company of armed men to southern Arizona to open the rich silver mines in that region.[21] Reaching the Rio Grande after a march through Texas, Poston and his companions remained at the town of Mesilla for some weeks, and late in the summer of 1856 came at last to the small village of Tucson in the southwestern part of the Territory of New Mexico.[22] Over the next few years, and especially after 1861, Poston's activities were to prove of great importance in the movement for territorial recognition of Arizona.

Delegates and Petitions

Even before Mowry and Poston had become active in behalf of territorial organization, some interest in the matter was manifest in the Southwest. It has been said that the legislature of New Mexico drafted a memorial as early as December, 1854, petitioning Congress to divide the territory,[23] and indeed James A. Lucas, a member of that legislature, introduced such a memorial on January 23, 1855.[24] Specific reference to this memorial was made by William Claude Jones, later to become speaker of Arizona's first territorial legislature, in an address before a secessionist convention in Mesilla on March 16, 1861.[25] On that occasion Jones turned to Lucas, who was the presiding officer, and said: "You, sir, know the facts. You, while a member of the Legislature of Doña Ana County, in the last week of December, 1854, in conjunction with myself, drew up a memorial to Congress, setting forth our wants and grievances, and asking for a Territorial organization. You, sir, introduced it into the Legislature, but the jealousy of New Mexico caused it to sleep the sleep of death."[26]

In the year 1856 two memorials were drafted in the Southwest for presentation to Congress. The second of these – and the only one indicated in Bancroft – was the document signed by residents of the southwestern portion of the Territory of New Mexico[27] in a convention held at Tucson on the 29th of August.[28] But many years later Poston told the story of a memorial drawn up at Mesilla before the Tucson convention for the creation of Arizona Territory (figure 4):

> ... in 1856, I met at El Paso, William Claud[e] Jones, the then Attorney General [United States Attorney] of New Mexico, and on a journey up the Rio Grande we discussed the propriety of making a petition to Congress for the organization of a territorial government between the Rio Grande and the Colorado. At La Mesilla, Jones, who was a lawyer and politician, wrote the petition, and when it came to giving the proposed Territory a name he wrote in ARIZONA. The petition was signed by everybody in Mesilla who could write and some who could not and sent by mail to Senator [Thomas J.] Rusk, at that time a Senator from Texas. This is the first time I knew of the word Arizona having been used in any official or government communication.[29]

Poston remarked that the petition was probably filed in the archives of the Senate, and he was right. This long forgotten memorial, written in

Spanish and signed by Jones and fifty-six others — many of whom, as Poston suspected, had their names written for them — was preserved and is now deposited in the National Archives.[30] In the manuscript the word "Arizona" is written over another undecipherable name, but it is noteworthy that a newspaper correspondent, writing from Fort Thorn on November 25, 1856, reported the election of Jones in September as delegate from the "Territory of *Mesilla*" [italics mine].[31] The Mesilla memorial was subsequently mentioned in a letter of March 11, 1858, from Sylvester Mowry to Stephen A. Douglas, chairman of the Senate Committee on Territories, in which Mowry explained that the pressure of official duties in New Mexico had prevented Delegate Jones from proceeding to Washington.[32]

The second memorial of 1856 did get to Washington. On July 15 the probate clerk of Doña Ana County, James A. Lucas, appointed Poston, who was then in Mesilla on his way to Tucson, as deputy clerk for the western portion of the Gadsden Purchase.[33] Poston's party reached Tucson on or about August 22, and here the leader of the expedition was reunited with Herman Ehrenberg, who had been making explorations in Sonora and southern Arizona during Poston's sojourn in the East. In light of the fact that he had participated in the territorial movement at Mesilla, it may be assumed that Poston himself now initiated similar action in Tucson, where a convention was held on August 29. The presiding officer was Mark Aldrich, *alcalde* and the first American merchant of the town. A committee, which included Ehrenberg, listed the grievances of the residents, who complained that they had no law, no courts, no vote, and no representation in any legislative body. For these reasons they petitioned Congress for a separate territorial government under the name of Arizona and specified the boundaries (figure 1).[34] The memorial bore more than two hundred and sixty signatures, including those of Aldrich, Ehrenberg, and Nathan P. Cook, but for some inexplicable reason not that of Charles D. Poston! Other signers were Edward E. Dunbar, one of the leading members of the Arizona Mining and Trading Company, which operated the Ajo copper mines, and at whose store on the American side of the international boundary four men of Henry A. Crabb's filibustering party would be executed by Mexican soldiers in April of the following year;[35] Solomon Warner, his partner Willis N. Bonner, and Edward Miles, early merchants of Tucson; Peter R. Brady, who had come in 1854 with the surveying party of the Texas Western Railroad under Andrew B. Gray;[36] Frederick Hulseman, Governor Gándara's former major-domo at Calabasas and later Poston's amanuensis and the storekeeper of the Sonora Exploring and Mining Company[37] and the first postmaster of Tubac.[38] Included also were such well-known pioneers as Frederick A. Ronstadt, Granville H. Oury, William H. Kirkland, Charles Schuchard, W. M. Rowlett, Hill de Armitt, Alfred L. Friar, Julius and Frederick Contzen, Juan Elias, and Ignacio Ortiz.[39]

In the Halls of Congress

On September 1 Nathan P. Cook, a former member of the Arizona Mining and Trading Company, was elected delegate and given a certificate by Deputy Probate Clerk Poston with instructions to present the memorial of the citizens of Tucson to the House of Representatives.[40] Cook was refused a seat and Congress later declined to pay for his transportation,[41] but the Arizona memorial was introduced in the House on December 11, 1856, by the delegate from New Mexico, Miguel A. Otero.[42] On January 20, 1857, Representative Justin S. Morrill of Vermont, as spokesman for the Committee on Territories to which the memorial had been referred, reported adversely on the question of organization, principally on the ground that the population was too small.[43] The evident plight of the residents, however, led the committee to introduce a bill on the same day to organize a judicial district south of the Gila (figure 3), to create the office of surveyor general, to provide for the adjudication of certain land claims, to grant donations to actual settlers, and to provide for representation in the territorial legislature of New Mexico.[44]

This unsuccessful bill was not the first measure dealing with the needs of Arizona to be introduced into Congress. On March 18, 1856 — months before the Tucson convention and while Poston was still in Cincinnati — Senator Thomas Jefferson Rusk of Texas had presented a similar bill (figure 2).[45] Not until February 7, 1857, however, was it reported by Senator Douglas with an amendment.[46] Speaking in opposition on the 21st of February, Senator John J. Crittenden of Kentucky called the bill one "of great perplexity and complexity."[47] The original version as framed by Rusk covered twenty-seven pages, and the amended bill as many more. Crittenden protested that it undertook to teach the Senate what the old Spanish law had been and established the Mexican law as seen through the eyes of Congress, and that on these interpretations the bill predicated the forfeiture of Spanish and Mexican claims that were guaranteed by the Treaty of Guadalupe Hidalgo.[48] He also

[*Library of Congress*]

THOMAS J. RUSK
(1803–1857)

This distinguished Texas statesman was a leading advocate of a southern transcontinental wagon road and railway, and the most aggressive supporter of the Gadsden Treaty in the Senate. In March, 1856 he introduced the first bill to create a separate judicial and surveying district for the Gadsden Purchase. He committed suicide in 1857.

[*Library of Congress*]

STEPHEN A. DOUGLAS
(1813–1861)

The "Little Giant" had a key role in passage of the fateful Kansas-Nebraska bill and in 1858 engaged in the famous debates with Lincoln. Douglas was chairman of the Committee on Territories when he successfully piloted Rusk's Arizona bill through the Senate in 1857 — a bill which failed in the House.

objected to the fees allowed the surveyor general.[49] Senator John Bell of Tennessee, admitting that the inhabitants of the region were entitled to the protection of the law, emphasized that it was the proposed railroad to the Pacific along the southern route which gave the bill its importance. His only motive in supporting the Gadsden Treaty, he said, was to acquire land through which it was practicable to build such a road. He feared, however, that if land in unlimited quantities were distributed to the settlers as proposed, there would be no desirable lands left to award to the railroads. Senator Judah P. Benjamin of Louisiana considered Bell's apprehensions unwarranted and appealed to all who were friendly to the construction of a railroad through the Gadsden Purchase to lend their support to the measure.[50] Senator Benjamin F. Wade of Ohio, who later would champion the bill by which Arizona finally became a territory, did not join in the debate on Rusk's bill but voted against it.[51] The measure, as amended, was passed by the Senate on February 21, but it failed in the House.[52] Sylvester Mowry was in error when he wrote that this bill had passed both chambers, but that owing to some minor difficulties and the lateness of the session it had failed to become a law.[53] Almost a year after the failure of Rusk's bill a third measure to provide a separate judicial district and representation in the New Mexico legislature was introduced by Delegate Otero (figure 6). Simpler in structure, Otero's bill of January 20, 1858, was not acted upon.[54]

Senator Rusk was the prime sponsor of federal wagon-road construction along the thirty-second parallel, the purpose of which was to secure a commercial outlet for his state to the west.[55] Rusk, who had played a distinguished part in the Texas Revolution, in the administration of the Republic of Texas, and in the proceedings which led to annexation by the United States, was also an ardent supporter of the proposed railroad through Texas to the Pacific. At home and in the Senate he made speeches promoting the construction of such a road.[56] For the successful passage of wagons or locomotives through the great unprotected stretches of the Gadsden Purchase, some semblance of government in that area seemed to him imperative. When designing his Arizona bill in March of 1856 he doubtless believed that the time was not yet ripe for separate territorial organization, and therefore sponsored a measure which in its lesser demands might have a better chance for success. But the time was not yet ripe even for the creation of a judicial district in Arizona.

On February 17, 1857, President Pierce signed the combined

measure which allotted funds for construction of wagon roads over a central route, a southern route, and one which would come to be known as Beale's route — all under the supervision of the Secretary of the Interior.[57] While Arizona's delegate Nathan P. Cook, a surveyor and civil engineer, was seeking support in Congress in behalf of organization, he also worked assiduously in behalf of the pending legislation on the wagon roads, and was rewarded with an appointment as assistant engineer of the El Paso-Fort Yuma road.[58] He owed this appointment to James B. Leach, who had been named superintendent of the road, and to Rusk and other members of Congress. It was the influential Texan who headed a list of signers in one of the letters of recommendation to Secretary of the Interior Jacob Thompson. This letter stated that Cook had "labored hard for such appropriations as would benefit his country, among which the appropriation for the Wagon Road from El Passo [*sic*] to Fort Yuma is the most prominent." The passage of this measure, the signers attested, was "owing greatly to his exertions."[59]

Bancroft calls specific attention to five different bills to organize a territorial government in Arizona, but indicates that others were introduced. In actual fact there were no less than fifteen such bills in addition to the three which proposed to create a judicial district.[60] The first bill to organize was the one presented in December, 1857, by Senator William M. Gwin of California, but it was not the product of Gwin's interest alone. The collaborator was Sylvester Mowry. As early as December of 1856, the very month that Delegate Cook was importuning Congress to be seated as the representative of the Gadsden Purchase, the ambitious lieutenant in a letter to Major Heintzelman announced his own desire to be chosen delegate.[61] On March 3, 1857, having succeeded to the command of Fort Yuma the previous month,[62] Mowry notified the Adjutant General that Henry A. Crabb's party of some one hundred and fifty men had arrived at the junction of the rivers and that reinforcements were expected from Texas, but the latter information proved to be untrue. On the 18th he reported that they had departed several days previously, but neither he nor the filibusters could foresee that they were marching to their death in Caborca.[63] In May Mowry left the post on sick leave,[64] but apparently his illness did not prevent him from continuing to work for organization, for in June a California newspaper announced that he would carry a petition to Washington.[65] Upon the recommendation of James Gadsden, Mowry was admitted as Arizona's delegate to the Southern Commercial Convention in Knoxville in the month of August. This assembly unanimously approved the resolutions which he drafted, urging the organization of the Territory of Arizona, the establishment of a Pacific railroad through the Gadsden Purchase, and the acquisition of a port on the Gulf of California.[66]

The Indefatigable Lieutenant

During his absence from Arizona, Mowry was chosen delegate to Congress in an election held at Tucson in the first week of September.[67] In that same month he wrote to Major Heintzelman requesting that officer's help in Washington. The major was then stationed at Newport Barracks, Kentucky, across the Ohio River from Cincinnati.[68] It was Heintzelman who, as commander of Fort Yuma, had welcomed Poston and Ehrenberg in 1854. Poston showed him specimens of mineral ore on that occasion, and this proved to be the first link in a chain of circumstances which led to Heintzelman's interest in the formation of the Sonora Exploring and Mining Company and his selection as its first president. This connection was to wed Heintzelman irrevocably to the territorial movement.[69] As the chief executive of the company in which he had a large personal investment, the major placed the highest importance on the opening of southern Arizona and the protection of its mines. Receiving a favorable response from Heintzelman, Mowry wrote that he would try to arrange for the major to go to Washington to give evidence before the Committee on Territories.[70] In the meantime the versatile lieutenant had prepared a long letter to Butterfield, Fargo, Spencer, and their associates, winners of the coveted mail contract. This communication contained the substance of Mowry's conversations with Spencer and the former boundary commissioner, John Russell Bartlett, and was published as a pamphlet.[71]

The nature of Mowry's intervention in the War Department can only be conjectured, but Heintzelman did obtain the desired leave and arrived in the capital on October 27, 1857.[72] Mowry, whose leave of absence had been unduly prolonged, was now threatened with a peremptory order to return to his military duties in Arizona. Favored treatment by the Secretary of War himself enabled Mowry to inform Heintzelman on November 5 that his leave had been extended, and it was not at all surprising that the Adjutant General was offended upon learning that the brash lieutenant had bypassed him.[73] Heintzelman was gratified when Mowry showed him the letter which Poston wrote from San Francisco reporting that specimens of silver ore from

Possessions and Prospects of the Sonora Silver Mining Co.

REPORT

OF THE

Sonora Exploring and Mining Co.,

MADE TO

THE STOCKHOLDERS.

SEPTEMBER, 1857.

These returns, although not quite so large as you anticipated, nevertheless, exhibit Silver Ores of very great value.—*Report of Assay by Prof. Booth, U. S. Mint.*

CINCINNATI:
RAILROAD RECORD PRINT.
1857.

[*Arizona Pioneers' Historical Society*]

Title page of second in a series of annual reports of the Sonora Exploring and Mining Company. The name "Sonora Silver Mining Company" *(top)* was not the official name. Thomas and William Wrightson, who were among the organizers and officials of this mining company, were editors of the Cincinnati *Railroad Record,* in whose plant this pamphlet was printed. This company, the history of which is indissolubly bound with preterritorial southern Arizona, ultimately owned eighty silver mines in the Santa Cruz Valley and in the Santa Rita Mountains. Production was discontinued when federal troops were withdrawn from Arizona in 1861, but later resumed.

OFFICERS OF THE COMPANY.

CINCINNATI.

MAJOR S. P. HEINTZELMAN, U. S. A., PRESIDENT.

W. WRIGHTSON, SECRETARY.

EDGAR CONKLING, GENERAL AGENT.

GADSDEN PURCHASE.

COL. CHARLES D. POSTON, COMMANDANT AND MANAGING AGENT, AT TUBAC.

HERMAN EHRENBURG, TOPOGRAPHICAL ENGINEER AND SURVEYOR AT TUBAC.

FREDERICK BRUNCKOW, GEOLOGIST, MINERALOGIST AND MINING ENGINEER, IN CHARGE OF CERRO COLORADO DISTRICT.

CHARLES SCHUCHARD, GEOLOGIST, MINERALOGIST AND MINING ENGINEER IN CHARGE OF LA ARIBAC AND SMELTING HACIENDAS.

[*Arizona Pioneers' Historical Society*]

List of officials in the 1857 report. Frederick Brunckow, who later resigned and acquired a mine of his own, was murdered by Mexican employees. In 1865 William Wrightson, then managing director of the Santa Rita Silver Mining Company, a subsidiary of the parent company, was murdered by Cochise's band of Chiricahua Apaches. The name of Poston's associate, Herman Ehrenberg, prominent Arizona pioneer who made the first map of the Gadsden Purchase, is misspelled.

the Heintzelman mine had won the first premium at the Mechanics' Fair.[74] But the major was soon confronted with financial difficulties arising from the failure of the Ohio Life Insurance and Trust Company, which had prepared his drafts.[75] The failure of this Cincinnati company, which had offices in New York, was one of the disastrous events which ushered in the grave financial crisis of 1857.[76] As it happened, financial relief soon came to the Sonora Exploring and Mining Company through the timely support of Samuel Colt of pistol fame.[77] Later, the armsmaker would succeed Heintzelman as president of the mining company.[78]

In the meantime Mowry had been working privately with a senator from California on the preparation of the first bill to organize Arizona.[79] This was William McKendree Gwin. Tall, squarely built, with a shock of white hair, his rough features seemed to one writer to have been hewn out of a block with an axe.[80] Trained as a physician, Gwin had abandoned the practice of medicine when his friend Andrew Jackson appointed him United States Marshal for the District of Mississippi. In 1849 he came to California, entered politics, served in the Senate until the outbreak of the Civil War, and for a period of years controlled the patronage in that state.[81] Gwin was an early advocate of the purchase of Alaska,[82] and the land bill which he sponsored was one of the most significant measures in the history of California.[83] In the heated Senate debates on the Gadsden Treaty, he had favored making a larger acquisition of Mexican territory and the securing of a port on the Gulf of California as a *sine qua non* for ratification.[84]

During Mowry's absence Ehrenberg and Edward E. Dunbar superintended the preparation of a memorial to Congress from the residents of the western portion of the Gadsden Purchase.[85] This document, which was signed with more than five hundred names and included those of the prominent pioneers, had been forwarded to Mowry in Washington. On December 17, 1857, Senator Gwin introduced this memorial,[86] and on the same day he reported a bill to organize the Territory of Arizona (figure 5).[87] This bill was excessively long and detailed, lacking the commendable simplicity of the territorial measure by which Arizona was ultimately organized. By its terms slavery was not prohibited, and the Fugitive Slave Law was to be enforced.[88] Both the memorial and the bill were referred to the Committee on Territories.

Mowry's certificate of election was presented to the House Committee on Territories on January 14, 1858, but a day later Representative Harris of Illinois objected that it had been improperly introduced and referred to the wrong committee. A long discussion ensued on the

[*California State Library*]

WILLIAM M. GWIN
(1805–1885)

United States Senator from California who introduced the first bill to organize the Territory of Arizona — a bill that was the product of collaboration with Lieutenant Mowry. Gwin, a former physician, was born in Tennessee and had long resided in Mississippi before moving to California.

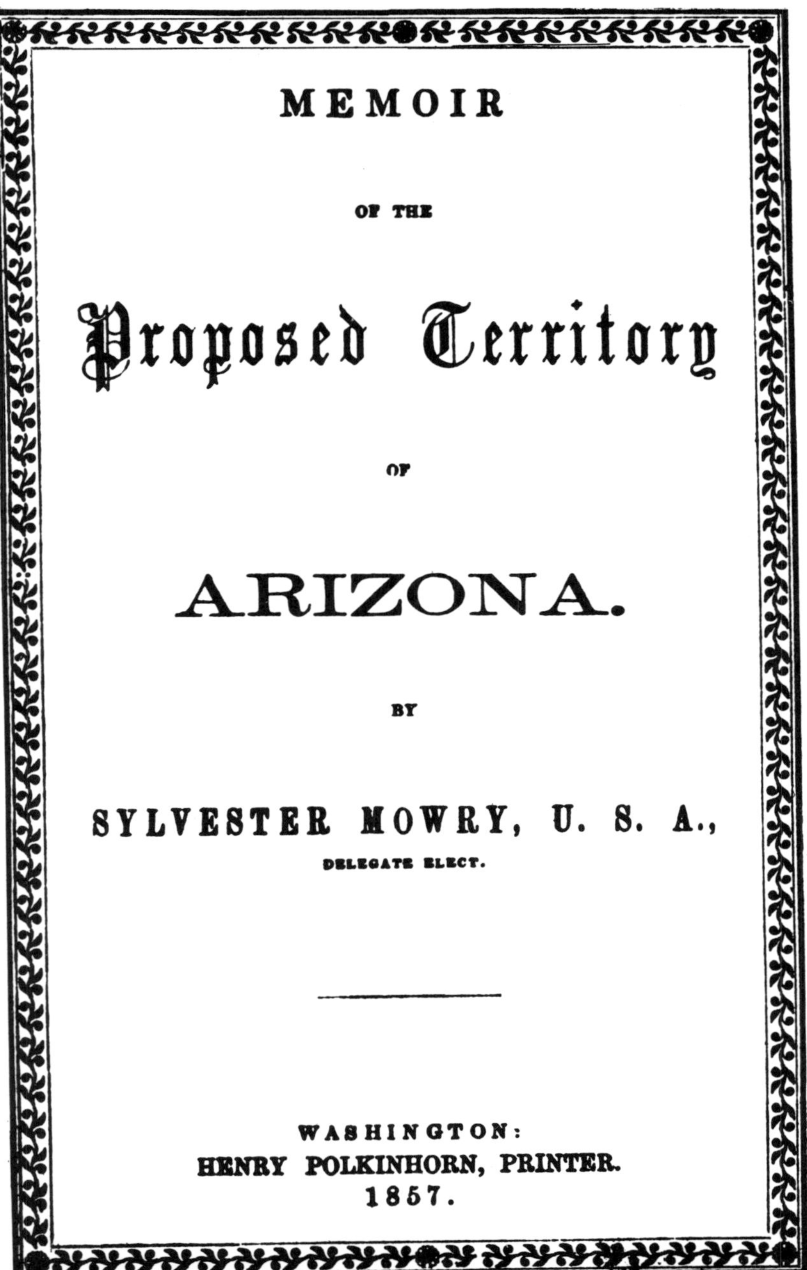
MEMOIR

OF THE

Proposed Territory

OF

ARIZONA.

BY

SYLVESTER MOWRY, U. S. A.,

DELEGATE ELECT.

WASHINGTON:

HENRY POLKINHORN, PRINTER.

1857.

[*Arizona Pioneers' Historical Society*]

Mowry's *Memoir* was first imprint devoted to the interests of Arizona. This promotional pamphlet was published by the lieutenant, apparently at his own expense. It contains a copy of the 1857 "Kippen Memorial" from the western section of the Gadsden Purchase, which is reproduced from the original in Appendix A, together with many of the signatures.

parliamentary question, and it was finally decided to return the certificate to Mowry, who, like his predecessor, Nathan P. Cook, was refused a seat.[89] On February 25 Heintzelman visited Gwin and showed him Herman Ehrenberg's map of the Gadsden Purchase, and the Senator took it to exhibit to some of his colleagues.[90] At other times the major provided Gwin with additional promotional material to be used if and when the bill came up for consideration in the Senate.[91] On March 1 Heintzelman accompanied Mowry to the Capitol where they showed reports of the Sonora Exploring and Mining Company to the chairman of the Committee of Territories, Senator Douglas, but the "Little Giant" merely remarked that mining was a poor business.[92] On March 10 the second memorial which Mowry received from New Mexico was introduced in the Senate.[93] This had been prepared on the Rio Grande and contained "nearly one thousand" signatures (figure 4).[94]

On the following day Mowry addressed a long letter to Douglas in which he reviewed Arizona's efforts to obtain an independent government and defended the boundaries which fixed the northern limit at about the thirty-fourth parallel, separating the entire southern segment from the parent territory.[95] These boundaries were very different from those which were stipulated when Arizona was finally established as a separate territory (figure a). Various boundaries proposed at one time or another between 1856 and 1861 caused inhabitants of the Mesilla Valley to consider themselves residents of Arizona, citizens who lived on the Rio Grande to attend conventions in Tucson as delegates of the proposed territory, and residents of Tucson to attend Arizona conventions in Mesilla. In 1862 and even as late as 1863 Brigadier General Joseph R. West of the California Volunteers, commanding the District of Arizona, addressed reports from Mesilla, *Arizona*.[96] In the original versions of both Senator Rusk's bill of March 18, 1856,[97] and that reported by Representative Morrill on January 20, 1857,[98] the northern limit was fixed at the thirty-third parallel or thereabouts. In each of these bills, the proposed judicial district was to extend eastward to the Rio Grande and no farther.[99] In Otero's similar bill of January 20, 1858, the eastern boundary extended to Texas at the one hundred and third meridian.[100]

Mowry's version of the Territory of Arizona was described in his Memoir of 1857 (figure 5)[101] and illustrated in Kelley's map of 1860 (figure 7).[102] In his letter to Senator Douglas, he gave his reasons for advocating the union of the eastern and western portions of southern New Mexico into a single territory. The southern district, he pointed

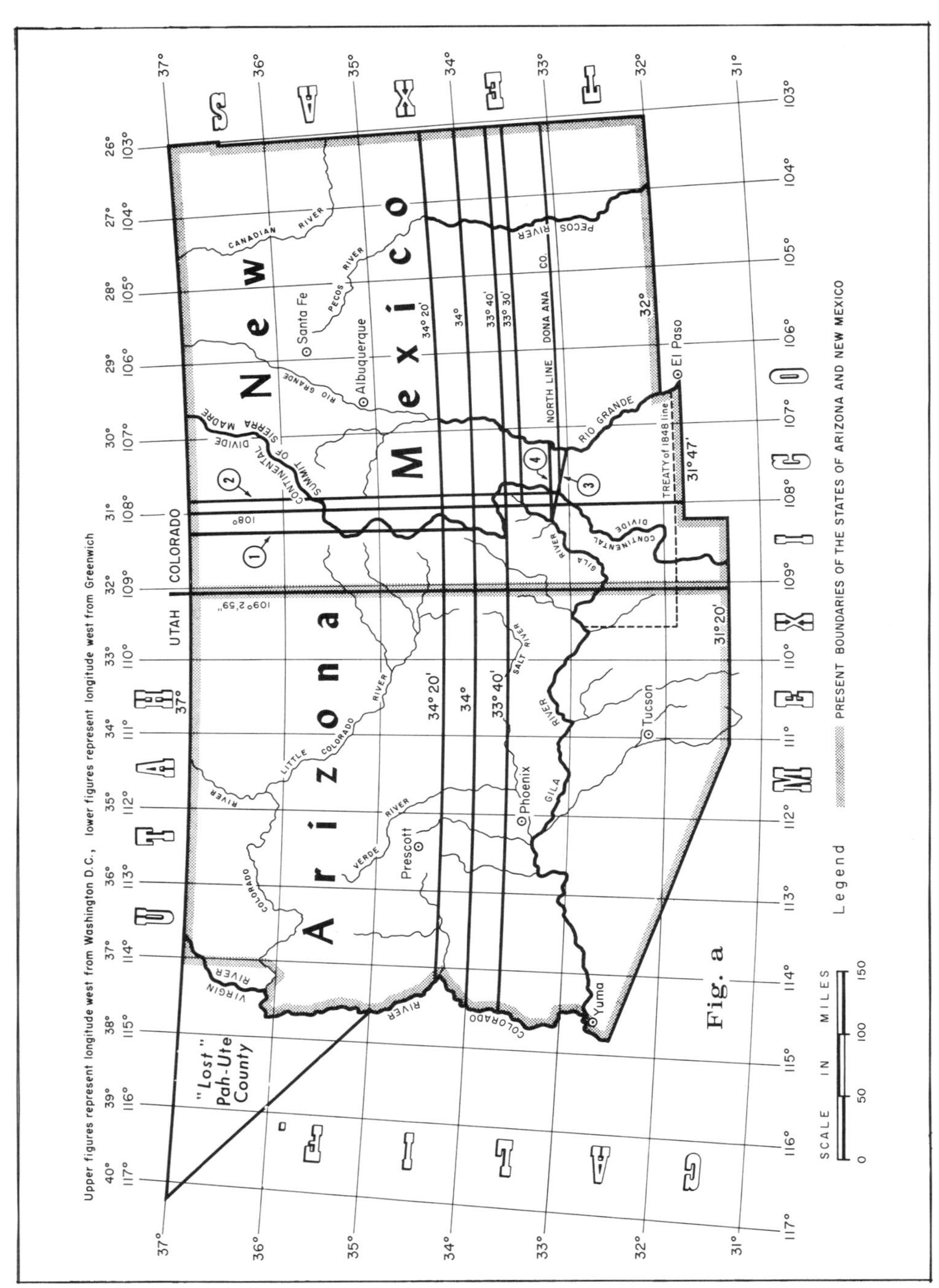
Upper figures represent longitude west from Washington D.C., lower figures represent longitude west from Greenwich
UTAH
COLORADO
Arizona
New Mexico
"Lost" Pah-Ute County
Santa Fe
Albuquerque
El Paso
Prescott
Phoenix
Tucson
Yuma
CANADIAN RIVER
PECOS RIVER
RIO GRANDE
SUMMIT OF SIERRA MADRE
CONTINENTAL DIVIDE
LITTLE COLORADO RIVER
VERDE RIVER
SALT RIVER
GILA RIVER
COLORADO RIVER
VIRGIN RIVER
NORTH LINE DONA ANA CO.
TREATY of 1848 line
109°2'59"
34°20'
34°
33°40'
33°30'
32°
31°47'
31°20'
37°
Legend
PRESENT BOUNDARIES OF THE STATES OF ARIZONA AND NEW MEXICO
SCALE IN MILES
0 50 100 150
Fig. a

Proposed Boundaries of Arizona, 1856-1863

DRAWN BY DON BUFKIN

Fig. a *(opposite page)* is key to maps that follow. Heavily shaded lines delineate present boundaries of Arizona and New Mexico. Triangular area *(upper left)* indicates the "lost Pah-Ute County" and a small segment of Mohave County transferred to Nevada by act of Congress, May 5, 1866, but the Arizona legislature did not concede the loss of this territory until February 18, 1871. Lines (2) and (3) refer to amended and unamended S. 176, respectively, in Fig 2. Lines (1) and (4) refer to amended and unamended H. R. 752, respectively, in Fig. 3. The horizontal lines mark various northern boundaries as shown in the figures to follow.

Fig. b. The limits of the Gadsden Purchase are those defined in the final version of the Gadsden Treaty, June 30, 1854, which also settled the dispute over the Mesilla Valley.

Figs. 2 & 3 show original and amended boundaries of separate judicial and surveying district as proposed in respective bills.

Fig. 4. The "Bradley Memorial" proposed to extend the eastern boundary of Arizona to the Texas border.

Fig. 5. In the four instances listed, the same boundaries were proposed for the federal and the Confederate Territory of Arizona.

Fig. 6. Judicial district proposed in Otero's H. R. 172.

Fig. 9. Largest area proposed for the Territory of Arizona.

Fig. 10. The boundaries in Watts' H. R. 171 were the same as in Ashley's successful H. R. 357.

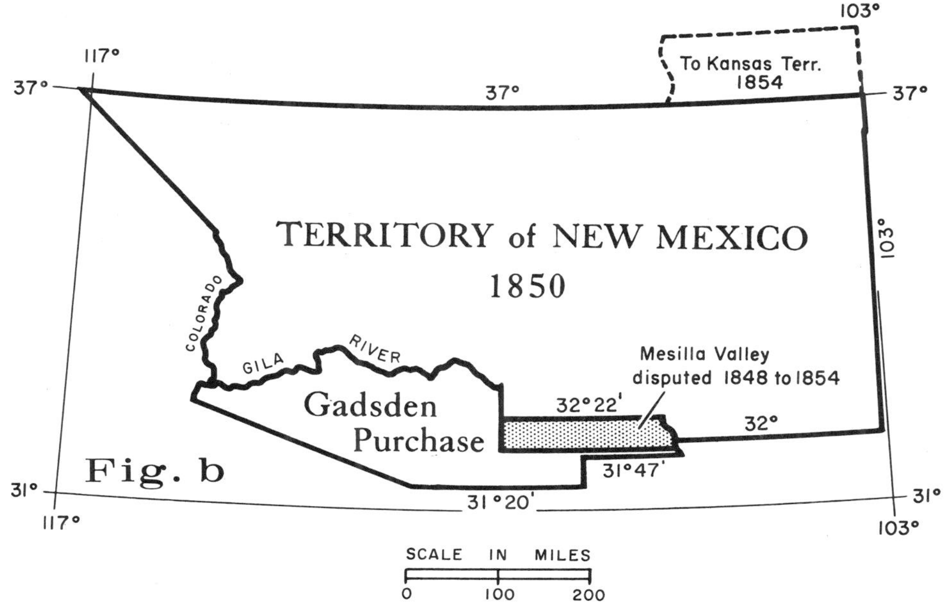

Fig. b

Memorial of the Tucson Convention of 1856

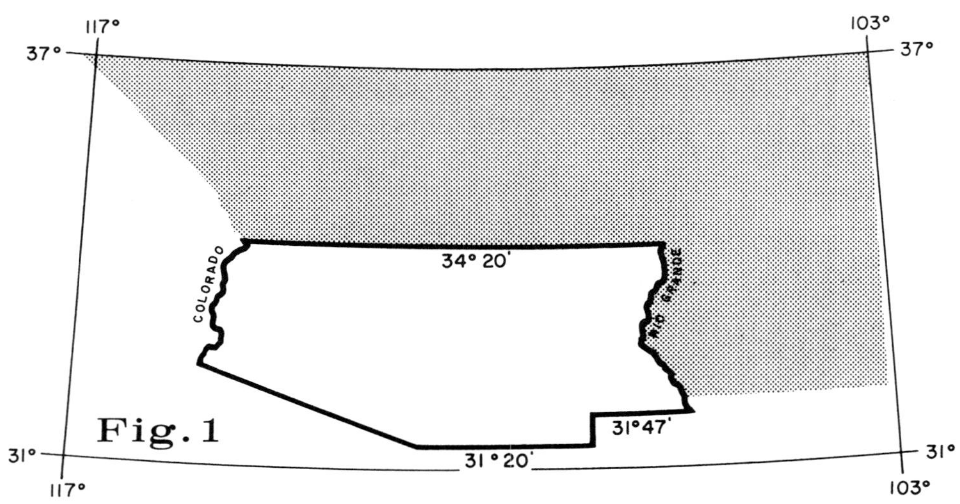

S 176 Mar. 18, 1856 34th Congress, 1st Session

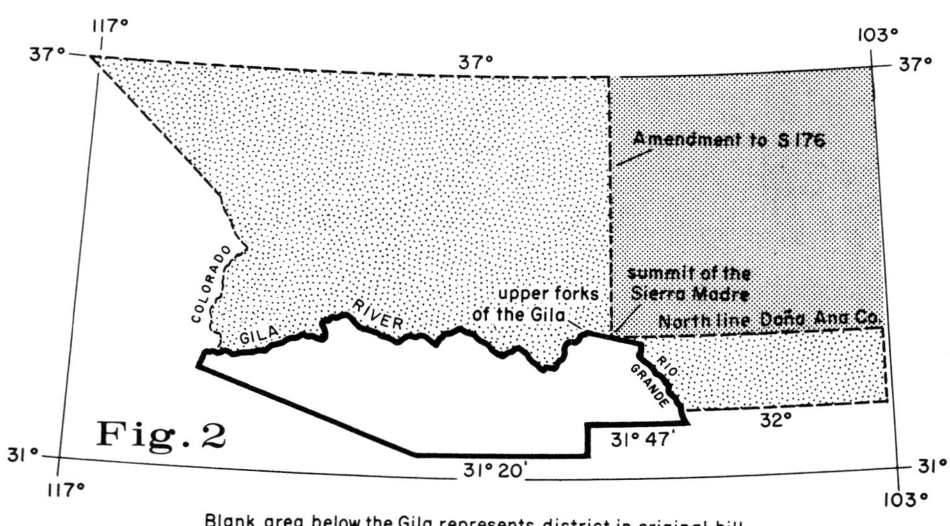

Blank area below the Gila represents district in original bill.

indicates area added to district in amended bill.

HR 752 Jan. 20, 1857 34th Congress, 3rd Session

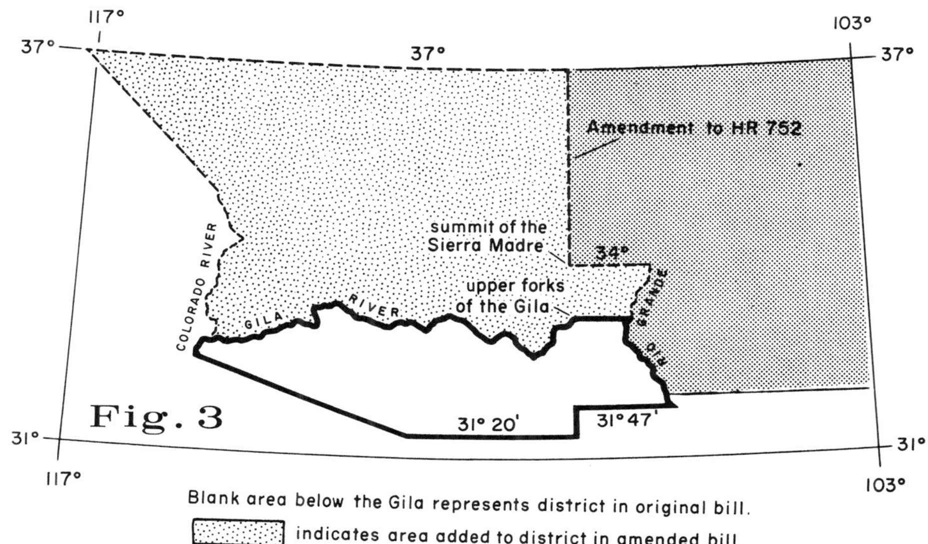

Blank area below the Gila represents district in original bill.

[dotted box] indicates area added to district in amended bill.

Jones Memorial Aug. 1856 (by Citizens of the Rio Grande Valley)
Bradley Memorial Mar. 10, 1858 (prepared in 1857)

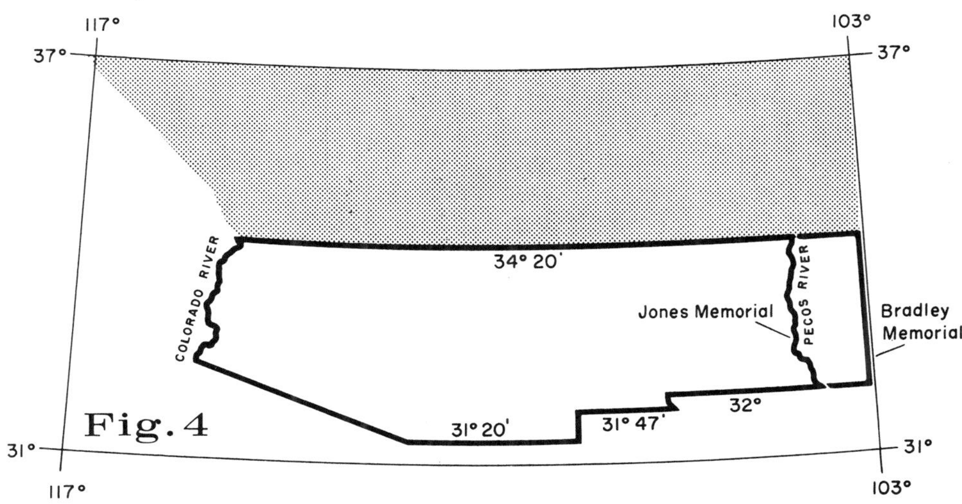

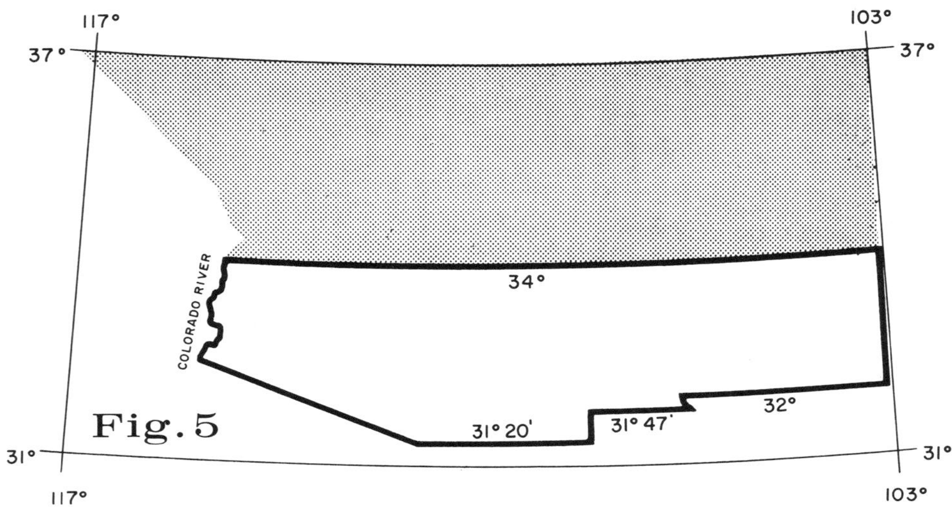
Mowry's Memoir of 1857
S 8 Dec. 17, 1857 35th Congress, 1st Session
Baylor's Proclamation Aug. 1, 1861
Confederate Territory Feb. 14, 1862
117°
103°
37°
37°
COLORADO RIVER
34°
32°
31° 20'
31° 47'
31°
31°
117°
103°

Fig. 5

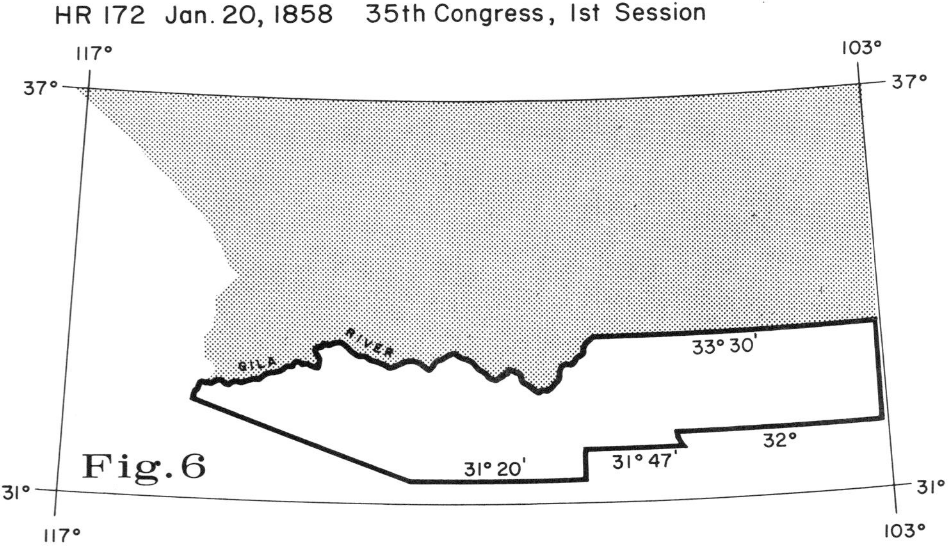
HR 172 Jan. 20, 1858 35th Congress, 1st Session
117°
103°
37°
37°
GILA
RIVER
33° 30'
32°
31° 20'
31° 47'
31°
31°
117°
103°

Fig. 6

HR 836 Jan. 28, 1859 35th Congress 2nd Session
S 555 Feb. 4, 1859 35th Congress 2nd Session
Memorial of the Tucson Convention of 1860
S 365 April 3, 1860 36th Congress 1st Session
Kelley's Map of 1860

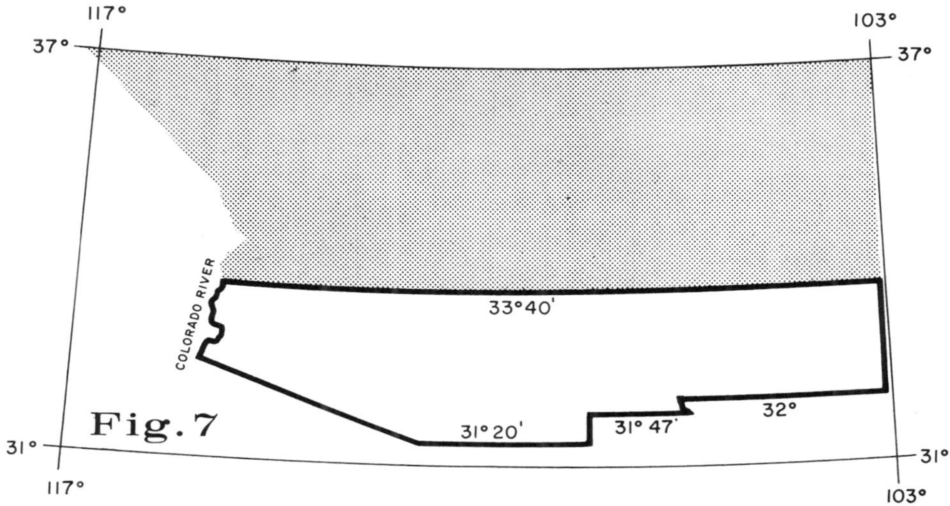

Fig. 7

HR 710 May 11, 1860 36th Congress 1st Session
HR— May 2, 1860 36th Congress 1st Session
HR— May 3, 1860 36th Congress 1st Session

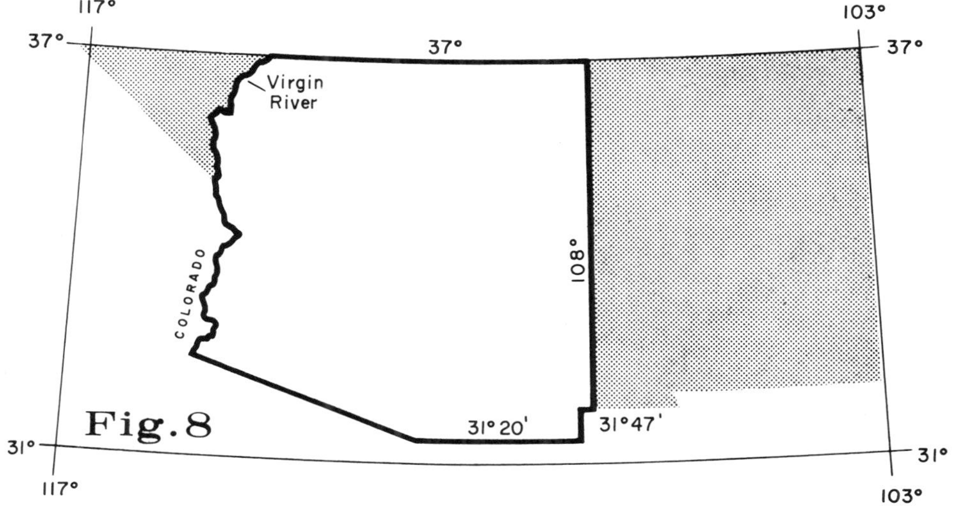

Fig. 8

HR 890 Dec. 1860 36th Congress 2nd Session

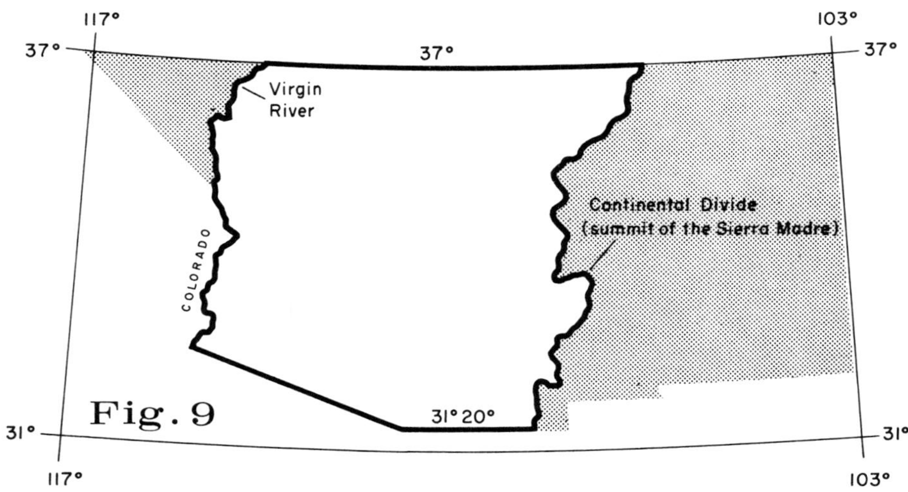

Fig. 9

HR 171 Dec. 23, 1861 37th Congress 2nd Session
HR 357 Mar. 12, 1862 37th Congress 2nd Session (Act of Feb. 24, 1863)

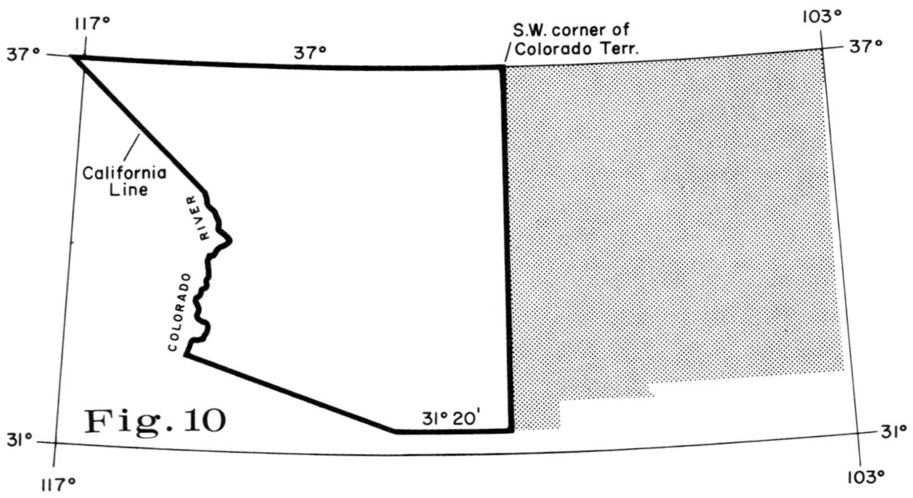

Fig. 10

out, was separated from the northeastern portion by the *Jornada del Muerto,* a natural barrier to intercourse and travel, and great stretches of Indian-infested country intervened between the western district and the seat of government in Santa Fé. Furthermore, the preponderance of Mexican Americans in the legislature of New Mexico prevented equitable legislation for the Anglos. Mowry gave as a further reason that the growing population in the Gadsden Purchase warranted autonomy, and, as the eastern and western sections formed a geographical unit and contained a natural highway of travel from Texas to California, they should be organized under a single government.[103]

On March 19, 1858, eight days after Mowry's letter to Douglas, Heintzelman had a long talk with Bartlett, the former boundary commissioner, and rejoiced that there was an extraordinary excitement about Arizona.[104] In the same month Mowry was troubled to learn of the arrival from Arizona of a rival delegate, a "Mr. McCartney."[105] By July Mowry lost all interest in his military career, resigned from the army,[106] and decided to return to the Southwest. On August 24 he left San Antonio for Mesilla,[107] where on September 3 he attended a meeting convened to consider again the matter of territorial organization.[108] A letter published in a Santa Fé newspaper announced that "Lieut. Mowry has been through here raising the devil about the Territory of Arizona. He has persuaded the people of Mesilla to hold no election under the laws of New Mexico, and to pay no attention whatever to our courts." The editor strongly disapproved this action. Should the dissidents persist, he wrote, "the mother Territory would doubtless much more willingly consent to the separation if Dona Ana would first send up to the Capitol the wherewith to liquidate certain accounts that stand against her unadjusted at the Treasury Department."[109] Mowry left Mesilla in company with James B. Leach, the superintendent of the El Paso-Fort Yuma Wagon Road. On the way they stopped to dress the wounds of Silas St. John, one of the victims of an attack by Mexican employees at the Overland Mail station then under construction at Dragoon Springs.[110] St. John had been left to die. But Assistant Surgeon B. J. D. Irwin of Fort Buchanan amputated his left arm, and the sturdy pioneer made a remarkable recovery.[111]

In the meantime Major Heintzelman had obtained a leave of absence for one year.[112] His object was to make a personal examination of the company's mines in Arizona and to relieve Poston, who was in poor health. Heintzelman arrived in San Francisco on June 28,[113] and took over the direction of the mines when he reached Tubac.[114] On

September 16 he met Mowry near the Sopori Ranch,[115] and two days later the ex-lieutenant arranged for an election for delegate. This was held on the 20th,[116] and Mowry, having received nearly all the votes, was elected to represent Arizona for the second time. His rival McCarty received eleven votes.[117] In December, 1858, having concluded that his private affairs would not permit him to prolong his visit, Heintzelman decided to leave, but not before the arrival of William Wrightson, who had been placed in charge of the Santa Rita mines, which had been transferred from the Sonora Exploring and Mining Company to its new subsidiary, the Santa Rita Silver Mining Company.[118] When Wrightson appeared early in January the direction of the mines of the parent company was turned over to Solon H. Lathrop, who had accompanied Heintzelman to Arizona.[119] The major left Tucson by the Butterfield stage on January 9.[120] Poston also returned to the East, though not in company with Heintzelman, and spent many months in New York for the treatment of a troublesome ailment of the eyes.[121]

Burnside Rifles at Forty Paces

The Thirty-fifth Congress adjourned on March 3, 1859. Since it first convened in December, 1857, six bills had been introduced to organize Arizona, with all but one being reported during the second session. On March 11 Mowry, who had returned to Washington a few months before, wrote to his friend Granville H. Oury in exasperation: "Congress adjourned leaving the country in a beautiful condition. The House not only defeated every Territorial bill — but [adjourned] without giving a single day to Territorial business. . . . I shall be out in May and arrange with you the plans of next sessions work. I have no idea of giving it up. We must succeed sometime and I still have a few thousands to spend. . . ."[122] Congress did, however, pass a bill which concerned Mowry. The act of February 28, 1859, appropriated $1,000 for a survey of the Pima and Maricopa Indian lands and provided $10,000 for gifts to these Indians.[123] Mowry, who since 1857 had been reporting directly to the Commissioner of Indian Affairs on the state of the various Indian tribes in Arizona,[124] was appointed as special agent to carry out the provisions of this statute, and he forwarded his bond on May 16.[125] By the end of the year the presents were distributed under his supervision, and the reservation was surveyed by Andrew B. Gray.[126]

Before Mowry's return to the Southwest, a meeting to urge territorial organization was held in Arizona City on May 7, 1859.[127] One of the leaders was the well-known pathfinder, Lansford Warren Hastings, attorney at law and postmaster of Arizona City, whom many still held responsible for the disaster to the Donner Party in 1846.[128] A few years later he would present Jefferson Davis with an elaborate plan for seizing Arizona and gaining control of California, and would be commissioned a major in the Confederate Army.[129] But his efforts came to naught. After the war his project to found a Confederate colony in Brazil also met with failure.[130] At the meeting in Arizona City, Hastings was a member of the committee to draft resolutions, and was probably the principal author of the preamble which painted this picture of horror:

> We have shown that Immigrant trains have been attacked by ruthless savages... leaving destitute women and children to wend their way back, in doubt, and dread, and... others, less fortunate, have all been slain. ... We have shown that... Mexican "cutthroats" and outlaws... have barbarously murdered and mangled the bodies of our citizens... and that marauding parties of ruthless savages and barbarous Mexicans, infest our Territory, deluging the country in blood... impoverishing our people, and depopulating our country....[131]

The resolutions explained the urgent need for a separate government, called for election of delegates to a convention in Tucson in June, and tendered thanks to Delegate Mowry for his able exertions in behalf of Arizona.

In June Mowry arrived in Mesilla and on the 19th he addressed a convention which passed resolutions reaffirming similar ones of the Mesilla meeting of September 3, 1858. It was agreed that the residents of the southern part of the territory would take no further part in the elections of New Mexico.[132] The resolutions also alleged that court had not been held for three years south of the *Jornada del Muerto,* but Kirby Benedict, one of the federal judges, denied this charge in a vigorous communication to the Attorney General: "I have now to state, that during the whole time, from the fall of 1853, up to the time of leaving that [judicial] District for this [district] . . . in 1858, I never failed going twice a year to the County of Dona Ana, to Las Cruces, or Mesilla to hold the terms of Court as fixed by Law, let the individual impediments, have been as numerous, or dangerous as they may. . . ."[133] Another convention was held at Tucson on July 3, 1859. Indian Agent John Walker presided, and Mowry, who addressed the delegates, expressed optimism that the next Congress would act more favorably than the last. It was resolved to act in concert with the residents along the Rio Grande in refusing to vote in New Mexican elections, and the

Tubac *Weekly Arizonian* was scored for taking a hostile stand toward organization.[134] Local differences along the Rio Grande on the subject of participation in territorial elections led to a second convention in Mesilla on August 7, and four days later citizens of Las Cruces met to protest the action of that convention.[135]

A journalistic battle of words between Mowry and a newspaper correspondent led to a physical encounter only a few days after the Tucson convention of July 3. In a dispatch dated at Tubac, January 30, 1859, Edward E. Cross, writing for the St. Louis *Missouri Republican* under the pseudonym of "Gila," questioned President Buchanan's estimate of the population of Arizona in his December message to Congress, and remarked that there had been *"an enormous amount of falsehood published concerning this country and its resources. As an agricultural country it is worthless."* [136] Cross had accompanied William Wrightson's party on the overland trip to the Gadsden Purchase, and when the Santa Rita Silver Mining Company, in cooperation with the parent company, established Arizona's first newspaper, the Tubac *Weekly Arizonian,* he became its editor.[137] Cross initially appeared to favor territorial organization, but when Congress did not act he advocated the establishment of a separate judicial district.[138] In retort to "Gila's" letter, Mowry wrote in a Washington paper that the delegate from New Mexico had certified the population in the Rio Grande Valley alone to be in excess of 8,000 in 1857. Mowry stoutly defended his claim that Arizona had "sufficient arable land" to support a large population, and added hotly: "I assert it, and have proved it by more evidence than it would be sufficient to hang twenty such fellows as the writer of this anonymous letter [Cross] if he was on trial — a fate, by the way, which will be apt to overtake him when his letter gets back to Arizona. . . ."[139] More letters were exchanged, and Mowry finally challenged the editor to a duel.[140] Cross, in accepting, chose Burnside carbines at forty paces.

In the presence of a gathering at a place near Tubac on July 8, each of the duelists fired three shots in a high wind without reaching a target. The editor's fourth shot failed, and Mowry, surrendering his right to shoot the defenseless man, who stood calmly with arms folded, discharged his rifle into the air ending the contest.[141] The antagonists shook hands and together with Solon H. Lathrop, managing director of the Sonora Exploring and Mining Company, led a procession to the company stores. A forty-two gallon barrel of prime Monongahela whiskey, purchased a few days before from the traders at Fort Buchanan, "melted before the fierce attacks like snow before the midday sun; besides mescal, and anisado, aguardienta [*sic*], etc., all disappeared as if by magic." The last traces of ill feeling were dissipated in the glow of ardent spirits.[142] This episode ended the publication of the *Arizonian* in Tubac. Mowry bought the press and removed it to Tucson where henceforth the paper was published as a Democratic organ under a new editor.[143]

Subsequently, Cross abandoned his opposition and actively favored organization. On New Year's Day of 1860 the *Missouri Republican* published a communication from him predicting that the current session of Congress would not organize any territories whatever, because, in his opinion, the legislators would approve no bill which increased the President's patronage. Cross told of an hour-long interview with President Buchanan in company with Mr. Otero, the delegate from New Mexico. Military and Indian affairs in Arizona were discussed. The correspondent advocated the transfer of all twelve companies of the First Dragoons to Arizona, but if this were not feasible, then provision should be made for stationing six companies of that regiment. His solution to the Apache problem was to place these Indians on a reservation where they would soon die away! Doubtless Buchanan's project for a protectorate over Sonora was discussed, for Cross ended his letter by stating: "I trust Congress will act wisely and promptly, so that within four months we may see the American flag waving over Guaymas and Hermosillo."[144]

Arizona Defies Congress

By February, 1860, ten Arizona bills had failed,[145] five elections for delegate had been held and admission to Congress consistently denied,[146] and resolutions of the legislatures of New Mexico and petitions from the Gadsden Purchase and other parts of the country ignored. Discouraged by these repeated rebuffs in Washington, residents of the Gadsden Purchase now decided to create a government of their own without benefit of congressional sanction. On April 2–5, 1860, a convention was held in Tucson,[147] presided over by James A. Lucas, who had officiated at the convention in Mesilla on June 19, 1859.[148] The secretaries were Granville H. Oury[149] and T. M. Turner, an Ohio journalist and attorney, and for a time editor of the Tucson *Arizonian*,[150] who would be brutally murdered in 1861. The Rio Grande was represented by delegates chiefly from Mesilla, Las Cruces, Doña Ana, and La Mesa. A seat of honor was given to Captain Richard S. Ewell, First Dragoons, the commanding officer of Fort Buchanan,[151] after whom the convention named a county.[152] Ewell was later the Confederate general concerning whom the poet, Stephen Vincent Benét, wrote:

> Ewell goes by,
> The little woodpecker, bald and quaint of speech,
> With his wooden leg stuck stiffly out from his saddle,
> He is muttering, "Sir, I'm a nervous Major-General,
> And whenever an aide rides up from General Jackson
> I fully expect an order to storm the North Pole."[163]

A provisional constitution was drafted to remain in force until Congress saw fit to organize a territorial government. The new "Territory of Arizona" was to comprise all of New Mexico south of 33° 40′ north latitude, and was divided by north and south lines into four counties to be known as Doña Ana, Mesilla, Ewell, and Castle Dome (figure 7).[154]

Lewis S. Owings, a physician and in later years the first mayor of Denison, Texas,[155] was elected governor and authorized to appoint a roster of officials. Judicial districts were to be created, a bicameral legislature was to be elected, provision made for organizing a militia with a full set of officers, and election of county officials called in May. Ignacio Orrantia, merchant of Mesilla, was chosen lieutenant-governor, with James A. Lucas as secretary, Granville H. Oury as chief justice, Mark Aldrich of Tucson as treasurer, Samuel G. Bean as marshal, Palatine Robinson as adjutant general, and William C. Wordsworth, a resident of the Sonoita Valley, as major-general of the militia. The hope was expressed that Mowry would continue to serve as delegate to Congress.

The Tucson proceedings, the constitution, and Doctor Owings' inaugural address were printed on the press of the *Arizonian* in the first imprint ever published in Arizona.[156] Although this government had a limited existence, it had officials who actually served — and these included justices of the peace and alcaldes who dealt with administrative and legal problems. It is not true, as Bancroft writes, that this government went unnoticed in Congress.[157] In actual fact a resolution was introduced in the House in 1860 to legalize the judicial proceedings of this government.[158] The formation of such a provisional government was not unique in the history of frontier areas and territories. When the federal government acted too slowly to meet impatient demands from pioneer settlements, the residents sometimes took matters into their own hands and erected extralegal provisional governments. Earlier there had been such governments in Michigan, California, and Oregon. When Congress refused to seat Dakota's delegate, Alpheus G. Fuller, and to organize

[*National Archives*]

RICHARD S. EWELL
(1817–1872)

A noted Indian fighter in the Gadsden Purchase, this captain of dragoons for a time was commander of Fort Buchanan. As a Confederate general he lost a leg at the Second Battle of Manassas in August, 1862, but returned to duty and succeeded Stonewall Jackson in command of the Second Corps of the Army of Northern Virginia.

[*Arizona Pioneers' Historical Society*]

GRANVILLE H. OURY
(1825–1891)

A native of Virginia and a prominent attorney in Tucson, Oury was the first chief justice of the provisional government. In 1857 he led an unsuccessful effort to rescue Henry A. Crabb's ill-fated filibustering expedition in Sonora. Elected in August, 1861, he served briefly as the first delegate from Arizona to the Confederate Congress in 1862. Later that year he entered the service of the Confederate army as captain of his own company. After Arizona was admitted as a federal territory, Oury served three terms in the territorial legislature and was speaker of the House in 1866 and 1873. In 1880 he was elected delegate to the United States Congress.

PROVISIONAL GOVERNMENT

—OF—

THE TERRITORY OF ARIZONA.

To all to whom these presents shall come—GREETING:

I, L. S. OWINGS, Governor of the Provisional Government of the Territory of Arizona, having confidence in the integrity and patriotism of Granville H. Oury, appoint and commission him the said Granville H. Oury Judge of the second Judicial district and chief Justice in the said Territory; and do authorize him to discharge, according to law, the duties of said office, and to hold and enjoy the same, together with all the powers, privileges and emoluments thereunto appertaining, until the legal termination thereof.

IN TESTIMONY WHEREOF, I have hereunto set my hand, and caused to be affixed the Great Seal of the Territory of Arizona. Done at Tucson, this 5th day of April in the year of our Lord, one thousand eight hundred and 61—

L. S. Owings

BY THE GOVERNOR.

Geo. A. Lucas
Secretary of the Territory.

[*Arizona Pioneers' Historical Society*]

The rarest extant document of the Provisional Government of 1860 is this certificate of appointment of Granville H. Oury, which is reproduced from the original in possession of the Arizona Pioneers' Historical Society. The embossed seal of the provisional government which appeared above the words "BY THE GOVERNOR" is not shown.

the territory, the Dakota Land Company in the autumn of 1858 established a squatter government with a governor and legislature.[159] Shortly thereafter a more formidable government of this kind was organized in Denver when miners met to create the "Territory of Jefferson," adopted a constitution, elected officials, convened an assembly and promulgated laws.[160]

Mowry, having completed his assignment as Special Indian Agent for the Pimas and Maricopas, was back in Washington by January, 1860. There, and in other cities on the east coast, private and public business relating to Arizona kept him too occupied to attend the constitutional convention at Tucson in April, 1860.[161] On the 22nd of that month, while in attendance at the Democratic National Convention at Charleston, South Carolina, Mowry wrote to his friend Granville H. Oury, with whom he collaborated closely on territorial affairs: "I hope you have put the Provisional Government through in good shape. It is going to help our cause very much."[162] On June 2 in Providence, Rhode Island, acting as agent of the Mexican owners, he conveyed a portion of the Sopori Grant to the newly-formed Sopori Land and Mining Company.[163] On July 17, 1860, President Buchanan appointed Mowry as commissioner to run the eastern boundary of California,[164] and Lieutenant Joseph Christmas Ives, the explorer of the Colorado River, was assigned as astronomer and surveyor. In a letter to Doctor Owings on August 20, Mowry resigned as Arizona's delegate without informing the provisional governor of his boundary appointment.[165] One month later Owings announced an election for November 6, and Edward ("Ubiquitous Ned") McGowan was chosen as Mowry's successor.[166]

Since the leaders of the movement which created the provisional government — men like Lewis S. Owings, James A. Lucas, and Granville H. Oury — were decidedly partial to the Southern cause, the provisional Territory of Arizona was in a sense the precursor of the later Confederate Territory of Arizona. In a letter dated at Mesilla, November 22, 1860, and published in the *San Francisco Herald,* the election of McGowan was reported with this comment: "It is not supposed, *now* that Lincoln is elected, that [the new delegate] can effect anything, as his constituents are in chief southern, and will not be willing to accept an organization under Republican rule. Should the South separate, he is instructed to attend the Southern Convention and pledge the Territory to the Southern Confederacy, and to ask for a Territorial organization under that Confederacy. . . ." Such was the prevailing sentiment eight months

[*Courtesy of Dr. Rex W. Strickland, El Paso*]

LEWIS S. OWINGS
(1820–1875)

A physician with mining interests, Dr. Owings was elected governor of the provisional Territory of Arizona in April of 1860. A Southern sympathizer, when the Confederate invasion of New Mexico and Arizona failed, he returned to Texas where he became the first mayor of Denison.

before Baylor proclaimed the Confederate Territory of Arizona in the summer of 1861.

Had he continued to serve as delegate, Mowry, a staunch Democrat with strong Southern leanings and the close associate of Arizona's future delegate to the Confederate Congress, Granville H. Oury, would have been placed in the same position as McGowan. During the Democratic administration Mowry wielded considerable influence in Washington, and even if it were not to become necessary to make a decision between the Confederacy and the Union he hardly could have expected the same partiality under Lincoln as under Buchanan. After his resignation Mowry ceased to exert any significant influence on the territorial movement. His later career was concerned largely with mining enterprises. On April 9, 1860, he negotiated the purchase of the valuable Patagonia Mine from Henry T. Titus of Kansas and Nicaragua notoriety, and Elias Brevoort, merchant of New Mexico and the former postmaster and sutler of Fort Buchanan.[167] Brevoort had bought the mine from a private company, the first members of which were James W. Douglas, formerly of the Mexican Army and then in occupation of the Sopori Ranch, Captain R. S. Ewell, Lieutenants Isaiah N. Moore, Richard S. C. Lord and Horace Randal of Fort Buchanan, and Richard M. Doss. The property had been acquired from a Mexican herder in 1857 for a trifling consideration.[168] The Patagonia, which came to be known as the Mowry mine, was seized and placed in the hands of a receiver when Mowry was arrested in June, 1862, on the charge of treason, tried by a military commission, and imprisoned at Fort Yuma.[169]

Not Arizona But Arizuma

Five unsuccessful bills to create Arizona Territory (figures 7–9) were reported in 1860, one of which deserves special notice. This was the measure which Senator James S. Green of Missouri, chairman of the Committee on Territories, introduced on April 3 to provide a temporary government for the "Territory of Arizuma." The proposed territory was to extend from the Colorado River to Texas, and northward to 33° 40′ (figure 7).[170] The debate on December 27 illustrated the degree to which the vexatious subject of slavery dominated Congressional deliberations on territorial bills during this period.[171] As soon as Senator Green listed reasons why organization was desirable, Albert G. Brown of Mississippi moved that the law passed by New Mexico in 1859 "to protect property in slaves" be extended to the proposed territory. This

[*Library of Congress*]

JEFFERSON DAVIS
(1808–1893)

A former Secretary of War and Southern expansionist, United States Senator Davis of Mississippi, in December, 1859 presented the first of two unsuccessful Senate bills to organize the "Territory of *Arizuma*." Later as President of the Confederacy he approved the bill which established Arizona as a Confederate territory.

motion caused Senator Lyman Trumbull of New York to demand the retention of the Mexican antislavery statute which prevailed at the time New Mexico was acquired by the United States. James R. Doolittle of Wisconsin, announcing that he would vote for Trumbull's amendment, sought to mollify the opposition. "We have lived together," he said, "under the Constitution . . . in slaveholding and non-slaveholding States for more than seventy years, and have lived together in peace. That peace, however, has rested upon two fundamental ideas: first, that the Federal Government and the citizens of the free States shall make no aggression upon slavery in the States; and the other, equally fundamental, that neither the Federal Government nor the slaveholders of the slave States shall make any aggressions upon or undertake to overturn freedom in the Territories. . . .[172] Doolittle made a special point of quoting the conciliatory views of President-elect Lincoln: "I have no purpose, directly or indirectly, to interfere with the institution of slavery in the States where it exists. I believe I have no lawful right to do so, and I have no inclination to do so."[173]

The debate was protracted and diffuse. There was discussion of the debts of Texas at the time of annexation, talk about the proposition to purchase Cuba, detailed treatment of the Dred Scott decision, and long disquisitions on other constitutional problems pertaining to slavery — but very little indeed on the merits of the Arizona question.[174] The discussions were not unlike those which inspired Andrew Johnson to comment on the recurrent intrusion of the slavery issue into Congressional deliberations: "Round and round this slavery agitation have we gone until our heads are reeling and our stomachs sick. . . . If some Senator from the South were to introduce the Lord's Prayer or . . . the Ten Commandments for consideration, some one would find a negro in it somewhere!"[175] Senator Green strove to keep his bill on course. "When I called up this bill," he declared, "it was not with a view to exciting any discussion whatever or introducing any of these exciting topics that divide one section from the other. I really think that the people of Arizuma . . . ought to be organized."[176] In its final form the bill stipulated that the proposed territory was eventually to be admitted to statehood with or without slavery, depending upon the constitution drafted at that time. Long before the speakers subsided, however, it was evident that Green's bill had no chance for passage even though it was to be considered again. Perhaps the only advantage which accrued to Arizona from these heated exchanges was that the future territory was to be spared the name "Arizuma."

But Why Not Arizona?

The elections of 1860 and the secession of the slave states left the Republicans in undisputed control of both House and Senate, and removed the principal impediment to the establishment of new territories. Even before the bitter sectional struggle was transferred to bloody battlefields, there was a rush to organize territories which had been knocking at the doors of Congress. While Buchanan was still in office Colorado, Nevada, and Dakota were organized — the first territories to be created since 1854.[177] By a strange inconsistency, which has been described as one of the singular contradictions in the political history of the country, the Republicans passed the pertinent bills without a mention of slavery. One historian has commented: "Radical Republicans and administration Democrats had agitated the territorial question for a decade, and had thus brought the country to the brink of war. By a profound irony, they now at last voted together, a few weeks before the bombardment of Fort Sumter."[178] In deciding to frame these bills as they did, leading Republicans apparently had agreed that the omission of the slavery clause not only would ensure passage but would conciliate the Democrats in those critical days before war erupted.[179]

It may be wondered why Arizona was not organized as a territory in 1861 together with Colorado, Nevada, and Dakota. With the resignation of Southern Democrats and the ensuing Republican control of both houses of Congress even before Lincoln had taken office, it would appear that Arizona could have been given an independent government at the same time as the other three. But at this moment there was scant enthusiasm for the organization of Arizona either in the Southwest or in the capital. Because most of the prominent Americans in both Tucson and Mesilla favored the South, aggressive activity in behalf of a territorial government under the Union had ceased in the Gadsden Purchase. In Washington, on the other hand, there was much lobbying in behalf of the sizable mining populations of Colorado and Nevada; and in the cause of Dakota the influence of Daniel M. Frost and J. B. S. Todd, cousin of Mary Todd Lincoln, probably was very great.[180] By contrast, there was in 1861 no strong lobbyist in the capital to plead the cause of Arizona. At the moment that the three successful territories were established, Mowry and Poston were both in Arizona — and if there were other interested parties in Washington they were otherwise occupied.

NOTES *for* PART ONE

[1] *San Diego Herald,* January 20, 1855.

[2] In 1854 Senator Thomas Hart Benton, in opposing the building of a railroad through the Gadsden Purchase, described the country as "so utterly desolate, desert, and God forsaken, that Kit Carson says a wolf could not make his living upon it." See Elbert B. Smith, *Magnificent Missourian* (Philadelphia, 1958), 299.

[3] For an extended treatment of the Ordinance, see Jay A. Barrett, *Evolution of the Ordinance of 1787* (New York, 1891); Max Farrand, *The Legislation of Congress for the Government of the Organized Territories of the United States, 1789–1895* (Newark: W. A. Baker, 1896); and Theodore C. Pease, "The Ordinance of 1787," *Mississippi Valley Historical Review,* XXV (September 1938), 638.

[4] See Earl S. Pomeroy, *The Territories and the United States, 1861–1891: Studies in Colonial Administration* (U. of Pennsylvania Press, 1947); and Howard R. Lamar, *Dakota Territory, 1861–1889: A Study of Frontier Politics* (Yale U. Press, 1956).

[5] Roy F. Nichols, "The Kansas-Nebraska Act: A Century of Historiography," *Mississippi Valley Historical Review,* XLIII (September 1956), 187–212.

[6] Examples are: Memorial of J. Grimes and others, citizens of Illinois, praying for protection for the overland mail route to California through the Arizona Territory, December 22, 1857; Memorial of W. T. Munday and others, members of the Tennessee Legislature, asking for protection to the overland mail route through Arizona, December 22, 1857; Memorial of James M. Wright and 239 others, citizens of Illinois, praying for protection for the overland mail route to California through the Arizona Territory, December 22, 1857. These memorials are in Records of the United States Senate, 35 Congress, 1 Session, RG 46, National Archives. Cited hereafter as Senate Records.

[7] See the resolutions of the legislature of New Mexico relative to the organization of the Territory of Arizona, and the removal of the wild Indians from the Territory of New Mexico, March 19, 1858, printed as *Sen. Misc. Doc.* 208, 35 Cong., I Sess., Serial 936. See also *Sen. Misc. Doc.* 21, 36 Cong., 1 Sess., Serial 1038. Resolutions of the legislature of New Mexico in favor of the organization of a territorial government for Arizona, February 27, 1860, Senate Records, 36 Congress, 1 Session. These resolutions are in the handwriting of Sylvester Mowry and were certified to be true copies by the delegate from New Mexico, Miguel A. Otero. The 1858 resolutions endorsed President Buchanan's recommendation to organize Arizona in his message of 1857, and contained the first published proposal which stipulated a north and south boundary at the 109th meridian for the separation of the proposed Territory of Arizona from New Mexico.

[8] James Buchanan and Abraham Lincoln. See Buchanan's recommendation in December, 1858, in *House Exec. Doc.* 2, 35 Cong., 2 Sess., 19.

[9] John B. Weller, *California Assembly Journal, 1858,* 56, cited in Hubert H. Bancroft, *History of Arizona and New Mexico, 1530–1888* (San Francisco, 1889), 506, note 25.

[10] *Supra,* 35–42, and pt. 2.

[11] W. A. Mowry, *The Descendants of Nathaniel Mowry of Rhode Island* (Providence: S. S. Rider, 1878), and supplement, published in Boston in 1900.

[12] George W. Cullum, *Biographical Register of the Officers and Graduates of the U.S. Military Academy. . . .* (3rd ed., 6 vols., Boston, 1891–1900), II, 483.

[13] W. Mulder and A. R. Mortensen (eds.), *Among the Mormons* (New York, 1958), 272 *et seq.*

[14] Document M 602, Letters Received, 1855, Records of the Adjutant General's Office, RG 94, National Archives. Cited hereafter as Adjutant General's Records.

[15] See "Charles D. Poston" in Allen Johnson and Dumas Malone (eds.), *Dictionary of American Biography* (22 vols., New York, 1928–44), XV, 121–22. Cited hereafter as *DAB.*

[16] Biographical data on Poston in the author's possession.

[17] Biographical data on Ehrenberg in the author's files.

[18] *San Francisco Herald,* February 20, 1854. The *Zoraida* cleared the port on February 17. Book of Naval Clearances for 1854 from the Port of San Francisco, General Records of the Treasury Department, RG 56, National Archives.

[19] C. D. Poston, "Reconnoissance in Sonora." Photostatic copy of manuscript in the Arizona Pioneers' Historical Society, Tucson. Noted hereafter as APHS. Also see Poston's narrative in J. Ross Browne, *Adventures in the Apache Country....* (New York, 1869), ch. 24.

[20] An article on the founding of Yuma is in preparation by the author.

[21] Byrd H. Granger (ed.), "Southwestern Chronicle: The Journal of Charles D. Poston, 1850–1899," *Arizona Quarterly,* XIII (Autumn 1957), 255.

[22] *Report of the Sonora Exploring and Mining Company, made to the stockholders, December, 1856* (Cincinnati, 1856).

[23] Thomas E. Farish, *History of Arizona* (8 vols., Phoenix [San Francisco], 1915–1918), I, 322.

[24] *Journal of House of Representatives, Territory of New Mexico, 1854–1855.* On January 23, 1855, the following entry appeared: "Mr. Lucas, by permission, introduced a memorial to Congress for the organization of a new territory in the southern part of the Territory of New Mexico which would be called 'Pimeria.' Read for the first time. On motion of Mr. Ortiz, the memorial was defeated." Copy of excerpt by courtesy of Myra Ellen Jenkins, Senior Archivist, State Records Center and Archives, Santa Fe, New Mexico.

[25] *Infra,* pt. 2.

[26] *Mesilla Times,* March 30, 1861. Jones, who was not a member of the territorial legislature of New Mexico, probably collaborated with Lucas in the preparation of this memorial. As Jones stated, the document may have been drafted in December of 1854. If this is correct, the memorial was prepared only six months or so after the Gadsden Purchase was proclaimed into law on June 30, 1854. It was introduced in the territorial legislature only five days after that body officially annexed the newly acquired country. See Section 227, January 18, 1855, in *New Mexico Compiled Laws, 1884.*

[27] The memorial prayed for the organization of a new territory "to be known as Arizona," and was prepared late in August. Records of the House of Representatives, 34 Congress, 3 Session, RG 233, National Archives. Cited hereafter as House Records. See also *House Report* 117, 34 Cong., 3 Sess., Serial 912; and *Congressional Globe,* 34 Cong., 3 Sess., 100, *Globe* cited hereafter as *Cong. Globe.*

[28] *Los Angeles Star,* October 25, 1856; *Sacramento Daily Union,* October 30, 1856; and Hayes' Scraps, Arizona, V, 244, Bancroft Library, University of California, Berkeley.

[29] Florence *Weekly Arizona Enterprise,* September 5, 1891.

[30] Petition in Spanish signed by W. Claude Jones, Rafael Ruelas, Remigio Saenz, Luis Garcia, and fifty-three other citizens of the Rio Grande Valley, "praying for a separate territorial organization under the name of Arizona." Territorial Papers of New Mexico, RG 46, National Archives. A translation in the handwriting of Sylvester Mowry is in this collection. The inability of many of the Mexicans to sign their own names to this memorial explains why a number of the signatures are in the same handwriting. It is probable that most, if not all, of these names were signed by permission of the individuals listed.

[31] *Santa Fe Weekly Gazette,* December 13, 1856.

[32] Mowry to Douglas, March 11, 1858, Territorial Papers of New Mexico, Senate Records.

[33] Record Book A [1856–1861], Recorder's Office, Pima County, Tucson, Arizona. A photostatic copy is in APHS.

[34] See notes 27 and 28.

[35] Robert H. Forbes, *Crabb's Filibustering Expedition into Sonora, 1857* (Tucson: Arizona Silhouettes, 1952).

[36] Peter R. Brady file in APHS; L. R. Bailey (ed.), *The A. B. Gray Report* (Los Angeles: Westernlore Press, 1963).

[37] Biographical data on Hulseman in possession of the author.

[38] John and Lillian Theobald, *Arizona Territory: Post Offices and Postmasters* (Phoenix: Arizona Historical Foundation, 1961), 76.

[39] Files on each of the signers named are in APHS.

[40] Hayes' Scraps, Arizona, V, 244.

[41] *Journal of the House of Representatives,* 34 Congress, 3 Session, 680. Cited hereafter as *House Journal.*

[42] *Cong. Globe,* 34 Cong., 3 Sess., 100.

[43] *Ibid.,* 386.

[44] This bill (H. R. 752), which failed to pass, is in House Records, 34 Congress, 3 Session.

[45] *Cong. Globe,* 34 Cong., 1 Sess., 676. See also *Journal of the Senate,* 34 Congress, 1 Session, 191. Cited hereafter as *Senate Journal.* A bill to establish a separate judicial district south of the Gila, and to create the office of surveyor general therein; to provide for the adjudication of certain land claims, to grant donations to actual settlers, to survey certain lands, and for other purposes, March 18, 1856. The original bill in manuscript is in Senate Records, 34 Congress, 1 Session.

[46] *Cong. Globe,* 34 Cong., 3 Sess., 613.

[47] *Ibid.,* 817.

[48] *Ibid.*

[49] *Ibid.,* 818.

[50] *Ibid.,* 821.

[51] *Ibid.*

[52] *Ibid.*

[53] Sylvester Mowry, *Memoir of the Proposed Territory of Arizona* (Washington: Henry Polkinhorn, Printer, 1857), 25.

[54] *House Journal,* 35 Congress, 1 Session, 210.

[55] W. Turrentine Jackson, *Wagon Roads West* (U. of California Press, 1952), 218.

[56] See "Thomas J. Rusk" in Walter P. Webb (ed.), *The Handbook of Texas* (2 vols., Austin: Texas State Historical Association, 1952), II, 516–17.

[57] *U.S. Statutes at Large,* XI (1857), 162.

[58] Pacific Wagon Road Office, El Paso-Fort Yuma Wagon Road, Records of the Department of the Interior, RG 48, National Archives.

[59] Rusk, Jones, Douglas, and others to Jacob Thompson, Secretary of the Interior, March 7, 1857, *ibid.*

[60] The following is a fairly complete list of the Arizona bills which were reported in the federal Congress from 1856 to 1862, some of which are reproduced in whole or in part in Appendix C:

(1) S. 176. Introduced by Senator Thomas J. Rusk of Texas on March 18, 1856. See *Cong. Globe,* 34 Cong., 1 Sess., 676; and *Senate Journal,* 34 Congress, 1 Session, 191. The original and amended bills are in Senate Records. See also note 99. The new district to be created first was given the name of "district of Gila," but in the amended bill was renamed "district of Arizona." The original bill stipulated that the surveyor's office as well as a proposed land office were to be located in Mesilla, but in subsequent amendments the revised bill located these offices first at Tucson, and in the final version as passed on February 21, 1857, at "a place to be designated by the Secretary of the Interior." This bill, which failed in the House, was the only Arizona bill passed in either chamber until 1862.

(2) H. R. 752. Reported by Representative Justin S. Morrill of Vermont on January 20, 1857, *Cong. Globe,* 34 Cong., 3 Sess., 386.

(3) S. 8. Reported by Senator William M. Gwin of California on December 17, 1857, *ibid.,* 35 Cong., 1 Sess., 62. This bill after much revision was finally reported adversely on February 8, 1859.

(4) H. R. 172. Reported by Delegate Miguel A. Otero of the Territory of New Mexico on January 20, 1858, *House Journal,* 35 Congress, 1 Session, 210. Arizona bills under (1), (2), and (4), unlike the others listed, were not designed to create a new territory, but to establish a separate judicial district, etc., within the Territory of New Mexico.

(5) H. R. [not given a number]. Reported by Representative Joseph C. McKibbin of California on December 10, 1858, *ibid.,* 35 Congress, 2 Session, 58.

(6) H. R. 836. Introduced by Representative Alexander H. Stephens of Georgia on January 28, 1859, *ibid.,* 35 Congress, 2 Session, 278, and *Cong. Globe,* 35 Cong., 2 Sess., 657.

(7) S. 555. Reported by Senator James S. Green of Missouri on February 4, 1859, *Cong. Globe,* 35 Cong., 2 Sess., 804. This was a bill "to provide for temporary governments for the Territories of Dacotah [*sic*] and Arizona. . . ."

(8) H. R. 876. Reported by Representative Alexander H. Stephens on February 16, 1859, *ibid.,* 1065, and *House Journal,* 35 Congress, 2 Session, 419.

(9) S. 24. Introduced by Senator Jefferson Davis of Mississippi on December 23, 1859, *Cong. Globe,* 36 Cong., 1 Sess., 222. Like S. 365, to which it was similar, this was a bill to organize the "Territory of Arizuma." There is no copy of S. 24 in the National Archives or in the Library of Congress.

(10) H. R. 192. Introduced by Delegate Otero on February 16, 1860, *ibid.,* 816. Unlike H. R. 172, which he reported on January 20, 1858, this was a bill to *organize* the Territory of Arizona. A copy has not been found.

(11) S. 365. Introduced by Senator Green on April 3, 1860, *ibid.,* 1501–1502. This bill, like that introduced by Senator Davis, was to organize the "Territory of Arizuma." The original bill is in Senate Records, 36 Congress, 1 Session, and the amended bill in *ibid.,* 36 Congress, 2 Session.

(12) H. R. [not given a number]. This bill was proposed by Representative Galusha A. Grow of Pennsylvania on May 2, 1860. Senate Records, 36 Congress, 1 Session. This may be the same as H. R. 710.

(13) H. R. [not given a number]. This bill was proposed by Representative Eli Thayer of Massachusetts on May 3, 1860, as a substitute for Grow's bill of the previous day. House Records, 36 Congress, 1 Session.

(14) H. R. 710. Reported by Representative Grow on May 11, 1860. *House Journal,* 36 Congress, 1 Session, 826, and *Cong. Globe,* 36 Cong., 1 Sess., 2069.

(15) H. R. 890. Reported by Representative Grow on December 18, 1860, *Cong. Globe,* 36 Cong., 2 Sess., 121.

(16) H. R. 171. Reported by Delegate John S. Watts of the Territory of New Mexico on December 23, 1861, *ibid.,* 37 Cong., 2 Sess., 167.

(17) H. R. 357. Reported by Representative James M. Ashley of Ohio on March 12, 1862, and passed by the House on May 8, 1862, *ibid.,* 1193, 2030. Passed by the Senate on February 20, 1863, and signed into law on February 24, 1863, *ibid.,* 37 Cong., 3 Sess., 1128.

(18) S. 254. Reported by Senator B. F. Wade of Ohio on March 31, 1862, *ibid.,* 37 Cong., 2 Sess., 1443. The National Archives does not have a copy of this bill.

[61] Journal of Samuel P. Heintzelman, February 18, 1857, Library of Congress. Cited hereafter as Heintzelman Journal. There is no doubt that Mowry also confided his ambition to the sutler at Fort Yuma, George F. Hooper, later a prominent Arizona merchant, with whom both Heintzelman and the lieutenant were on intimate terms. A letter from the sutler, dated December 28, 1856, was mentioned by Heintzelman on the same day that he referred to Mowry's communication. *Ibid.* After leaving Fort Yuma, the major, a partner in the

profitable Colorado Ferry, continued his business association with L. J. F. Jaeger, the ferryman, and also with Hooper.

[62] Post Returns, February, 1857, Fort Yuma, Adjutant General's Records.

[63] Forbes, *Crabb's Expedition,* 22 *et seq.*

[64] Special Orders 61, May 15, 1857, Department of the Pacific. Mowry's leave was extended by Special Orders 104, July 20, 1857, Adjutant General's Office.

[65] *San Francisco Herald,* June 30, 1857.

[66] *Ibid.,* October 2, 1857; Knoxville *Register,* August 15, 1857, cited in *San Diego Herald,* October 10, 1857.

[67] Mowry, *Memoir,* 22.

[68] Heintzelman Journal, September 22, 1857.

[69] Biographical data on Poston in the author's possession.

[70] Heintzelman Journal, October 3, 1857.

[71] *Letter of Lieutenant Mowry, U.S.A., to the U.S. Mail Contractors upon the Overland Mail Route to California* (New York, 1857). Pamphlet in 12 pages.

[72] Heintzelman Journal, October 27, 1857.

[73] *Ibid.,* November 5, 1857.

[74] *Ibid.*

[75] *Ibid.,* November – December, 1857, *passim.*

[76] Otto C. Lightner, *The History of Business Depressions* (New York, 1922), 141–47.

[77] Heintzelman Journal, December, 1857 – January, 1858, *passim.*

[78] Tubac *Weekly Arizonian,* April 21, 1859. See also *Fourth Annual Report of the Sonora Exploring and Mining Company, March, 1860* (New York, 1860).

[79] Heintzelman Journal, December 21, 1857.

[80] Sara Yorke Stevenson, *Maximilian in Mexico* (New York, 1899), 178.

[81] See "William M. Gwin" in *DAB,* VIII, 64–65.

[82] Hallie M. McPherson, "The Interest of William McKendree Gwin in the Purchase of Alaska, 1854–1861," *Pacific Historical Review,* III (March 1934), 28–38.

[83] Robert G. Cleland, *The Cattle on a Thousand Hills* (San Marino: The Huntington Library, 1941), 37 *et seq.*

[84] Paul N. Garber, *The Gadsden Purchase* (Philadelphia: U. of Pennsylvania Press, 1923), 121. During the Civil War Gwin represented the Confederate government at the French court. A singular chapter of Gwin's career concerned his negotiations with Napoleon III to establish an American colony in northern Mexico, in reward for which he was to be made the Duke of Sonora. His plan failed. See the article by his son-in-law, Evan J. Coleman, "Senator Gwin's Plan for the Colonization of Sonora," *Overland Monthly,* XVII (May 1891), 497–519, 593–607; and XVIII (August 1891), 203–13; Hallie M. McPherson, "The Plan of William McKendree Gwin for a Colony in North Mexico, 1863–1865," *Pacific Historical Review,* II (December 1933), 357–86; and Stevenson, *Maximilian in Mexico,* 178.

[85] Poston to Mowry, August 15, 1857, in Mowry, *Memoir,* 21.

[86] Memorial of George Kippen, Wm. H. Martin, B. H. Darmint [De Armitt], Eugene Wakefield, and five hundred and fifteen other residents of southern New Mexico, praying for a separate territorial organization under the name of Arizona, December 17, 1857. *Senate Journal,* 35 Congress, 1 Session, 41. Senator Gwin requested leave to withdraw this memorial on January 4, 1858, and two days later it was returned to Mowry. Delegate Otero of New Mexico, to whom the memorial was transferred, presented it to the House on January 12. House Records, 35 Congress, 1 Session.

[87] S. 8. A bill to organize the Territory of Arizona, and to create the office of surveyor general therein; to provide for the examination of private land claims, to grant donations to

actual settlers, to survey the public and private lands, and for other purposes, December 17, 1857. Senate Records, 35 Congress, 1 Session.

88 *Ibid.*

89 *Cong. Globe,* 35 Cong., 1 Sess., 312–13.

90 Heintzelman Journal, February 26, 1858.

91 *Ibid.,* 1857–1858, *passim.*

92 *Ibid.,* March 1, 1858.

93 Petition of M. E. Bradley and others, citizens of the U.S. and residents of the country known as the Gadsden Purchase, and the southern portion of the territory of New Mexico, praying a separate organization under the name of Arizona, March 10, 1858. Senate Records, 35 Congress, 1 Session.

94 *Ibid.* See also Mowry to Douglas, March 11, 1858, Territorial Papers of New Mexico.

95 *Ibid.*

96 Letters Received [from J. R. West], 1862–1863, Department of New Mexico, Records of the United States Army Commands, RG 98, National Archives. Cited hereafter as Records of Army Commands.

97 See item (1) in note 60.

98 See item (2) in note 60.

99 In Rusk's bill (S. 176) as amended, the boundaries of the proposed district were greatly enlarged. The new boundaries began "at a point on the boundary line between Texas and New Mexico, at a point where the north line of the county of Dona Ana in New Mexico, strikes said boundary line, thence west with said line . . . to the summit of the Sierra Madre mountains; thence north to the boundary line of the Territory of Utah; thence west . . . to the eastern boundary of California; thence southeasterly along said boundary line to the point at which the line between the United States and Mexico intersects it; thence along the several lines between the United States and Mexico and between New Mexico and Texas to the beginning." Figs. a and 2.

In the amended version of H. R. 752, the proposed district was enlarged by extending the boundary from a point on the Rio Grande due east of the upper forks of the Gila River northward along the former river to the 34th parallel, thence west to "the summit of the Sierra Madre, thence north to the south line of Utah, thence west to the east line of California," thence along the California boundary to the point where it joins the district as defined in the original bill. Figs. a and 3.

100 H. R. 172. A bill to establish a separate judicial district south of the Gila, and to provide for the representation of the inhabitants of the Gadsden Purchase in the Territorial legislature of New Mexico, and for other purposes, January 20, 1858. House Records, 35 Congress, 1 Session.

101 The proposed territory as described in Mowry's *Memoir,* 4, consisted of all of New Mexico from the Colorado River to Texas that lay south of the 34th parallel. The eastern boundary on the map which was included in some copies of his *Memoir* extended only to the 106th meridian. See *Map of the Proposed Arizona Territory from explorations by A. B. Gray & others, to accompany memoir by Lieut. Mowry, U.S. Army, Delegate elect* (Cincinnati: Middleton, Wallace & Company, [1857]).

102 R. P. Kelley's *Map of the Territory of Arizona . . . 1860* (St. Louis: Engraved and published by Theodore Schrader). Mowry's endorsement read: "The most elaborate and correct map of Arizona yet compiled – SYLVESTER MOWRY, Delegate to Congress from Arizona." The boundaries depicted on this map are the same as those described in Mowry's *Memoir,* except for the northern line at 33° 40′, rather than at 34 degrees. Original copies of this map are in possession of APHS and Dr. Rex W. Strickland of El Paso.

103 Mowry to Douglas, March 11, 1858, Territorial Papers of New Mexico.

104 Heintzelman Journal, March 19, 1858.

105 *Ibid.,* March 20, 1858. "McCartney" was Justus I. McCarty.

106 Mowry to Major General Irvin McDowell, July 3, 1858 [M 256], Letters Received, 1858, Adjutant General's Records; E. D. Townsend, Assistant Adjutant General, to Mowry, July 12, 1858, in Letter Book, 1858, II, 418, *ibid*. The official date of Mowry's resignation was July 30, 1858.

107 San Francisco *Daily Evening Bulletin,* September 28, 1858; *San Diego Herald,* September 18, 1858.

108 The date of this convention is given in Hayes' Scraps, Arizona, V, 253.

109 *Santa Fe Weekly Gazette,* October 9, 1858.

110 A newspaper correspondent, writing from Tucson, told what happened when the stage carrying the two men arrived at the station: "The first sight which met their eyes was the dead body of old Mr. Burr [one of the murdered employees]. Thinking that perhaps the Indians had made an attack, they approached carefully, but were hailed by St. John, who cried out for God's sake to bring him water. Lieutenant Mowry and Colonel Leech [*sic*], of the road commission, tendered all assistance in their power, and were five hours dressing St. John's wounds. The sight was so horrible that Colonel Leech, a man of tremendous physique, fainted. . . ." See Philadelphia *Press,* October 21, 1858.

111 Roscoe P. and Margaret B. Conkling, *The Butterfield Overland Mail, 1857–1869* (3 vols., Glendale: The Arthur H. Clark Co., 1947), II, 141–47. For medical and other details, see B. J. D. Irwin, "Amputation at the Shoulder-Joint," *American Journal of Medical Sciences,* October, 1859.

112 Heintzelman Journal, April 29, 1858.

113 *Ibid.,* June 28, 1858.

114 *Ibid.,* August 17, 1858, *et seq.*

115 *Ibid.,* September 16, 1858.

116 *Ibid.,* September 20, 1858; William A. Duffen (ed.), "Overland Via 'Jackass Mail' in 1858: The Diary of Phocian R. Way," *Arizona and the West,* II (Winter 1960), 367.

117 *Sacramento Daily Union,* October 11, 13, 1858; *San Diego Herald,* November 13, 1858.

118 Heintzelman Journal, December 22, 1858.

119 *Ibid.,* January 6, 1859.

120 *Ibid.,* January 9, 1859.

121 Biographical data on Poston in the author's possession.

122 Cornelius C. Smith, "Some Unpublished History of the Southwest," *Arizona Historical Review,* IV (July 1931), 15.

123 Mowry to A. B. Greenwood, Commissioner of Indian Affairs, November 21, 1859, in *Sen. Exec. Doc.* 2, 36 Cong., 1 Sess., Serial 1023. See also Tucson *Weekly Arizonian,* August 4, 1859.

124 Mowry to Commissioner of Indian Affairs, February 14, 1857 [enclosure in M 191], Letters Received, 1857, Adjutant General's Records; Mowry to J. W. Denver, November 10, 1857, in *House Exec. Doc.* 2, 35 Cong., 1 Sess., 586. See also Mowry to C. E. Mix, September 14, 1858 [M 518], Letters Received, New Mexico, 1858; and Mowry to Commissioner, April 26, 1859 [M 611], Letters Received, Pimo, 1859. Both documents are in Records of the Office of Indian Affairs, RG 75, National Archives. Cited hereafter as Indian Office Records.

125 Mowry to Greenwood, May 16, 1859 [M 622], Letters Received, Pimo, 1859, Indian Office Records.

126 See note 123.

127 *San Diego Herald,* May 23, 1859.

128 Bernard De Voto, *The Year of Decision: 1846* (Boston, 1942), 313, 402, 429, 444, 463.

129 *Journal of the Confederate States of America, 1861–1865,* III, 653-54, published as *Sen. Doc.* 234, 58 Cong., 2 Sess., Serial 4612.

[130] W. J. Hunsaker, "Lansford W. Hastings' Project for the Invasion and Conquest of Arizona and New Mexico, for the Southern Confederacy," *Arizona Historical Review,* IV (July 1931), 5–12; and L. F. Hill, "The Confederate Exodus to Latin America," *Southwestern Historical Quarterly,* XXXIX (1935–36), 100–34, 161–99.

[131] *San Diego Herald,* May 23, 1859.

[132] St. Louis *Daily Missouri Republican,* July 6, 1859; Hayes' Scraps, Arizona, V, 253–54.

[133] Benedict to J. S. Black, August 18, 1859, Attorney General's Papers, New Mexico, Records of the Department of Justice, RG 60, National Archives. Also see Benedict to Garland, May 9, 1856 [B 39], Letters Received, 1856, Department of New Mexico, Records of Army Commands.

[134] Tubac *Weekly Arizonian,* July 14, 1859; St. Louis *Daily Missouri Republican,* July 21, 1859; Hayes' Scraps, Arizona, V, 260.

[135] Tucson *Weekly Arizonian,* August 18, 1859.

[136] Reprinted in Washington (D. C.) *States,* February 20, 1859.

[137] Tubac *Weekly Arizonian,* March 3, 1859, reprinted in Estelle Lutrell, *Newspapers and Periodicals of Arizona, 1859–1911* (U. of Arizona, 1949), opposite the preface.

[138] Tubac *Weekly Arizonian,* March 10, 1859.

[139] Mowry to Editor, Washington *States,* March 1, 1859. The letter was dated February 27, 1859, at Washington, D. C.

[140] See Cross' letter of April 24, 1859, in *ibid.,* May 24, 1859, and Mowry's letter of July 2, 1859, dated at Tucson, that appeared in *ibid.,* July 23, 1859.

[141] Jo Ann Schmitt, *Fighting Editors* (San Antonio: The Naylor Company, 1958), 18–19.

[142] Tucson *Arizona Enterprise,* March 3, 1892. This newspaper was moved from Florence to Tucson early in 1892.

[143] Lutrell, *Newspapers of Arizona,* 63–64. See also Tubac *Weekly Arizonian,* July 21, 1859, and Tucson *Weekly Arizonian,* August 4, 1859.

[144] St. Louis *Daily Missouri Republican,* January 1, 1860.

[145] See the first ten bills listed in note 60.

[146] W. Claude Jones and Nathan P. Cook were elected delegates in September of 1856 from the Mesilla Valley and the western section of the Gadsden Purchase, respectively. Mowry was elected on September 7, 1857, and re-elected on September 20, 1858 and September 5, 1859. In reporting the election of Mowry for the third time, a California newspaper commented: "The proposed return to the position of a Territory on the part of the southern counties of this State may prove to be the one thing necessary to enable the people of Arizona to procure a Territorial Government. . . . " The editor was not too certain, however, that this proposal would be acceptable, for he added: "Perhaps . . . annexation to Southern California might prove as objectionable to the people of the territory as their present connection with New Mexico – a connection which they are daily and steadily striving to sever." *San Diego Herald,* October 15, 1859.

[147] *The Constitution and Schedule of the Provisional Government of the Territory of Arizona, and the Proceedings of the Convention held at Tucson* (Tucson: J. Howard Wells, Publisher, 1860), *passim.* Appendix B.

[148] Tubac *Weekly Arizonian,* June 30, 1859.

[149] Biographical files on Granville H. Oury are at APHS. Oury's photograph was also reproduced in Charles F. Parker, "Arizona's Provisional Government of 1860," *Arizona Highways,* XXVIII (September 1962), 36.

[150] See Tucson *Arizonian,* February 9, 1861.

[151] For biographical data on Ewell, see Percy Gatling Hamlin (ed.), *The Making of a Soldier: Letters of General R. S. Ewell, 1817–1872* (Richmond: Whillet & Shepperson, 1935); and his *"Old Bald Head"* (Strasbourg, Va.: Shenandoah Publishing House, 1940). See also James S. Hutchins, " 'Bald Head' Ewell, Frontier Dragoon," *Arizoniana,* III (Spring 1962), 18–23.

[152] See note 147.

[153] Stephen Vincent Benét, *John Brown's Body* (Garden City: The Country Life Press, 1927), 192.

[154] See note 147.

[155] Biographical data on Owings in the files of the author.

[156] See note 147.

[157] Bancroft, *Arizona and New Mexico,* 508, note 29.

[158] *House Journal,* 36 Congress, 1 Session, 1208–1209; and *ibid.,* 36 Congress, 2 Session, 287. The committee to which this resolution was referred reported adversely.

[159] Lamar, *Dakota Territory,* 44.

[160] Frederic L. Paxson, "The Territory of Colorado," *University of Colorado Studies,* IV (February 1907), 68–76; and *ibid.,* "The Territory of Jefferson: A Spontaneous Commonwealth," *ibid.,* III (November 1905), 15–18.

[161] Biographical data on Mowry in the author's files.

[162] Mowry to Oury, in Smith, "Some Unpublished History," *Arizona Historical Review,* IV, 16–17.

[163] Biographical data on Mowry in the author's files.

[164] Mowry's appointment as commissioner, May 26, 1860, is in Records of Explorations and Surveys, RG 48, National Archives.

[165] *Mesilla Times,* October 18, 1860.

[166] *Ibid.,* November 1, 1860.

[167] Deed Record B, Doña Ana County, Las Cruces, New Mexico, 613–14. Biographical data on Brevoort are in the author's files.

[168] Hamlin, *"Old Bald Head,"* 49.

[169] See Bert Fireman, "What Comprises Treason?" *Arizoniana,* I (Winter 1960), 5–10; B. Sacks, "Sylvester Mowry: Artilleryman, Libertine, and Entrepreneur," a paper read at the annual meeting of the Western History Association, Salt Lake City, October 18, 1963, to be published in *The American West.*

[170] S. 365. The amended bill was ordered printed, January 2, 1861. Senate Records, 36 Congress, 1 Session.

[171] *Cong. Globe,* 36 Cong., 2 Sess., 195–205.

[172] *Ibid.,* 195.

[173] *Ibid.,* 196.

[174] *Ibid.,* 195–205, *passim.*

[175] Quoted in J. T. DuBois and G. S. Mathews, *Galusha A. Grow* (Boston, 1917), 213.

[176] *Cong. Globe,* 36 Cong., 2 Sess., 202.

[177] The Territory of Colorado was created by act of February 28, 1861; the Territory of Nevada, by act of March 2, 1861; and the Territory of Dakota, by act of March 2, 1861. *U.S. Statutes at Large,* XII (1861), 172, 209, 239.

[178] David N. Potter, *Lincoln and His Party in the Secession Crisis* (Yale U. Press, 1942), 278.

[179] See also James G. Blaine, *Twenty Years of Congress* (2 vols., Norwich, Conn.: The Henry Bill Publishing Co., 1884–1886), I, 269–70; and II, 677–78.

[180] Lamar, *Dakota Territory,* 65.

PART TWO

Originally published in *ARIZONA and the WEST*
VOLUME 5 NUMBER 2 SUMMER 1963

Rebellion in the Southwest

Lincoln's election in November, 1860, precipitated drastic action in the South and led to a series of events which prepared the soil for a new and dramatic development in the Southwest. At the same time that the secession crisis brought an apparent halt to the movement for organization of Arizona as a federal territory, it served to amplify the importance of Arizona in the minds of Confederate leaders. The Gadsden Purchase had long been a focal point of interest for Southerners because of the evident merits of the thirty-second parallel for the construction of a wagon road and a railway to the Pacific — projects which earlier had been ardently advocated by nationalists like Jefferson Davis and Texas expansionists like Senator Rusk. With secession came a revival of the proposal to erect a transcontinental highway of commerce linking Southern states to Pacific ports and leading to the coveted gold fields of California. With the outbreak of war the acquisition of the mineral wealth of Arizona became an added objective of the Confederacy, and there was renewed hope among Texans that their state might regain the western lands which had been relinquished to New Mexico in the compromise measures of 1850.

Many Southerners and especially Texans confidently believed that the entire Territory of New Mexico would side with the Confederate States. Among the reasons which supported this conviction was the fact that the principal civil officials of the territory, Governor Abraham Rencher and Secretary Alexander M. Jackson, and many of the Army officers — including the commander of the department — were Southerners and could naturally be expected to espouse the aims of the Confederacy. The adoption of a slave code in New Mexico in 1859 and its strong advocacy by the territorial delegate, Miguel A. Otero, seemed to indicate another bond with Southern principles.[181] Moreover, Doctor Owings and other prominent men of the Mesilla Valley were sure that the predominant sentiment in southern New Mexico, from the Rio Grande to the Colorado, was sympathetic to the South. But Secretary Jackson himself was not sanguine. Taking a realistic view of the state of affairs in a letter to a political acquaintance early in 1861, Jackson made it clear that he did not share the hopes of many Texans that the people of New Mexico would gather at a constitutional convention and petition for statehood under the Confederate government. The natives, he predicted, would not make this move for fear of increased taxation; and the "Pike's Peakers" in the legislature at Santa Fé, though comprising a small minority, would influence their colleagues by vocal denunciation of the South. The decisive factor, Jackson believed, was the old economic connection between New Mexicans and Missouri traders. He prophesied that the action of Missouri in the secession crisis would largely determine the course of New Mexico, but in the meantime he hoped that strong action would be taken to acquire the rich lands of the Southwest before Lincoln appointed territorial officials inimical to Southern interests.[182]

After Governor Sam Houston refused to call the legislature into special session to consider the position of Texas in the impending crisis, secessionists in that state decided as early as December, 1860, to take independent action and called for a convention to meet at Austin. On the 29th of January, 1861, the delegates voted to withdraw from the Union, and on March 2 Texas became the seventh state to secede.[183] At the instance of Simeon Hart, wealthy merchant and miller of El Paso and an ardent supporter of the South, the secession convention appointed him and the El Paso attorney Philemon T. Herbert as commissioners to invite the people of the Territory of New Mexico to join hands with the Confederate government. Hart was assigned as agent to New Mexico proper; Herbert, an erstwhile Congressman of California,[184] was instructed to use his influence in the Rio Grande Valley. To mobilize interest the Austin secessionists formally recommended that the people of New Mexico draft a constitution recognizing slavery and make application at Montgomery for admission to the "confederacy of Southern States."[185]

Commissioner Herbert lost no time in launching his campaign. From Austin on the first day of February he dispatched a declaratory letter which was printed three weeks later in the *Mesilla Times* together with a call, carrying sixty-one signatures, for a secession convention to be held at Mesilla on March 16.[186] In a subsequent letter to Doctor Owings, the chief executive of the provisional government of Arizona, Herbert urged the people of the Gadsden Purchase to unite their fortunes with "those who have ever sympathized with you" against "the black fanaticism of the North."[187] In reply, Governor Owings extended to the commissioner a warm invitation to attend the important meeting of the 16th of March.[188]

Conspicuous among the promoters of the Mesilla convention were men who had been officials of the provisional government — Owings, James A. Lucas, and Granville H. Oury — and such fervid Southern sympathizers as Robert P. Kelley, principal owner of the *Mesilla Times,* W. Claude Jones of El Paso, who in 1856 had prepared one of the earliest of the Arizona memorials,[189] and Samuel J. Jones, the notorious former sheriff of Kansas and now sutler of Fort Fillmore.[190] The convention was held on schedule with Lucas, secretary of the provisional government, presiding. Commissioner Herbert addressed the meeting, but his oratory was exceeded by that of his law partner, W. Claude Jones,[191] who protested strenuously against Northern injustice. "Has not [the North] treated us with cold and criminal neglect," he thundered, "and has this corrupt sectional party [the Republicans] . . . taken any steps toward our organization? . . . They have organized Colorado, Dacotah [*sic*] and Nevada . . . and passed over our claims . . . . For six years we have petitioned, pleaded, prayed for protection and some kind of organization. . . ." He closed with this exhortation: "The hell of abolitionism glooms to the north — the Eden of liberty, equality, and right smiles upon you from the south! Choose ye between them." Unanimous resolutions were passed to repudiate the "Black Republican" administration of Lincoln, to sever all ties with the Union, and to unite with the Confederacy.[192]

On the 18th of March the preamble and resolutions of the Mesilla convention were forwarded by Lucas to Howell Cobb, president of the Provisional Congress of the Confederate States then in session at Montgomery.[193] In Tucson on the 23rd the prominent merchant Mark Aldrich, an early advocate of the organization of Arizona,[194] presided over a meeting similar to that held in Mesilla. Pro-Southern delegates excitedly joined the citizens of the Rio Grande in emphatic denunciation of the North. All past experience had shown, the Tucsonans declared, that they had "nothing to hope for from Northern legislation," and therefore they earnestly desired the Confederacy to extend to them "the protection necessary to the proper development and advancement of the Territory."[195]

News of the outbreak of hostilities in Charleston harbor reached the Rio Grande in the middle of May. The exuberant endorsement of

THE MESILLA TIMES.

VOL. I. {B. C. MURRAY & CO., Publishers.} CITY OF MESILLA, ARIZONA, SATURDAY, MARCH 30, 1861. {TERMS: $3 00 per Year, in Advance.} NO. 24.

POLITICAL POSITION OF ARIZONA.

[Synopsis of a speech of Gen. W. CLAUDE JONES, in the Mesilla Convention, March 16th, 1861.]

The question being on the adoption of the Resolutions, Gen. Jones said:

MR. PRESIDENT:—The time for delay has passed, and the time for action has come. Vigorous, decided action on the part of the people of Arizona is now demanded, in order to secure our rights, and that government protection which has been so ardently desired and so long sought in vain. We must now make our choice for evil or for good. We must either cling to the North, with the Black Republican banner waving over our people, unprotected and neglected, denied their Constitutional rights and down-trodden and oppressed by a government alien to our principles, with which we have no sympathies, and which rules over us without our consent; or we must unite with the South and ask that protection and equality of legal right which is the birthright of our citizens. We must go to that South which is endeared to us by the holiest sympathies of our nature, and the manly rectitude of whose conduct our reason approves—that South, in the path of whose glorious destiny we must follow, or be lost in the gloom of neglect and oppression from a power we hate. Northward, insult, wrong and oppression are frowning upon us; Southward a brilliant and glorious pathway of hope, leads to the star of empire smiling loose, trampled upon, because you are not north of 36 30, and do not bow down and worship the Baals of Northern fanatacism — the idols of the negro worshippers. Are we to have no mails? Are we to be deprived of postal benefits? Sir; the Confederate States of America possess a vital energy—they have all the elements of greatness, power and durability—they have vast interests—and the indomitable ability and will to protect all, and the roads of their commercial prosperity, and their means of rapid communication, will not be blocked up. They will open extended and new facilities for the transportation of the mails. The shortest route from the Atlantic to the Pacific, is from Indianola, through our Territory to Guymas; and I venture to predict that before twelve months, we will have a tri-weekly line of coaches between the two points, with branches to San Diego and San Francisco. We will have troops here for our protection—rangers—the hardy sons of the South, and not the prebold, mungrel materials of the present U. S. Army. And are we under obligations for this deprival of mail facilities?

And has this corrupt sectional party of the North taken any steps toward our organization, or even noticed our Territory? They have organized Colorado, Dacotah and Nevada, all free Territories, and passed over our claims, notwithstanding they knew the neglect with which they had treated us — the wrongs ... North has folded her meshes around you, and you are secure in the net? Will you worship at the Juggernaut of the North, with the blind faith of the Hindoo, till the deadly wheels of the idol's car, crush you hopelessly beneath?

The crisis is upon us — there is no escape. Let us meet it calmly, manfully and independently. Let us *act* and pass the Resolutions. If we succeed in our object and we are organized as a Territory of the confederate States, a bright future is before us. Emigration will be incited to our rich mineral mountains and fertile agricultural valleys. Across our Territory will be the Southern pathway to the Pacific, and an extensive commerce will go hand in hand with the development of our resources.

Arizona constitutes the greatest portion of the northern border of the State of Texas. Your destiny is linked with hers. You must be made a bulwark against the fell tide of Northern encroachment and fanatacism, or you must be a seething den for abolitionists, from which they can hurl their incendiary bolts into the heart of the South. You must be a hot-bed for Northern upas-like exotics, poisonous to Southern institutions, or you must be the home of independent freeman, growing and prospering under the seven starred banner of the South as it waves protectingly above you.— The ... nor' ... r'

[*National Archives*]

Part of page from *Mesilla Times* reporting fiery speech of W. Claude Jones at Mesilla convention on March 16, 1861.

the Southern cause in Mesilla was exemplified by the celebration which attended the presentation of a Confederate flag to Captain George M. Frazer's "Arizona Rangers."[196] Headed by a military band and joined by the citizens generally, the troops marched to the residence of a Mr. Patton where W. Claude Jones delivered a stirring address and presented the flag in behalf of the Patton girls. The flag was received by Philemon T. Herbert, later to become a lieutenant colonel in the Confederate service, who promised in behalf of the company that it would never be surrendered "while one was living to tell the tale." The band then struck up "Dixie's Land" and the crowd marched through the plaza and principal streets to Joshua S. Sledd's billiard saloon, in front of which a flagstaff was erected and the seven-starred banner raised aloft "with music, cheering and speeches."[197]

Army officers stationed in New Mexico did nothing to discourage such secessionist demonstrations or to interfere with the publication of the *Mesilla Times*, which in its inflammatory columns reviled the Union and openly demanded annexation of the "Territory of Arizona" by the Confederacy. By the time the Confederate flag was flying at Mesilla, many of the ranking officers of the Department of New Mexico already had resigned their commissions in the United States Army. Colonel William Wing Loring, a noted cavalryman then commanding the department, was a native of North Carolina; he submitted his resignation on May 13[198] and Colonel Thomas T. Fauntleroy of Virginia, a former commander of the department, resigned on the same day. Among others who surrendered their commissions to offer their services to the Confederacy were Lieutenant Colonels George B. Crittenden and John B. Grayson of Kentucky, Majors James Longstreet of Alabama, R. B. Reynolds of Tennessee, and Henry Hopkins Sibley of Louisiana, and Captains Dabney H. Maury and Richard S. Ewell of Virginia. By the middle of June it was widely rumored in Santa Fé that a Confederate military force was preparing to enter New Mexico from the direction of El Paso, and Lieutenant Colonel Edward R. S. Canby of the Nineteenth U.S. Infantry, who succeeded Loring in command of the department, now ordered Major Isaac Lynde to abandon Fort McLane and move his companies from that small post to Fort Fillmore opposite the seat of Southern sympathy at Mesilla.[199]

Fearing a sudden invasion from Texas, Canby took steps to consolidate the troops of his far-flung command at the principal posts on the Rio Grande. Forts Breckenridge and Buchanan, situated in the southwestern corner of the department, were abandoned and their companies ordered east to Fort Fillmore. What supplies could not easily be transported were to be destroyed, and the installations leveled by fire.[200] The evacuation and destruction of the posts on the Arivaipa and the Sonoita left southern Arizona without military protection, and by the end of July the whole country south of Tucson was at the mercy of savage Apaches and lawless Mexicans. Murders were frequent, and occupancy of the mines in the vicinity of Tubac became untenable. Charles D. Poston's younger brother, John Lee, was one of a number of mining officials who were killed, and Poston and Raphael Pumpelly, engineer of the Santa Rita Silver Mining Company, barely escaped with their lives.[201] Taking a circuitous route westward, the fugitives arrived at Fort Yuma on August 17, and on the following day Poston sent to Cincinnati the melancholy report of the murder of his brother at the Heintzelman Mine and the abandonment of the company properties in the Gadsden Purchase.[202]

Arizona Turns Confederate

The Confederate penetration of New Mexico was not long in coming.[203] From San Antonio in June the Texas frontiersman John R. Baylor, newly commissioned by the Confederacy as lieutenant colonel of mounted rifles,[204] led a "flying squad" of daredevil volunteers across the plains to El Paso, reaching that stronghold of Southern sentiment on the first day of July. On July 23 Baylor marched his three hundred Texans up the Rio Grande toward Mesilla for the purpose of "protecting the citizens of Arizona" from the large federal force which had assembled at Fort Fillmore under Major Lynde. Thwarted in his plan to deliver a surprise attack on the fort at daylight on the 25th, Baylor moved his troops across the river and into Mesilla where they were received with "vivas and hurrahs" by the citizenry. Lynde advanced on the town, but retreated after a few shots were exchanged and three of his men killed. In the early hours of the morning of the 27th the timorous major, overestimating the strength of the Texans, started his numerically superior force of eleven regular companies in great confusion northeastward toward Fort Stanton, but was overtaken at San Augustine Pass some twenty-two miles distant and surrendered unconditionally to Baylor without firing a shot.[205]

On the 1st of August, 1861, Baylor formally took possession of the "Territory of Arizona" in the name of the Confederate States of America, organized it as a military government with himself as governor, and designated Mesilla as the capital. His proclamation read in part: "The social and political condition of Arizona being little short of general anarchy, and the people being literally destitute of law, order, and protection, the said Territory . . . is hereby declared temporarily organized as a military government, until such time as Congress may otherwise provide. . . . All offices, both civil and military, heretofore existing . . . either under the laws of the late United States, or the Territory of New Mexico, are hereby declared vacant, and from the date hereof shall forever cease to exist. . . ." The new territory was to comprise "all that portion of the recent Territory of New Mexico lying south of the thirty-fourth parallel of North latitude." The next day Baylor published the list of his appointees to territorial office, principal among whom were James A. Lucas as secretary and the Mesilla lawyer M. H. MacWillie as attorney general. On August 14 he informed his military superior at San Antonio, Brigadier General Earl Van Dorn, of the establishment of a provisional government for Arizona and announced that he had extended the northern limits of the territory from 34° to 36° 30′.[206]

Before Baylor's Territory of Arizona was a week old it had, as a result of a mass meeting in Tucson, a duly elected delegate to the Confederate Congress in the person of Granville H. Oury, who a year earlier had been chief justice in Doctor Owings' provisional government.[207] Oury soon left for Richmond to take up his duties, and there on November 22, 1861, John H. Reagan of Texas presented a bill to ratify the military government proclaimed by Baylor and thereby to organize the Territory of Arizona under the Confederacy.[208] Although not yet officially qualified, Oury was invited on December 18 to address the Congress on the subject of organization.[209] On the 24th Josiah A. Campbell of Mississippi sought to establish the northern boundary of the proposed territory at 36° 30′ instead of 34°, but he was voted down.[210] On the same day Reagan's bill was passed,[211] but a successful motion to reconsider sent the bill back to committee on January 2, 1862.[212] The Arizona bill was passed in amended form on January 13,[213] signed by President Davis on the 18th,[214] and proclaimed to be in force on February 14.[215] By this statute the boundaries of the Territory of Arizona were to be those originally stipulated in Baylor's proclamation, but the Confederate States of America reserved the right to acquire all or any part of New Mexico north of the thirty-fourth parallel. Slave ownership was to be protected by the territorial legislature, and it was stipulated that when the Territory of Arizona was admitted as a state of the Confederacy her constitution must provide for the permanent maintenance of slavery.[216]

President Davis confirmed Baylor as governor and named his friend and private secretary, Robert Josselyn of Mississippi, as secretary of the new territory. Alexander M. Jackson, another Mississippian and former secretary of the Territory of New Mexico, was appointed chief justice, with Columbus Upson of Texas as associate justice, Russel Howard of Arizona as attorney general, and the boisterous Samuel J. Jones as marshal. Oury had taken his seat as delegate in the Confederate Congress on January 24, 1862,[217] but as a result of the machinations of Baylor he was replaced on the 11th of March by M. H. MacWillie.[218] At about the same time Baylor's reign as governor came to an end when Davis discovered that the impetuous colonel had ordered the extermination of all "hostile" Indians in the territory. By now, however, it scarcely mattered who represented the Territory of Arizona in the coun-

PROCLAMATION.

To the People of the Territory of Arizona:

I, John R. Baylor, Lieut. Col. commanding the Confederate Army in the Territory of Arizona, hereby take passession of the said Territory in the name and behalf of the Confederate States of America.

The social and political condition of Arizona being little short of general anarchy, and the people being literally destitute of law, order and protection, the said Territory from the date hereof, is hereby declared temporarily organized as a military government, until such time as Congress may otherwise provide.

For all the purposes herein specified, and until otherwise decreed or provided, the Territory of Arizona shall comprise all that portion of the recent Territory of New Mexico lying south of the thirty-fourth parallel of North latitude.

All offices, both civil and military, heretofore existing in this Territory, either under the laws of the late United States,or the Territory of New Mexico, are hereby declared vacant, and from the date hereof shall forever cease to exist.

That the people of this Territory may enjoy the full benefits of law, order and protection, and as far as possible, the blessings and advantages of a free government, it is hereby decreed that the laws and enactments existing in this Territory prior to the date of this Proclamation, and consistent with the Constitution and Laws of the Confederate States of America, and the provisions of this decree, shall continue in full force and effect, without interruption, until such time as the Confederate Congress may otherwise provide.

The said Government shall be divided into two separate and distinct departments, to wit: the Executive and Judicial.

The Executive authority of this Territory shall be vested in the Commandant of the Confederate Army in Arizona.

The Judicial power of this Territory shall be vested in a Supreme Court, two District Courts, two Probate Courts and Justices of the Peace, together with such municipal and other inferior Courts, as the wants of the people may from time to time require.

The two District Judges shall constitute the Supreme Court, each of whom shall determine all appeals, exceptions, and writs of error removed from the District Court wherein the other presides. One of the said Judges shall be designated as the Chief Justice of the Supreme Court. There shall be but one session each year, which shall be holden at the seat of Government.

The District Jndges shall hold two terms of Court every year in their respective Judicial Districts. They may likewise hold special terms, whenever in their opinion, the ends of public justice require it.

The Judicial Districts of this Territory shall be divided as follows: The First Judicial District shall comprise all that portion of Arizona lying east of the Apache Pass, the District and Probate Courts whereof shall be holden at La Mesilla. The Second Judicial District shall comprise the remainder of the Territory; the District and Probate Courts shall be holden at Tucson. The Governor shall likewise appoint one Probate Judge and Sheriff, and the necessary Justices of the Peace in and for each Judicial District. The Constables shall be appointed by the respective Justices of the Peace.

Each District Judge shall appoint his own Clerk who shall be *ex-officio*, Clerk of the Probate Court within such District.

The District and Probate Courts of the two Districts shall be holden at such times as heretofore provided by the Legislature of New Mexico for the Counties of Doña Ana and Arisona.

All suits and other business now pending in any of the late Courts of New Mexico within this Territory, shall be immediately transferred to the corresponding Courts of this Territory as herein established.

The style of all process shall be 'The Territory of Arizona," and all prosecutions shall be carried on in the name of the Territory of Arizona.

There shall likewise be appointed by the Governor, an Attorney General, Secretary of the Territory, Treasurer, and Marshal, whose duties and compensation shall be the same as herotofore under the laws of New Mexico.

The City of Mesilla is hereby designated as the seat of Government of this Territory.

All Territorial officers shall hold their respective terms of office until otherwise provided by Congress, unless sooner removed by the power appointing them.

The salaries, fees and compensation of all Territorial officers shall remain the same as heretofore in the Territory of New Mexico.

The Treasurer, Marshall, Sheriffs and Constables, before acting as such, shall execute to the Territory a bond, with good and sufficient securities, conditioned for the faithful discharge of their official duties, in the same manner as heretofore provided under the laws of New Mexico.

All Territorial officers, before entering upon their official duties, shall take an oath or affirmation to support the Constitution and laws of the Confederate States and of this Territory, and faithfully to discharge all duties incumbant upon them.

The Bill of Rights of the Territory of New Mexico, so far as consistent with the Constitution and laws of the Confederate States and the provisions of this Decree, are hereby declared in full force and effect in the Territory of Arizona.

Given under my hand, at Mesilla, this 1st day of August, 1861. **JNO. R. BAYLOR,**
Lt. Col. Com. Mtd. Rifles, C. S. A.

Appointments.

In accordance with the provisions of a Proclamation dated August 1st, 1861, organizing temporarily the Territory of Arizona, I, John R. Baylor, Governor of the said Territory, do hereby publish and declare the following appointments. All appointees are requested to qualify, and enter upon their respective official duties without delay:

Secretary of the Territory, James A. Lucas;
Attorney General, M. H. Macwillie;
Treasurer, E. Angerstein;
Marshall, Geo. M. Frazer;
Judge 1st Judical District, H. C. Cook,
Probate Judge, 1st Judicial District, Frank Higgins;
Sheriff " J. A. Roberts,
Justice of the Peace, Dona Ana Louis W. Geck;
do do Mesilla, 4th Prct., M. A. Veremendi;
do do do 5th do Henry L. Dexter;
do do La Mesa, Theo. J. Miller;
do do Pino Alto, M. M. Steinthal;
do do Santo Tomas, Cristobal Sanches,
do do Las Cruces, John G. Ward.

Given under my hand, at Mesilla, this 2nd day of August, A. D. 1861. **JNO. R. BAYLOR,**
Gov. and Lieut. Col. Comdg. Mtd. Rifles, C. S. A.

[*National Archives*]

Lieutenant Colonel John R. Baylor's proclamation establishing the *military government* of the Territory of Arizona. Printed document also shows list of Baylor's appointments.

[*Courtesy of George W. Baylor, Jr.*]

JOHN R. BAYLOR
(1822–1894)

Shortly before his departure from San Antonio in 1861 to lead his Texan Confederates in an invasion of southern New Mexico, Lieutenant Colonel John R. Baylor, then 39, sat for this oil portrait by Iwanski. Baylor was attired in the handsome dress uniform of the Republic of Texas – blue jacket, gray trousers, and red sash. His belt-buckle, emblazoned with the Lone Star, was fashioned from a silver hair-piece taken from a Comanche he killed on the Brazos in 1858. The painting, owned by his grandson, George W. Baylor, Jr., of Tucson, is on loan and exhibit at the Alamo.

cils of the Confederacy or who held the office of governor at Mesilla. The whole Southwest was fast slipping out of Confederate control. On the very day that MacWillie assumed Oury's seat in Richmond, a fresh regiment of Colorado volunteers arrived at Fort Union to reinforce Canby's depleted regulars on the upper Rio Grande; and simultaneously Colonel James H. Carleton was leading a large column of California volunteers eastward into the Gadsden Purchase. The dream of Confederate leaders for a Southern Southwest and for a highway to the Pacific was about to disappear in the capricious winds of war.

For a brief moment that dream had been bright and seemingly close to realization. Early in 1862 the Confederates mounted a full-scale campaign against the defenders of the Rio Grande.[219] To follow up Baylor's entry at Mesilla and drive the Union forces from all their posts in New Mexico, President Davis had authorized a brigade-sized invasion under the command of the gifted but erratic Henry Hopkins Sibley, a veteran cavalryman who had exchanged his majority in the United States Army for the star of a brigadier general in the Confederacy. Organizing his "Army of New Mexico" at San Antonio in the autumn of 1861, Sibley marched to El Paso and in January, 1862, occupied the abandoned Fort Thorn about forty miles north of Mesilla. After sending Captain Sherod Hunter's company of "Arizona Volunteers" west to take post at Tucson, Sibley pushed up the Rio Grande, met Canby's troops at Valverde on February 20–21 and drove them in retreat to Fort Craig, and proceeded north to occupy Albuquerque and Santa Fé. Then, on the 28th of March, the tide turned as elements of Canby's command and Colorado volunteers under Major John M. Chivington trapped Sibley's army at Glorieta Pass, east of Santa Fé, in the decisive engagement of the Civil War in the southwestern theater.[220] Having lost almost all their supplies, the Confederates fled in pathetic disarray down the Rio Grande, and on May 14 at El Paso the disillusioned Sibley delivered a sad valedictory to his beaten brigade. A month earlier a detachment of Captain Hunter's company succeeded in ambushing a few troops of the advance guard of the "Column from California" at Picacho Pass, some forty-two miles northwest of Tucson,[221] but by the second week of May the Confederates in that town fully realized the hopelessness of their precarious hold on southern Arizona and hastily evacuated. On the 20th Lieutenant Colonel Joseph R. West led the first units of the California volunteers into Tucson and raised the Union flag in the plaza.

[*Museum of New Mexico*]

JAMES H. CARLETON
(1814–1873)

A strict disciplinarian, this experienced Regular Army officer was the commander of the impressive Column from California, composed of some 2,000 volunteers. His advance into southern Arizona led to the withdrawal of Captain Sherod Hunter's Confederate forces to the Rio Grande. The march of Carleton's column to that river precipitated the flight of the last elements of General Sibley's "Army of New Mexico."

To all whom it may Concern:

The Congress of the United States has set apart a portion of New Mexico, and organized it into a Territory complete of itself. This is known as the TERRITORY OF ARIZONA. It comprises within its limits all the country eastward from the Colorado river, which is now occupied by the forces of the United States known as "The Column from California;" and, as the flag of the United States shall be carried by this column still further eastward, these limits will extend in that direction until they reach the furthest geographical boundary of this Territory. Now, in the present chaotic state in which Arizona is found to be: with no civil officers to administer the laws: indeed with an utter absence of all civil authority: and with no security of life or property within its borders: it becomes the duty of the undersigned to represent the authority of the United States over the people of Arizona, as well as over all those who compose or are connected with the Column from California.

Thus, by virtue of his office as Military Commander of the United States forces now here, and to meet the fact, that wherever within our boundaries our colors fly, THERE the sovereign power of our country must at once be acknowledged, and law and order at once prevail, the undersigned as a Military Governor assumes control of this Territory until such time as the President of the United States shall otherwise direct.

Thus, also, it is hereby declared that until civil officers shall be sent by the Government to organize the Civil Courts for the administration of justice, the Territory of Arizona is hereby placed under Martial Law.

Trials for capital offences shall be held by a Military Commission to be composed of not more than thirteen nor less than nine commissioned officers.

The rules of evidence shall be those customary in practice under the Common Law.

The trials shall be public, and shall be trials of record: and the mode of procedure shall be strictly in accordance with that of Courts Martial in the Army of the United States.—Unless the public safety absolutely requires it, no execution shall follow conviction until the orders in the case by the President shall be known.

Trials for minor offences shall be held under the same rules, except that for these a commission of not more than five nor less than three commissioned officers may sit; and a vote of a majority determine the issue.

In these cases the orders of the officer organizing the commission shall be final.

All matters in relation to rights in property and lands which may be in dispute, shall be determined FOR THE TIME BEING by a Military Commission, to be composed of not more than five nor less than three commissioned officers. Of course, appeals from the decision of such commission can be taken to the Civil Courts when once the latter have been established.

There are certain fundamental rules for the government of the people of this Territory which will be rigidly enforced.

I . . . No man who has arrived at lawful age shall be permitted to reside within this Territory who does not without delay subscribe to the oath of allegiance to the United States.

II . . . No words or acts, calculated to impair that veneration which all good patriots should feel for our country and Government, will be tolerated within this Territory, or go unpunished if sufficient proof can be had of them.

III . . . No man who does not pursue some lawful calling or have some legitimate means of support shall be permitted to remain in the Territory.

Having no thought or motive in all this but the good of the people, and aiming only to do right, the undersigned confidently hopes, and expects, in all he does to further these ends, to have the hearty co-operation of every good citizen and soldier in Arizona.

All this is to go into effect from and after this date, and will continue in force unless disapproved or modified by General George Wright, United States Army, commanding the Department of the Pacific, under whose orders the Column from California has taken the field.

Done at the Head Quarters of the Column from California in Tucson, Arizona, this the eighth day of June, A. D. 1862.

(Signed) **JAMES H. CARLETON,**
COL. 1ST CAL. VOL'S.,
Commanding

[*National Archives*]

Carleton's proclamation, issued at Tucson on June 8, 1862, by which he assumed authority over the "Territory of Arizona" as military governor. His regulations under martial law were exceptionally severe.

Even before the last elements of Sibley's brigade under Colonel William Steele had departed from New Mexico in July, 1862, the Confederate Territory of Arizona had collapsed.[222] Thus passed the second of the four "Territories of Arizona," the first of these having been established at Tucson in April of 1860.[223] The third "Territory of Arizona" was proclaimed by the commander of the imposing Column from California, Colonel James H. Carleton, on June 8, 1862, the day after he reached Tucson. In his proclamation Carleton announced that Congress had "set apart a portion of New Mexico, and organized it into a Territory complete of itself," and declared martial law in the exercise of federal jurisdiction "until such time as the President of the United States shall otherwise direct."[224] Although the proclamation of June 8 received the endorsement of Carleton's superior, Brigadier General George Wright, commander of the Department of the Pacific, this territorial government had no sanction in federal law. At this moment only the House of Representatives had approved the bill which was intended to achieve organization, and it would be many months before the fourth and definitive "Territory of Arizona" would be signed into law by President Lincoln.

Ashley Reports A Bill

On March 12, 1862, less than a month after Jefferson Davis had proclaimed the Confederate Territory of Arizona, the chairman of the House Committee on Territories, James M. Ashley, Republican of Ohio, introduced the bill (H.R. 357) which was destined to organize Arizona as a territory of the United States.[225] Ashley's measure stipulated that the new territory be separated from New Mexico by a north and south line at approximately 109° west of Greenwich, though that meridian was not specifically mentioned. The territory was to comprise "all that part of the present Territory of New Mexico situated west of a line running due south from the point where the southwest corner of the Territory of Colorado joins the northern boundary of the Territory of New Mexico. . . ."[226] A similar north and south boundary at the 108th meridian was proposed in Galusha A. Grow's bills of 1860, and the boundaries defined in the measure which Delegate John S. Watts of New Mexico introduced late in 1861 were exactly the same as in the bill which Ashley now presented.[227]

[*Library of Congress*]

JAMES M. ASHLEY
(1824–1896)

A strong supporter of the general territorial movement and friend of officers of the Sonora Mining and Exploring Company, Ashley of Ohio, chairman of the House Committee on Territories, introduced in 1862 the bill which ultimately created the definitive Territory of Arizona (H. R. 357).

The Arizona bill received the close scrutiny of the House of Representatives. On March 24 the venerable "Duke" of Kentucky, Charles A. Wickliffe, a former governor of Missouri and at one time postmaster general, joined the debate now underway. Wickliffe saw no reason to appoint civil officers in Arizona when they would be prevented from entering the proposed territory by Confederate troops.[228] Rebel occupation was denied by Ashley,[229] who apparently had not learned that Captain Sherod Hunter and his Confederate company of "Arizona Volunteers" had taken possession of Tucson on February 28. Another aspect of the bill which provoked controversy was the perennial slavery question. Unlike the territorial bills which organized Colorado, Dakota, and Nevada in 1861, the present measure expressly prohibited slavery, and this provision led Samuel S. Cox, Democrat of Ohio, to demand that consideration of the entire bill be postponed indefinitely.[230] The motion of James A. Cravens, Democrat of Indiana, to lay the Arizona bill on the table was defeated by a count of 76 to 49, but when Abram B. Olin, Republican of New York, called for an immediate decision on the main question he was refused by an equally emphatic vote.[231]

On May 8 William A. Wheeler, Republican of New York serving his first term,[232] reopened the debate as the leader of the opposition. He reminded his colleagues that when Congress organized three new territories the year before, it was considered neither necessary nor expedient to include Arizona. Then he exclaimed: "What change of circumstances may have occurred in the interim to render it now necessary, I know not." Wheeler's next remark must have surprised those members of the House who recalled the past arrival of delegates from the Gadsden Purchase bearing petitions for organization of an independent government. "So far as the records of the House throw any light upon the subject," he declared, "no single inhabitant within its proposed bounds has asked for this organization."[233] Wheeler gave the white population of the region as 2,401, in response to an inquiry by Wickliffe, who then asked leave to mention that a gentleman from Kentucky, an agent of a large mining company, had called on him in connection with the bill and stated that "renegades from the South" and Indians had driven away every white resident. The reference was clearly to Charles D. Poston, whose appeal to his fellow-Kentuckian seems to have boomeranged, for after this comment on a territory without settlers the lordly Wickliffe challenged Congress to organize such an area "if it chooses."[234]

Wheeler, continuing the assault, denied that the region ever had a permanent population, protesting that it was "the home not of those seeking to make farms and build school houses, but of the adventurous miner who seeks sudden wealth . . . to be enjoyed elsewhere." Protection of persons and property, he insisted, must come from the military, and "it matters not whether it be extended to any remaining inhabitants of Arizona, as citizens of Arizona or of New Mexico." It was the opinion of the Representative from New York that the government had never organized a territory for so small a white population. "Assuming the statement of the Delegate from New Mexico as the correct basis," he said, "there are not now one thousand whites in the whole of Arizona. We are asked to incur . . . an expenditure [of] at least $50,000. . . . Sir, a territorial government at fifty dollars per head . . . is an expense which the people of this country are just now not in a mood to indulge."[235]

When Wheeler yielded the floor, Delegate John S. Watts of New Mexico[236] rose to contradict the New Yorker's statement that not a single person within the proposed boundaries had asked for organization. He himself, Watts said, had introduced a bill to provide for the desired government; and previous administrations had agitated the question, presidents had recommended affirmative action, and for years the residents of Arizona had "petitioned and prayed and asked and knocked at the doors of Congress. . . ." But now, he added, "they have got disheartened and are almost ashamed to come back."[237] When Watts remarked that Wheeler was mistaken in his reading of the census returns, the Congressman from New York handed him the document to check for himself. Upon examination, Watts found no support for Wheeler's contention that there were too few inhabitants to warrant a separate government. The delegate declared that the official returns of 1860 showed that Arizona County, which had been created that year by the New Mexico legislature[238] and which lay within the limits of the proposed territory, had 6,462 whites, 4,040 Indians, and 21 free colored — a total of 10,523 inhabitants.[239]

When these figures were challenged by William E. Lehman, Democrat of Pennsylvania, Watts retorted that the numbers did not matter. If there was "but one solitary white man there," he should be entitled to civil law and protection. As to the question of color which had entered the debate, he brought laughter to the House when he said that "there may be a well-grounded dispute in the minds of some people as to who are white, and who are black." Watts wished to emphasize, however, that regardless of color the treaty obligations between the United States and Mexico had invested the adopted citizens of the area with all "the privileges and immunities" of citizens of the United States. There was, he said, a border of seven hundred miles facing the Mexican states of Sonora and Chihuahua, and across this line Indian hordes rode with impunity.

> ...we have not a single fort, a single soldier, or a single man with which to enforce our treaty stipulations.... Our troops have been withdrawn, and this vast frontier is opened to these ten thousand savages to plunder the citizens of Arizona and Sonora. Is there any fair and candid man, any just man, who can for a moment pretend that it is not a serious and solemn duty to extend protection to that country?[240]

Another Republican now rose to support the Arizona bill. He was the handsome John Addison Gurley of Ohio, former Universalist minister and newspaper publisher of Cincinnati,[241] who reported that more than a million dollars had been expended to open the gold and silver mines of Arizona. Was not the federal government bound by honor to protect those who went there to undertake these operations?[242] When Wheeler of New York countered that a new territorial government could not provide more effective protection than the existing one, Watts in denial pointed out that the great distances from the seat of government at Santa Fé prevented rapid communication with the mining regions. Moreover, he said, a man had to go into this country at his own risk and "run the gauntlet of ten thousand Indians" to appreciate the dangers of Arizona.

> If the outrages perpetrated on the people of that territory had been perpetrated upon the constituents of the gentleman from New York [Wheeler] or those of the gentleman from Kentucky [Wickliffe] – if one hundred and fifty or two hundred of the people of their districts had been chained to wagon wheels and burned, along with their property, or hung up by the heels and roasted to death – the eloquence of the gentleman [*sic*] would ring through this Hall and through the country until it would have nerved the hearts of the people as hearts of steel to avenge such outrages.[243]

The debate was in full swing when Watts presented an argument better calculated to impress the House. Holding in his hand a specimen of silver ore – admittedly a choice sample worth $5,000 a ton and derived from the Heintzelman Mine, one of the richest in southern Arizona – he read a letter from the director of the Philadelphia mint to Charles D. Poston, giving the results of assays of average specimens from the same mine. One of these assayed $1,600 a ton.[244] If the mineral resources of Arizona could be developed, Watts asserted, millions of

[*Department of Library and Archives, Phoenix*]

JOHN A. GURLEY
(1813–1863)

This Congressman from Ohio and former Universalist minister was a warm advocate of territorial organization for Arizona in the 37th Congress. One of Poston's "Lame Ducks," he was rewarded for his efforts by being appointed as governor of the new territory, but he died before he was able to leave for Arizona.

dollars would be added to the circulating medium. Whereas the California mines had increased the national currency by perhaps $75,000,000, Arizona was prevented from contributing her wealth because savages roamed the land. In his belief that this remote region was not sufficiently understood in Congress, Watts eulogized Arizona:

> An Italian sunset never threw its gentle rays over more lovely valleys or heaven-kissing hills, valleys harmonious with the music of a thousand sparkling rills, mountains shining with untold millions of mineral wealth, wooing the hand of capital and labor to possess and use it. The virgin rays of the morning sun first kiss the brow of its lofty mountains, and the parting beams of the setting sun linger fondly around their sublime summits, unwilling to leave the darkness and to night such beauty and such grandeur. If there be a single thought which lights up the oft times gloomy pathway of the faithful legislator, it is the sweet reflection that he has been instrumental in protecting the rights of a distant, feeble, and oppressed people against the merciless barbarities of a powerful and treacherous foe. Let it not be said of us that, while we are ready to spend untold millions of money and thousands of lives to protect our own lives and property, the appeal of this distant people falls upon our bosoms
>
> "Cold as moonbeams on the barren heath."
>
> Let it not be said of us that we have the power to conquer and annex provinces, but not to protect or defend them.[245]

When given an hour to close the debate on his bill, Ashley spoke with earnest conviction. Revealing his familiarity with the Cincinnati companies which had operated the silver mines of southern Arizona, he declared that citizens of his own state "and of my own acquaintance" had "gone into this territory with the positive assurance of the late Administration that they would be protected," but not only had they "sacrificed all their wealth invested there, but many of them have lost their lives." His information concerning Arizona, he said, had been derived from friends who had been there and from men who had called on him to urge the necessity of organization. Ashley indicated in various ways that he leaned heavily on the statements of General Samuel P. Heintzelman, former commander of Fort Yuma and the first president of the Sonora Exploring and Mining Company, whose opinions he apparently respected. He referred to the importance which earlier Democratic legislators – "men who have been regarded as statesmen" – had placed on the organization of Arizona, and he did not hesitate to mention the efforts of Senators Gwin of California, Douglas of Illinois, Green of Missouri, and Jefferson Davis of Mississippi.[246]

At one point Ashley unrolled a map to show what an immense area would be carved from New Mexico to constitute the new territory.

Here was an area "larger than Nevada, larger than Utah, larger than the State of New York, and larger than any other state in the Union except Texas." The House of Representatives, he said, had a solemn duty to pass this bill, and he warned of the great and irrevocable loss in treasure to the nation should Congress fail to organize the proposed territory.[247] Gurley then interposed that he saw a gentleman in the gallery who had spent $50,000 of his own money to develop mines in Arizona before being driven off by the Indians. If the necessary protection were provided, this gentleman and his associates could make available to the Union millions in silver.[248] To dispel any suspicion that he himself might have a personal motive in supporting the bill, Gurley made it clear that he owned "nary gold mine or silver mine in the Territory." Ashley similarly disclaimed a personal interest and spoke again of the imperative need to organize.[249]

Unimpressed by the arguments of his colleagues from Ohio, Wheeler called for the yeas and nays on the motion to postpone. It was defeated by the slender margin of 59 to 54, and the closeness of the count undoubtedly gave the advocates of the Arizona bill an uneasy moment. There was more discussion, and after a few minor amendments were accepted Cravens of Indiana, who had attempted to table the measure on March 24, again proposed this disposition of the bill. Here was the crucial test, but Cravens' motion failed decisively by a vote of 72 to 52.[250] Minutes later the House passed the bill.[251] The affirmative decision was made without recording the individual yeas and nays, because, in view of the comfortable majority who refused to table, a roll call apparently was not necessary.[252] As the political affiliations of those who determined the fate of the bill were not placed on record, it is of interest to analyze the composition of the preceding vote to lay the bill on the table. Of the fifty-two who voted for Cravens' motion, thirty were Democrats, twelve were Republicans, and ten were "Old Line" Whigs. Not a single Democrat opposed the tabling motion. Probably it will never be known whether any Democrats joined the Republican majority in acceptance of Ashley's bill on May 8, 1862. If any did, it may be surmised that this was because passage of the bill had become inevitable.

"*Bluff Ben*" *Takes Charge*

The Senate did not concur at once with the House. On June 5 four amendments were added to the Arizona bill.[253] The first of these required the governor of the proposed territory to serve *ex officio* as Superintendent of Indian Affairs without additional salary;[254] the second located the seat of government at Tucson;[255] the third stipulated that the territorial officers receive no more than three months' pay before taking up their duties within the territory; and the fourth prohibited the legislative assembly from sitting more than forty days in a single session. Spearheading the opposition was a respected and influential Republican, Lyman Trumbull of Illinois.[256] Now that Congress had the power to organize territories with a ban on slavery, Trumbull remarked, he was unwilling to create the Territory of Arizona merely to affirm this principle. He repeated the argument that there were too few inhabitants in Arizona to justify the establishment of a new territorial government.[257] Now a Democrat came to the support of the bill. Acknowledging that the population of Arizona was indeed greatly reduced, Senator James A. McDougall of California explained that thousands from his state who had gone there had been driven off by the savages.[258]

Debate was resumed on July 3 after the amended bill had been read.[259] Trumbull announced that since making his earlier estimate he had learned that there were 6,482 inhabitants in the proposed territory, but insisted that even this number was too small. It seemed to him that the purpose of the bill was to find berths for office-seekers. If there was a clear need to establish authority in Arizona, he thought it could be done by force of arms as easily without territorial officials as with them. When Trumbull moved to postpone further consideration of the bill until the next session,[260] the chairman of the Senate Committee on Territories entered the arena in its defense. He was the obdurate, courageous, and profane Benjamin Franklin Wade of Ohio, familiarly known as "Bluff Ben," a muscular man of sixty-one years with iron-gray hair and sharp eyes. A former Whig, he was now one of the leaders of the "Radical Republicans."[261] He dismissed as trifling Trumbull's contention that organization was a costly matter. Always the practical politician, Wade was not worried that new offices would be created. "If it is necessary to organize a civil government there," he said impatiently, "the fact that some persons will be appointed to office does not form a very formidable objection against the proposition." He informed the Senators that the members of his committee had made a careful study of the question, had held hearings, and were unanimously in favor of prompt legislation. He also reported that the Department of State, which had the principal jurisdiction over territorial affairs, had urged upon him the absolute necessity of securing a good government in Arizona and had strongly recommended organization.[262]

McDougall joined Wade in defense of the bill. He referred to Arizona as one of "the finest parts of the world, rich in mineral wealth, rich in agricultural resources," and reiterated that "thousands of our people who adventured their fortunes there have been driven out. That is their misfortune and the nation's loss. . . . The country which it is proposed to be organized now would be worth three times New Mexico if there was a government there." The Senator from California explained that it took a fortnight for fast riders from Santa Fé to find Tucson, and that judges of the courts of New Mexico could not travel there without escort.[263] Senator James H. Lane of Kansas now declared that his constituents had a great deal of interest in the subject under debate. He hoped that his colleagues would not be deterred by Trumbull's statement that there now were only 6,000 residents in the proposed territory. States like Missouri, Kentucky, and Virginia once had equally small populations. When Lane remarked that the people of Arizona had been driven out by the Confederates, Trumbull retorted that even before the war there were only 6,482 inhabitants in the region. "You will never settle up a Territory," Lane replied, "if you wait to get the population."[264] Despite these arguments, Trumbull's motion to postpone further consideration until the next session was passed by a vote of 25 to 13.[265]

The Arizona bill was not discussed again until the 19th of February, 1863. Senator McDougall of California, who had come to regard the organization of Arizona as of major importance, now accused his colleagues of ignorance and of unwillingness to accept advice from men who understood conditions in the West. The Senators, he said, had deliberately made themselves "blind and dumb" on the question.[266] On the 20th Senator Wade announced that the Committee on Territories had decided to withdraw the various amendments, including the one to locate the seat of government at Tucson. In view of the fact that the mining interests seemed to be establishing themselves elsewhere in the proposed territory, it was agreed to let the people of Arizona decide the location of the capital for themselves.[267] Willard Saulsbury, Democrat of Delaware, now moved to delete the antislavery clause, but his motion was denied. The Senate then proceeded to strike out all the amend-

[*National Archives*]

BENJAMIN F. WADE
(1800–1878)

This United States Senator from Ohio, as chairman of the Committee on Territories, had dominant role in piloting successful Arizona bill through the Senate. "Bluff Ben" advanced Congressman Ashley's H.R. 357, without several amendments he had hoped to make.

ments,[268] as Wade had suggested, and the formidable Senator from Ohio stood again to speak.

Wade made a strong plea for organization. Reviewing the respective populations of seven earlier territories at the time they were given independent government, he called attention to the fact that in the instance of only one of these did the inhabitants number more than 6,857. It had always been necessary to organize a territory in order to attract settlers, he said, because people hesitated to make their homes in a country "entirely unprotected by law." He pointed to the Territory of Nevada, which he believed now had more than 45,000 inhabitants, as against only 5,000 two years earlier. The question of organizing Arizona was one that had been under consideration by the committee as long as he had been a member; he had no wish to prolong the argument unduly since he believed that the bill would pass "without even a call for yeas and nays." Trumbull's continued objections seemed to irritate Wade, and he now exclaimed truculently:

> ...the richest country in the world, we are told, should not be organized so that the American people can feel safe and be under the protection of the law when they go there. The Senator thinks, because we have a civil war on our hands, we ought to give up everything.... Let me say to the Senator right here that I do not like this croaking about civil war. It certainly has not pinched the toes of the northern people much yet.... Are we to be told that we must not organize our Territories, that we must not develop our wealth, because we are involved in civil war?[269]

There was further debate on the question of population, especially as to the number of whites, and some doubt was expressed as to which Mexicans were "white" and which were not. Senator James R. Doolittle, Republican of Wisconsin, took occasion to excoriate "the traitors, the confederates, as they style themselves," who sought to organize Arizona in their own behalf, and expressed the opinion that the presence of loyal officials would discourage disloyalty.[270] At this point, however, it did not seem to matter what was being said, for the opposition to the Arizona bill apparently had collapsed. Trumbull's motion to postpone consideration of the bill indefinitely was defeated by a count of 26 to 14, and without further delay the Senate passed the bill by a vote of 25 to 12.[271] Two Democrats joined the twenty-three Republicans who voted in the affirmative; six Republicans, four Democrats, and two "Old Line" Whigs opposed. Four days later, on February 24, 1863, President Lincoln signed the statute which created the Territory of Arizona.[272]

[*Library of Congress*]

ABRAHAM LINCOLN
(1809–1865)

Photograph of Abraham Lincoln taken by Mathew B. Brady, probably shortly after the President approved the act organizing the Territory of Arizona. Lincoln and Poston were born in the same section of Kentucky, and a personal link with Poston's father-in-law, Samuel Haycraft of Elizabethtown, is indicated by the Haycraft-Lincoln correspondence.

Behind the Scenes With Poston

The organization of Arizona as a territory of the United Sttaes was not achieved solely through the exertions of legislators. Rather it was the product of a collaborative effort on the part of men both in and out of Congress. Among the individuals who early had been active in the Gadsden Purchase and were still promoting the cause of Arizona in 1862 and 1863, the pioneer Charles D. Poston was especially conspicuous. In various reminiscences Poston described his personal labors in the national capital to obtain a government for Arizona independent of the Territory of New Mexico. His manuscript journal contained short entries relating to his activities in Washington,[273] and he published more detailed accounts in the Tucson *Arizona Citizen* in 1884,[274] the Florence *Arizona Enterprise* in 1891,[275] the *Phoenix Herald* in 1893,[276] and the *Overland Monthly* in 1894.[277] There were also brief allusions in the "Christmas Lecture" which Poston delivered at Phoenix in 1895.[278]

Poston departed from Arizona early in 1859, and did not return until the autumn of 1860 when he again took over the operations of the Sonora Exploring and Mining Company.[279] He remained until the evacuation of the military posts in southern Arizona compelled him to close the mines and make his escape in the summer of 1861.[280] That fall he visited his family in Kentucky and subsequently went to Washington to promote the cause of organization. From his reminiscences it is not entirely certain when he reached the capital, for in different accounts he named the year variously as 1861, 1862, and 1863. In all probability he made visits to Washington in each of these years.

In the *Phoenix Herald* in 1893 Poston recalled that he had helped the delegate from New Mexico to draw up the Arizona bill which was eventually enacted into law, but he made no mention of the date of the bill and did not name the delegate. Poston wrote:

> In a little room on Capital [*sic*] Hill the delegate from New Mexico and myself sat at a table and drew a line of boundary dividing New Mexico into nearly equal parts by the 111th [109th] degree of longitude. He drafted a bill which soon became an act of Congress organizing "The Territory of Arizona" which was approved by President Lincoln [on the] 23rd [24th of] February, 1863.[281]

Poston was in error in assuming that the bill reported by Delegate John S. Watts of New Mexico on December 23, 1861 (H.R. 171) was the one finally passed, for it was Ashley's bill of March 12, 1862 (H.R.

357) which was enacted into law.[282] Despite Poston's misstatement there is little reason to doubt the pioneer's specific recollection, and it may be assumed that he was in Washington late in 1861 not very long after his flight from Arizona. According to his journal, Poston brought his family to New York and spent most of the year 1862 in that city.[283] That he interviewed Representatives Ashley, Gurley, and Wickliffe, as well as Delegate Watts, in Washington in the course of that year is proven by their remarks in the House during the debates on Ashley's bill.[284]

One such visit by Poston to the chairman of the House Committee on Territories early in 1862 was recorded by General Samuel P. Heintzelman in a significant entry in his diary. On February 24 Heintzelman wrote that he and Poston had gone that day to see Congressman Ashley. "He will report a bill for the Ter. of Arizona," the general noted, "with different boundaries and the Wilmot Proviso." Prepared to make concessions if necessary in the details of organization, Heintzelman added wearily: "Anything for a government."[285] The general's reference to "different boundaries" was to the north and south line at approximately the 109th meridian, which was the eastern boundary as described in the bill introduced by Ashley on March 12; the reference to the Wilmot Proviso was in anticipation of the clause banning slavery. What bearing the visit of Poston and Heintzelman on February 24 may have had on Ashley's decision to introduce his Arizona bill three weeks later is, of course, a matter of conjecture.

In the Florence newspaper in 1891 and in his magazine article in 1894 Poston told of an interview with President Lincoln, to whom he explained his mission. The President, he wrote,

> listened to my tale of woe like a martyr, and finally said, "Well, you must see Ben Wade about that." I subsequently called upon Senator Wade of Ohio, the chairman of the Committee on Territories, and repeated my story of Arizona. The bluff old Senator said, "O, yes, I have heard of that country—it is just like hell—all it lacks is water and good society." He finally consented to attend a meeting at the President's, to discuss the subject.[286]

No record has been bequeathed by Poston of his first visit to the President, but when he introduced himself or was introduced the name of his father-in-law, Samuel Haycraft, a well-known personality in Kentucky and for many years the clerk of Hardin County Court, unquestionably entered the conversation. The Haycrafts, father and son, knew Lincoln's father in Elizabethtown, the county seat, and Thomas Lincoln in fact

Private

Springfield, Ills. June 4. 1860

Hon. Saml. Haycraft.

Dear Sir.

Your second letter, dated May 31st is received— You suggest that a visit to the place of my nativity might be pleasant to me— Indeed it would— But would it be safe? Would not the people Lynch me?

The place on Knob Creek, mentioned by Mr. Read, I remember very well; but I was not born there— As my parents have told me, I was born on Nolin very much nearer Hodgin's-Mill than the Knob Creek place is— My earliest recollection, however, is of the Knob Creek place—

Like yourself I belonged to the Whig party from its origin to its close— I never belonged to the American party organization; nor ever to a party called a Union party; though I hope I neither am, or ever have been, less devoted to the Union than yourself, or any other patriotic man. It may not be altogether without interest to let you know that my wife is a daughter of the late Robert S. Todd, of Lexington Ky– and that a half sister of hers is the wife of Ben. Hardin Helm, born and raised at your town, but residing at Louisville now, as I believe.

Yours very truly
A. Lincoln.

[*Henry E. Huntington Library, San Marino*]

This is one of the letters exchanged by Lincoln and Samuel Haycraft, the father-in-law of Charles D. Poston. Lincoln's casual remark about being lynched was misrepresented in a newspaper and caused him much embarrassment. Fearing that the adverse publicity might have disturbed Haycraft, the future President later sent his regrets. Ben Hardin Helm was the future Confederate general who died of wounds received at the Battle of Chicamauga in September, 1863. Although Lincoln did not know it when he wrote this letter, Helm was a cousin of Mrs. Haycraft.

was employed for a time by the senior Haycraft.[287] Lincoln's family moved away from Kentucky in 1816 when Abe was seven, and this may be the reason why Samuel Haycraft had never met him. On the other hand, the two men became well acquainted in 1860 through a notable exchange of letters.[288] A further basis for rapport between Poston and Lincoln could have been the fact that a half-sister of Lincoln's wife was married to the Confederate general, Ben Hardin Helm, a native of Elizabethtown, and Poston's mother-in-law, Mrs. Haycraft, was of the Helm family.[289] It is certain, in any case, that Poston's admiration for the President was unbounded,[290] and he frequently expressed it with fervor and eloquence.[291]

[*Library of Congress*]

This elaborate inkstand, fashioned by Tiffany from silver mined in Arizona, was Charles D. Poston's gift to Abraham Lincoln in gratitude for his friendship to the cause of the Territory. The President's name was engraved on one panel and Poston's name on the opposite side.

The Oyster Supper and The Lame Ducks

It has become traditional to apply the name of "Father of Arizona" to Charles D. Poston. The appraisal of his personal exertions which inspired this designation rests principally upon his own story of "wire-pulling" in Washington at the time the successful bill was under consideration in Congress. This story, which doubtless was embellished by Poston in numerous private conversations, has been repeated often in print and has not been seriously challenged.[292] The familiar account of Poston's maneuvers in Washington was first published in the Tucson *Citizen* in April, 1884, thirty years after his first venture into the Gadsden Purchase[293] and twenty-one years after the creation of the Territory of Arizona. In an article entitled "SCRAPS OF HISTORY FURNISHED BY ONE WHO HELPED TO MAKE THE SCRAPS," Poston told the amusing story of the "lame ducks" and the famous "oyster supper." This is the pertinent passage:

> At the meeting of Congress in December 1862, I returned to Washington, made friends with Lincoln, and proposed the organization of the Territory of Arizona.... There was no other person in Washington (save General Heintzelman) who took any interest in Arizona affairs, they had something else to occupy their attention, and did not know where Arizona was.
>
> Old Ben Wade, the chairman of the Senate Committee on Territories, took a lively and bold interest in the organization of the Territory, and Ashley, the chairman of the Committee in the House, told me how to accomplish the object. He said there were a number of members of the expiring Congress who wanted to go West, and offer their political services to the "galoots," and if they could be grouped, and a satisfactory slate made, they would have influence enough to carry the bill through Congress. Consequently an "oyster supper" was organized to which the "lame ducks" were invited, and there and then the slate was made and the territory virtually organized.
>
> Gourley [Gurley] of Ohio (Lincoln man), was to be Governor; Goodwin of Maine (Blaine man), was to be Chief Justice; Allyn of Connecticut (Secretary Welles' man), was to be Associate Justice; Turner of Iowa (Senator Grymes' [Grimes'] man), was to be Associate Justice; McCormick of New York (Senator Morgan's man), was to be Secretary of the Territory and prospective Premier; Bashford (Wisconsin man), was to be Surveyor General; Duffield (Senator Pomeroy's man), was to be United States Marshal, to represent the African element.
>
> So the slate was made and the bargain concluded, but towards the last it occurred to my obfusticated [*sic*] brain that my name did not appear on the slate, and in the language of Daniel Webster, I exclaimed, "Gentlemen, what is to become of me?" Gourley [*sic*] politely replied, "O! We will make you Indian agent."

> So the bill passed and Lincoln signed all the commissions, and the oyster supper was paid for and we were all happy, and Arizona was launched upon the political sea under command of as
>
> "Mild mannered men
> As ever cut a throat or scuttled a ship."[294]

Upon analysis, Poston's account of 1884 is found to contain some interesting discrepancies. At the time of the "oyster supper" the territorial contest was being waged in the Senate and not in the House, which had passed the Arizona bill the previous May. While there is little reason to question that Representative Ashley, to whom Poston referred as his "political guardian,"[295] had advised him to court the "lame ducks," it is very doubtful that their help was of decisive importance. Five of the territorial appointees named — Joseph P. Allyn, William F. Turner, Richard C. McCormick, Levi Bashford, and Milton B. Duffield — were not themselves members of Congress; nor were their sponsors, as named by Poston, in any sense "lame ducks." Edwin D. Morgan did not take his seat as Senator from New York until March 4, 1863 — two weeks after the bill had passed the Senate. It is possible of course that even at an earlier date Morgan, in the capacity of Senator-elect, was in a position to campaign in behalf of McCormick.[296] Since only two "lame ducks" were involved in any way in these negotiations — Representatives John A. Gurley of Ohio and John N. Goodwin —[297] and only one, Gurley, was a vocal advocate of the territorial bill, it is evident that Poston greatly exaggerated this aspect of the subject. As for the listing of "Turner of Iowa (Senator Grymes' man)" among those who presumably were present or discussed at the "oyster supper," it is possible that Senator James W. Grimes of Iowa — one of the six Republicans who voted against the Arizona bill — may have had a hand in this appointment. But Poston's memory was at fault here, for William F. Turner was not nominated for a post in the territorial supreme court until after the death of Gurley, Lincoln's first gubernatorial appointee, in August of 1863.[298] At that time John N. Goodwin was named as governor, and Turner was appointed in Goodwin's place as chief justice.[299] Poston also had forgotten that Levi Bashford was not at once named to the post of surveyor-general, for John N. Francis was nominated for this office by the President on March 7, 1863, and rejected by the Senate four days later.[300] Before Bashford was appointed, moreover, Poston signed his name in March to a letter recommending Colonel Alfred W. Gilbert, who failed to be nominated.[301]

However misleading may be some features of Poston's story of "wire-pulling," it is altogether fitting to applaud the sentiment expressed in a statement which Senator Wade added to a letter recommending Poston for appointment as Superintendent of Indian Affairs in the new territory. This letter, apparently composed on the very day that President Lincoln approved the organic act, was signed by General Heintzelman, William Wrightson, Gurley, and Delegate John S. Watts of New Mexico. Below these names Wade wrote: "I cordially indorse [*sic*] the above and hope Mr. Poston may receive the appointment as an acknowledgment for his long and faithful services in the Territory."[302] Yet, in giving recognition to the highly significant exertions of Poston in behalf of organization, the earlier activities of Sylvester Mowry[303] and the devoted efforts of the legislators should likewise be remembered – and the notable labors of Samuel P. Heintzelman and William Wrightson not underestimated. It is especially the role of the general that has been insufficiently understood and appreciated.

Another Father of Arizona?

Although Poston made mention of General Heintzelman in the newspaper article of 1884, the soldier was not given the credit he richly deserved for his work in behalf of Arizona. It is true that an exhaustive examination of all the writings of Poston discloses a somewhat more equitable recognition of the participation of both Heintzelman and Wrightson than in the passage most often quoted. In 1880, for example, Poston noted that William Wrightson "exercised great influence in getting the territorial organization of 1863 passed through Congress and approved by the President, without, however, claiming any official reward for his great and acknowledged public services."[304] Poston's most explicit statement concerning Heintzelman – one which also mentions Wrightson – was made in 1892:

> At the breaking out of the civil war in 1861 I went to Washington and remained in that vicinity until 1863, when the chances seemed favorable for the organization of a civil government for Arizona. General Heintzelman and William Wrightson were the only people in Washington who had ever been in Arizona, capable of rendering any assistance, and they did so nobly.[305]

This reference is in sharp contrast, however, to the ungenerous declaration which Poston made in 1893: "It is thirty-three years this winter since I went to Washington *unaided and alone* [emphasis added] endeavoring to get the government to organize a civil government for Arizona. . . ."[306]

Heintzelman died in Washington, D.C., on May 1, 1880, at the age of seventy-four. Of all the men who played a part in the creation of the Territory of Arizona, it may be truly said that none desired organization more fervently than the founder of Fort Yuma, distinguished Regular Army officer, and Civil War major general of volunteers.[307] As one of the principal promoters of the Sonora Exploring and Mining Company in 1856 and its first president,[308] Heintzelman was vitally interested in Arizona — and especially so because much of his life's savings was invested in its mines. A little known fact is that Poston failed in his efforts to obtain financial support in the East in 1855 and 1856, and it was Heintzelman who arranged meetings with the editors of the *Railroad Record,* William and Thomas Wrightson, and other Cincinnati investors. It was this intervention that led to the formation of the company which played so prominent a role in the early history of the Gadsden Purchase. The entries in Heintzelman's diary disclose the extent of his exertions in 1862 and 1863 in the cause of territorial organization. While Poston's journal is sketchy, with many of the entries made long after the events recorded, the daybook kept by Heintzelman is detailed and far more revealing. His meetings and correspondence with men in public life and with members of the mining company — and more especially his association with Mowry, Poston, and the Wrightsons — are treated fully but without embellishment. Whatever Heintzelman's journal may lack in literary luster is more than compensated for by the precise information it supplies.

In the account which Poston published in 1884 he stated that he arrived in Washington in December, 1862, and indeed he may have, though Heintzelman made no mention of him during that month. On the 21st, however, the general wrote to William Wrightson, then in Cincinnati, urging him to come to the capital and lend his influence in behalf of the Arizona bill.[309] During the month of January, 1863, Heintzelman was occupied with military duties and with efforts to have his son Charles admitted to the military academy at West Point,[310] but on February 3 Representative and Mrs. Gurley spent the evening with the Heintzelmans. The talk began with the war and ended with the silver mines of Arizona.[311] On the 8th the Ohio Congressman called again and examined Heintzelman's silver specimens.[312] "We are making an effort to have the bill pass for a Govt. for Arizona," the general noted in his journal on February 10. That evening he went to the National Hotel to call on Senator Wade and Senator James Harlan of Iowa, a friend of the President, and there saw also Senator Morton S. Wilkinson of Minnesota; later the general and his wife called at the White House and had a "pleasant visit" with Mrs. Lincoln.[313] On the 14th Heintzelman and Poston accompanied Gurley to see Senator Lyman Trumbull, the principal opponent of the bill, and the same evening Heintzelman visited Senators Ira Harris of New York and Henry S. Lane of Indiana, who gave assurances that they would vote in the affirmative.[314] On the night of February 15 the general, together with Poston and Gurley, called again to see Senator Wade, who now promised to bring up the bill when the moment was auspicious. Heintzelman was sanguine, and in a revealing passage he confided to his journal: "After the bill has passed I hope we will be able to sell out [the mines] on favorable terms."[315]

William Wrightson arrived in Washington on February 16. That evening Heintzelman went to the capitol to see the Senators from Michigan, Zachariah Chandler and Jacob M. Howard, both of whom promised to support the bill. "I have invited a party to dinner tomorrow," Heintzelman wrote, "to talk Arizona."[316] Various entries in his journal reveal that the general was extremely fond of oysters and seldom missed an opportunity to partake of them wherever he happened to be. There is little doubt that the historic "oyster supper" took place on February 17 with Heintzelman as host, for his entry under that date is explicit:

> I had an Arizona dinner party – Mr. Gurley of the House, Col. Cross and Poston, Wrightson, Jarvis and Lathrop, and Col. Puleston. All interested or desiring to be. It passed off quite pleasantly.[317]

The following day it rained and the streets were a sea of mud. Heintzelman met Wrightson and Poston and together they went to Gurley's room.[318] Two days later, on February 20, Poston called on Heintzelman to report that the Senate had just passed the Arizona bill "near two to one."[319] It was planned the next day for Heintzelman, Poston, and Wrightson to accompany Senator Wade to the White House to request the President "to put the Arizona Government in motion as soon as possible,"[320] and on the 24th Lincoln signed the document which brought to a successful conclusion Arizona's long struggle to achieve territorial status.[321]

We then called & saw Col. Pulaski who is quite taken with Arizona. After the bill has passed I hope we will be able to sell out on favourable terms.

Washington Feb. 16. 1863.

Beautiful day. Went to the funeral of Gen. Custin [illegible] child.

Mr. Wrightson has arrived. I have invited a party to dinner tomorrow to talk Arizona.

After dark went to see Sen. Chandler & Howard. Dr. Summers & family were here & he wanted me to see Howard about his confirmation. I met Mr. Clark the executive clerk of the Senate & he told me the Senate was in session so I went to the Capitol & saw both there. Both promised favourably as to the Doctor & the Arizona bill. Col. Lathrop came up & we stopped & saw Col. Forney.

On our way back we called on Mr & Mrs Mann. I had agreed to go to Mr. Corcorans with him. He did not come till after 11 P.M. I went into the room with Mrs. Heintz. It was not a large party. The house of Corcoran is a fine one the dancing was in the picture gallery. I got home at 2 a.m.

Tues. Feb. 17. 1863.

When I got up this morning we had considerable snow on the ground & it continued steadily most of the day.

At 12 M. I went to the Capitol to

appear before the Sen. committee on the Conduct of the War. I found Gen. Sumner there & waited half an hour. I then had a long examination, lasting from 1½ P.M. till 4½ P.M. — on the Peninsular campaign. From the questions they asked they have a very good idea of the operations. They however forgot some very important ones. They were a little surprised that Gen. McClellan did not more consult with me & at his absence from the battlefields. They had heard that he was on board the Galena, whilst the battle was progressing.

I learned from them, what expedition Gen. Franklin sent Newton & Cochran to see the President about & which he countermanded after it had gone twenty miles. It was a grand cavalry raid & could not have failed to cut all the rail communications. Our cavalry would have brought up at Suffolk. What an unfortunate interference! The risk was nothing to the promised advantages.

I had an Arizona dinner party — Mr. Gurley of the House, Cols. Brown & Poston — Wrightson Jarvis & Lathrop & Col. Robertson. All interested or desiring to be. It passed off quite pleasantly.

[Library of Congress]

Pages from Heintzelman's Journal. Significant passages are indicated by arrows.

[*Brady Collection, National Archives*]

SAMUEL P. HEINTZELMAN
(1805–1880)

This distinguished army officer was the founder of Fort Yuma and the first president of the Sonora Exploring and Mining Company, which pioneered silver mining in the Gadsden Purchase. Like Charles D. Poston, he was one of the principal sponsors of territorial organization for Arizona.

In Brief Review

In an elegant suite in Mexico City on December 30, 1853, the American diplomat James Gadsden signed the treaty which brought under the jurisdiction of the United States a vast domain in the Southwest. On a windswept plateau in Arizona on the 29th of December, 1863 – a decade later almost to the day – the civil authority of the federal government was finally proclaimed over the soil of a new territory[322] which included within its limits ninety-two percent of the 29,670 square miles of the Gadsden Purchase.[323] Through the intervening years many earnest men – among them soldiers, entrepreneurs, investors, members of Congress, cabinet officers, and even Presidents of the United States – contributed in diverse ways to the creation of the Territory of Arizona. In summary, it may be said that the motives which animated the advocates of Arizona were varied and complex. Early settlers of the Gadsden Purchase, isolated and desperately afraid of the savage Apache, desired military and judicial protection for the peaceful pursuit of their sundry occupations. Southern statesmen dreamed of the sectional advantages of a southwestern railway to the Pacific. Young Lieutenant Mowry, afire with ambition, envisaged a rich mineral and agricultural country and coveted a position of prestige in its affairs, but the slavery controversy frustrated his hopes just as it defeated every effort to organize any new territory between 1854 and 1861. Promoters like Poston, Heintzelman, and Wrightson were motivated largely by their financial stake in mining, though in Poston's case there were also other considerations. Office seekers exerted a certain amount of influence, but in the conclusive deliberations of 1862 and 1863 the prospect of adding the gold and silver of Arizona to the war chest of the Union was the most effective argument in shaping the decision of the legislators; and it was the masterly captainship of the committee chairmen, Representative Ashley and Senator Wade, which piloted the Arizona bill to succcessful passage in both houses of Congress. Among the southwestern pioneers who championed the cause of organization for Arizona, the figure of Charles D. Poston continues to occupy a place of prominence and high importance. Yet throughout the drama, and especially in the closing scenes, the "Father of Arizona" received substantial support from the spirited and insufficiently acknowledged efforts of others, pre-eminent among whom, as the new findings demonstrate, was Samuel P. Heintzelman.

A postscript may be added concerning the fate of the four special friends of Arizona. Sylvester Mowry, who aspired to wealth and a place of vantage under the Arizona sun, was discredited during the Civil War, failed to regain his former acclaim, and died in London when not yet forty.[324] William Wrightson, intelligent and amiable, sought happiness more than fame, but was brutally murdered by Chiricahua Apaches belonging to the band of Cochise. Samuel Peter Heintzelman, who desired comfort and security for his family, lost his investment in the mining company he had helped to found; and Charles Debrille Poston, who never ceased to promote Arizona and who craved admiration as much as affluence and position, died years later in squalid poverty, a frustrated and embittered man.[325] In a sense, then, each of the four lost his individual battle. But there was a winner — it was Arizona.

NOTES *for* PART TWO

[181] For an analysis of the situation at this time in Santa Fe, see L. M. Ganaway, *New Mexico and the Sectional Controversy, 1846–1861* (U. of New Mexico Press, 1944), ch. 4.

[182] Jackson to Orlando Davis, February 17, 1861, John T. Pickett Papers, Box 108A, Library of Congress, as given in Martin H. Hall, *Sibley's New Mexico Campaign* (U. of Texas Press, 1960), 13–16. A month after the bombardment of Fort Sumter, a Santa Fe editor emphasized that New Mexico wished to remain neutral. The Territory, he said, was represented both as belonging to the North and as naturally allied with the interests of the South, but the truth was that "New Mexico desires to be let alone.... In her own good time she will say her say, and choose for herself the position she wishes to occupy...." *Santa-Fe Gazette,* May 11, 1861.

[183] Ernest W. Winkler (ed.), *Journal of the Secession Convention of Texas, 1861* (Austin: Texas State Library, 1912), 87–88.

[184] On May 8, 1856, while serving as a member of the House from California, Herbert shot and killed a waiter after a trifling argument in the dining room of Willard's Hotel in Washington. He was acquitted, but the episode ended his career in California. See Aurora Hunt, *Major General James Henry Carleton, Western Frontier Dragoon* (Glendale: Arthur H. Clark, 1958), 257–59; and Walter Noble Burns, *Robin Hood of Eldorado* (New York, 1932), 285. For Herbert's Confederate military service, see *The War of the Rebellion: A Compilation of the Official Records of the Union and Confederate Armies* (128 vols., Washington, 1880–1901), Series 1, XV, 678; XXXIV, pt. 1, 515 and pt. 2, 910, 1063. Cited hereafter as *O.R.* with all citations to Series 1. His service record and the muster rolls of Herbert's Battalion of Arizona Cavalry, also known as Herbert's Battalion of Arizona Mounted Volunteers and as the First Texas Arizona Battalion of Mounted Rifles, are in War Department Collection of Confederate Records, RG 109, National Archives. Cited hereafter as Confederate Records.

[185] *Journal of the Secession Convention of Texas,* 67.

[186] *Mesilla Times,* February 23, 1861.

[187] Letter of February 26 from El Paso, *ibid.,* March 2, 1861.

[188] Letter of February 28, 1861, *ibid.*

[189] *Supra,* pt. 1, 10.

[190] A native of Virginia, Samuel John Jones removed to the Missouri frontier in the early 1850s and soon displayed his violent nature in the sectional strife which beset "bleeding Kansas." Typical of his behavior was his participation in an election at Bloomington, Kansas, on March 30, 1855, while he was postmaster of Westport, Missouri. Early that morning five or six hundred Missourians arrived at Bloomington on horseback, in carriages, and in wagons. When two of the three election judges refused to permit the Missourians to vote without swearing to their residence, a boisterous group led by Jones rushed in with cocked pistols and bowie knives. Jones, with watch in hand, gave the judges five minutes to resign, and later threatened the two newly chosen judges with death if the Missourians were not permitted to vote. See J. N. Holloway, *History of Kansas* (Lafayette, Indiana, 1868), 144–46. Jones soon was made sheriff of Douglas County, Kansas, and became notorious for his actions in the Wakarusa War and the sacking of Lawrence. A staunch Democrat, he was appointed in 1858 as collector of customs for the District of Paso del Norte and as such had jurisdiction in New Mexico; but on July 12, 1860, he forwarded to Washington his resignation as collector to take effect at the end of President Buchanan's term if Lincoln, Douglas, or Bell were elected in November. On September 22, 1860, he was appointed sutler at Fort Fillmore and

even before war was declared he was in communication with key men of Southern origin and sympathy. Late in 1861 Jones served briefly as acting civil governor of the Confederate Territory of Arizona and was recommended by Granville H. Oury for the governorship, but Jefferson Davis confirmed John R. Baylor in this office and appointed Jones as marshal of the territory. After the departure of Confederate troops in 1862 he was twice placed in custody by federal military authorities, but each time was released after taking the oath of allegiance to the Union. His subsequent activities included contracting for the government, mining, and farming, and he developed a local reputation as an apple grower. According to a personal communication to the author from Mrs. J. Paul Taylor of Mesilla, New Mexico, the gentlemanly Virginian with whom the people of Mesilla were familiar in his mature years could scarcely be recognized as the fiery sheriff who had earned a reputation for violence in Kansas. In 1873 Jones became paralyzed and died ten years later. A biographical study is in preparation by the author.

[191] Advertisements of this partnership appeared in the *Mesilla Times,* June 8 and December 19, 1861.

[192] *Ibid.,* March 23, 1861; and "Report of Mesilla Convention" in *O.R.,* IV, 39.

[193] These papers are in Confederate Records. They were presented to the Confederate Congress on April 29, 1861, and referred to the Committee on Territories. *Journal of the Congress of the Confederate States of America, 1861–1865* (7 vols., Sen. Doc. 234, 58 Cong., 2 Sess., Serials 4610–4616), I, 159. Titles of the individual volumes vary. The first volume of this set carries the title *Journal of the Provisional Congress of the Confederate States of America.*

[194] *Supra,* pt. 1, 11. See the sketch on Aldrich in Frank C. Lockwood, *Life in Old Tucson, 1854–1864* (Tucson: Tucson Civic Committee, 1943), 16–23. Further data are in his biographical file at APHS.

[195] *Mesilla Times,* March 30, 1861.

[196] Captain Frazer's military service record and the muster rolls of his company are in Confederate Records. The members of the company are listed in Hall, *Sibley's New Mexico Campaign,* 324–25.

[197] *Mesilla Times,* May 17 [18], 1861.

[198] Loring, a veteran of more than twenty-five years in the Army, had gained his reputation in the Mexican War as leader of the newly organized Regiment of Mounted Riflemen. In the spring of 1861 Lieutenant John V. DuBois confided to his diary that he doubted Loring's loyalty to the Union, and other officers shared this view. See George P. Hammond (ed.), *Campaigns in the West, 1856–1861: The Journal and Letters of Colonel John Van Deusen DuBois* (Tucson: Arizona Pioneers' Historical Society, 1949), 111. After service in the Confederate armies as a brigadier and major general, Loring spent ten years in Egypt in the army of the khedive as general of brigade.

[199] The order to Lynde was dated June 16, but Canby did not formally assume command until June 23.

[200] In pursuance of special orders from Washington under date of May 17, 1861, instructions were issued from Santa Fe on June 14 for a march of the two companies of dragoons from Fort Breckenridge southward to Fort Buchanan. On June 30 the dragoons, together with the companies of the 7th Infantry at Fort Buchanan, were ordered to march to the Rio Grande. Special Orders No. 85 and No. 97, Headquarters, Department of New Mexico, Santa Fe, June 14 and 30, 1861, Adjutant General's Records. Lieutenants Isaiah N. Moore and R. S. C. Lord were instructed to remove the remaining supplies and destroy the posts. Forts Breckenridge and Buchanan were burned on July 10 and July 23, 1861, respectively. When information was received by Moore that Fort Fillmore also had been evacuated, the troops were re-routed to Fort Craig where they arrived on or about August 10. The Confederate commander, Lieutenant Colonel John R. Baylor, and Brigadier General Albert Sidney Johnston, who joined him briefly at Mesilla, were chagrined at their failure to capture these troops and the valuable public property which they carried. See Martin H. Hall, "Albert Sidney Johnston's First Confederate Command," *McNeese Review* (McNeese State College, Lake Charles, La.), XIII (1962), 3–12. A detailed study of the evacuation of the posts in southern Arizona will be found in a history of Fort Buchanan now in preparation by the

author in collaboration with Ray Brandes. Fort Breckenridge was named in honor of Buchanan's vice president, John C. Breckinridge, but in contemporary military reports was generally spelled "Breckenridge."

[201] Raphael Pumpelly, *My Reminiscences* (2 vols., New York: Holt, 1918), I, 222 *et seq.*

[202] Poston's letter of August 18, 1861, was published at Cincinnati in the *Railroad Record,* IX (October 3, 1861), 425–26. For excerpts see B. Sacks, *Charles Debrille Poston: Prince of Arizona Pioneers* (Smoke Signal No. 7, Tucson Westerners, Spring 1963), 7.

[203] A review of the reasons is in Charles S. Walker, Jr. "Causes of the Confederate Invasion of New Mexico," *New Mexico Historical Review,* VIII (April 1933), 76–96.

[204] For biographical data on Baylor, together with selected references, see *Handbook of Texas,* I, 124, and W. A. Keleher, *Turmoil in New Mexico, 1846–1868* (Santa Fe: Rydal Press, 1952), 195–96, note 7.

[205] For further details see Martin H. Hall, "The Skirmish at Mesilla," *Arizona and the West,* I (Winter 1959), 343–51, and Martin L. Crimmins, "Fort Fillmore," *New Mexico Historical Review,* VI (October 1931), 327–33. The primary accounts are in *Mesilla Times,* July 27, 1861, and *O.R.,* IV, 4–15. In 1878 a Union officer, Assistant Surgeon J. Cooper McKee, wrote his *Narrative of the Surrender of a Command of U.S. Forces at Fort Fillmore, New Mexico,* and published it privately in Prescott. This pamphlet of fifteen pages, which is highly critical of Major Lynde, has recently been reprinted by the Stagecoach Press, Houston. On November 25, 1861, Lynde was dropped from the rolls of the Union army "for abandoning his post . . . and subsequently surrendering his command to an inferior force of insurgents." Lynde worked diligently to have his rank restored, and in an act of mercy in 1866 General Grant requested that Lynde be reinstated and immediately retired. This was done on President Johnson's order of November 27 of that year. Keleher, *Turmoil in New Mexico,* 198, note 16.

[206] *O.R.,* IV, 20–22. A copy of the printed proclamation is in Confederate Records. The literature on Baylor's government includes specialized articles by Charles S. Walker, Jr., "Confederate Government in Doña Ana County," *New Mexico Historical Review,* VI (July 1931), 253–302, and F. S. Donnell, "The Confederate Territory of Arizona," *ibid.,* XVII (April 1942), 148–63.

[207] *Supra,* pt. 1, 35–36. An important biographical source is C. C. Smith's typescript "History of the Oury Family" in APHS. Oury's election on August 5 was reported in the Tucson *Arizonian* on August 10, 1861. A photostat of this rare issue is in the author's possession; copies of the photostat are in APHS and the University of Arizona Library. Excerpts from the August 10 issue of the *Arizonian* appeared in the San Francisco *Daily Alta California* on September 2, 1861.

[208] *Journal of the Congress of the Confederate States,* I, 475.

[209] *Ibid.,* 585.

[210] *Ibid.,* 613.

[211] *Ibid.,* 620. A manuscript copy of the bill is in Entry 163, No. 151, Confederate Records.

[212] *Journal of the Congress of the Confederate States,* I, 635.

[213] *Ibid.,* 660–61.

[214] *Ibid.,* 691.

[215] For a brief discussion of the legalities of organization, see Robert L. Rodgers, "The Confederate States Organized Arizona in 1862," *Southern Historical Society Papers,* XXXVIII (1900), 222–27.

[216] The text of the act to organize the Territory of Arizona, as approved on January 18, 1862, is in James M. Matthews (ed.), *The Statutes at Large of the Provisional Government of the Confederate States of America. . . .* (Richmond, 1864), 242–47.

[217] *Journal of the Congress of the Confederate States,* I, 701.

[218] *Journal of the House of Representatives of the First Congress of the Confederate States of America* (Senate Doc. 234, 58 Cong., 2 Sess., Serial 4614), V, 80. MacWillie was

apparently one of the more intelligent and influential citizens of Mesilla Valley. Before his appointment as attorney general by Baylor, he had served in Doctor Owings' government as district judge and as chief justice. The *Mesilla Times* of October 18, 1860, gave an account of his speech to miners at the gold camp of "Pino Alto" on September 30, 1860, in which he lauded the provisional government that the California newspapers reported to have failed. Hayes' Scraps, Arizona, V, 286. Baylor called for a second election for delegate and on December 30, 1861, MacWillie was chosen in Oury's place. *Mesilla Times,* January 1 [2], 1862. In order to insure MacWillie's election, Baylor caused letters to be dispatched over his own signature to the justices of the peace of the various precincts to instruct them how to vote. One such letter has been preserved. Dated at Mesilla on December 28, it was written in Spanish to the justice of the peace of the precinct of Amoles, who was informed of the urgent necessity of choosing a delegate who would protect the interests of the territory. The person best suited to fill the position, said Baylor, was MacWillie. Oury's friends resented this maneuver and refused to vote, viewing the election as illegal because due notice had not been given. Baylor's arbitrary action had the effect of disfranchising the residents of a large part of the territory. Smith, "Some Unpublished History," *Arizona Historical Review,* IV, 25. Whether the fatal shooting earlier in December of Robert P. Kelley, the principal owner of the *Mesilla Times,* had some connection with Baylor's endorsement of the attorney general is debatable. The paper had been critical of Baylor in its columns. See Martin H. Hall, "The Baylor-Kelley Fight: A Civil War Incident in Old Mesilla," *Password,* V (July 1960), 83–90; and Nona Barrick and Mary H. Taylor, "Murder in Mesilla," *New Mexico Magazine,* XXXVIII (November 1960), 3–5, 34. See also *Mesilla Times,* December 19, 1861, and January 1 [2], 1862.

219 No attempt need be made here to recount in detail the military adventures of the Confederates and their Union antagonists in the Southwest during the early months of 1862. The literature is abundant. The most extensive treatment will be found in Hall's thorough study, *Sibley's New Mexico Campaign,* but see also Robert L. Kerby, *The Confederate Invasion of New Mexico and Arizona, 1861–1862* (Los Angeles: Westernlore Press, 1958) and Ray C. Colton, *The Civil War in the Western Territories* (U. of Oklahoma Press, 1959). Important particulars are in Keleher's *Turmoil in New Mexico* and in Aurora Hunt, *The Army of the Pacific* (Glendale: Arthur H. Clark, 1951). See also Miss Hunt's *James Henry Carleton, Western Frontier Dragoon* and Max L. Heymann, *Prudent Soldier: A Biography of Major General Edward R. S. Canby* (Glendale: Arthur H. Clark, 1959). Among useful older articles are A. A. Hayes, "The New Mexican Campaign of 1862," *Magazine of American History,* February 1886, 171–84, and Ralph E. Twitchell, "The Confederate Invasion of New Mexico," *Old Santa Fe,* III (January 1916), 5–43. Among the recent are Rufus K. Wyllys, "Arizona and the Civil War," *Arizona Highways,* XXVII (January 1951), 34–39; William I. Waldrip, "New Mexico during the Civil War," *New Mexico Historical Review,* XXVIII (October 1953), 251–90; and a survey in three parts entitled "War in the Southwestern Desert," *Montana: The Magazine of Western History,* XII (Spring 1962), 12–34. For a convenient introduction to the whole subject, see James Lee Neeley, *The Desert Dream of the South* (Smoke Signal No. 4, Tucson Westerners, Fall 1961).

220 For particulars see J. F. Santee, "The Battle of La Glorieta Pass," *New Mexico Historical Review,* VI (January 1931), 66–75.

221 For particulars see Martin H. Hall, "The Skirmish at Picacho," *Civil War History,* IV (March 1958), 27–36. More recent studies by the author disprove the statement by Bancroft and subsequent writers that the Confederate picket at Picacho Pass was under the command of Lieutenant John W. Swilling. These findings were incorporated in a paper, "Jack Swilling: The Tarnished Hero," read by Mark Shields at the Fourth Annual Arizona Historical Convention, March 15, 1963.

222 It is a matter of record, however, that the agile M. H. MacWillie was able to retain his seat in the Confederate Congress until the end of the Civil War. On January 8, 1864, he introduced a bill (H.R. 124) to amend the act which had organized the Territory of Arizona in 1862. MacWillie's measure was passed by the House on February 12, concurred in by the Senate, and approved by President Davis. Since the amending act called for the present delegate to continue in office until a new one was elected and qualified, and since a successor could scarcely be chosen as long as the Gadsden Purchase was in Union control, MacWillie

had found a way to represent the nonexistent Confederate Territory of Arizona as delegate for the life of the Confederate Congress. See *Journal of the House of Representatives of the First Congress of the Confederate States,* V, 802, 825, 851. The act is printed in James M. Matthews (ed.), *Public Laws of the Confederate States of America Passed at the Fourth Session of the First Congress, 1863–1864* (Richmond, 1864), 191. Other officials of the Confederate Territory also managed to continue in office. A voucher in the National Archives shows that as late as 1864 the former private secretary of President Davis, Robert Josselyn, submitted an account as "Secretary and Acting Governor and Indian Commissioner of Arizona Territory" for $500, "worth in the old issue $750," which was his salary for the quarter ending June 30 of that year. The attorney general of the Confederate government decided that Josselyn was entitled to a salary as territorial secretary but not as governor, and the amount was correspondingly reduced. Despite this ruling Josselyn signed a receipt for the original sum. These documents are in the "Arizona" bundle in Records of the Treasury Department.

[223] *Supra,* pt. 1, 35–40.

[224] The text of Carleton's proclamation appears in *O.R.,* L, pt. 1, 96–97. A copy of the printed original is filed in Enclosure A, Letters Received, 334N – 1863, Adjutant General's Records. A manuscript copy was enclosed in Carleton's letter of June 10, 1862, to R. C. Drum, assistant adjutant general of the Department of the Pacific, which is preserved in Letters Received, Department of the Pacific, C137 – 1862, Records of Army Commands. An unusual provision was the flexibility of certain of the boundaries of this third "Territory of Arizona." It was to comprise "within its limits all the country eastward from the Colorado river, which is now occupied by the forces of the United States known as 'The Column from California;' and, as the flag of the United States shall be carried by this column still farther eastward, these limits will extend in that direction until they reach the farthest geographical boundary of this Territory." Inasmuch as the successive areas of occupation would determine the eastern boundary, it could be assumed in accordance with this definition that El Paso, Texas, fell within the geographical limits of the Territory of Arizona at a time when the headquarters of the military department of Arizona were in Franklin, an early name for El Paso. See William J. Glasgow, "On the Confusion Caused by the Name of El Paso," *Password,* I (May 1956), 65–67, and Rex W. Strickland, "Six Who Came to El Paso," *Southwestern Studies,* I (Fall 1963), 7–8.

[225] *Cong. Globe,* 37 Cong., 2 Sess., 1193. James Mitchell Ashley (1824-1896) had a varied career. A native of Pennsylvania, he taught himself the elementary subjects while serving as a clerk on boats on the Ohio and the Mississippi. As a young man he edited newspapers in Portsmouth, Ohio, and in 1849 was admitted to the bar but never practiced. After engaging in the wholesale drug business in Toledo, Ohio, he was elected to the House in 1859 for the first of five terms. An unsuccessful candidate in 1868, he was appointed the next year to the governorship of the Territory of Montana by President Grant, but his tenure was brief. Later he constructed the Toledo, Ann Arbor and Northern Railroad and served as its president from 1877 to 1893. See Clarence E. Carter's sketch in *DAB,* I, 389–90, and Charles S. Ashley, "Governor Ashley's Biography and Messages," Historical Society of Montana *Contributions,* VI (1907), 143–289.

[226] *Cong. Globe,* 37 Cong., 2 Sess., 3093. See also *ibid.,* 37 Cong., 3 Sess., Appendix, 189, and *U.S. Statutes at Large,* XII, 664–65. Later surveys fixed the eastern boundary more precisely at 109° 2′ 59.25″ and the northern boundary at 36° 41′ 40.3″. The proposal to establish the Territory of Arizona with a north-south boundary at the 109th meridian meant the surrender of the earlier concept of a territory derived from lands in southern New Mexico only. After the end of the Civil War this concept was revived in different form when a petition was presented to Congress to separate all of southern New Mexico east of the 109th meridian and south of 33° 30′ and organize it as the "Territory of Montezuma." This petition was referred to the House Committee on Territories on July 9, 1865. House Records.

[227] Bancroft (*Arizona and New Mexico,* 508) states erroneously that this bill differed from all earlier ones in delineating such a boundary. For Grow's bills of May 11, 1860 (H.R. 710) and December 18, 1860 (H.R. 890), see *Cong. Globe,* 36 Cong., 1 Sess., 2069 and *ibid.,* 36 Cong., 2 Sess., 121. For Watts' bill of December 23, 1861 (H.R. 171), see *ibid.,* 37 Cong., 2 Sess., 167. Ashley implied in a subsequent statement that the bill reported by Watts would have been acceptable had it been shorter and less complex. *Ibid.,* 2027.

[228] *Ibid.*, 2023. Wickliffe, a Union Whig, had served as postmaster general under President Tyler. See Robert S. Cotterill's sketch in *DAB*, XX, 182–83.

[229] *Cong. Globe*, 37 Cong., 2 Sess., 2023.

[230] *Ibid.*, 1341.

[231] *Ibid.*, 1342.

[232] *DAB*, XX, 57–58. In 1876 Wheeler was elected Vice President on the Republican ticket with Rutherford B. Hayes.

[233] *Cong. Globe*, 37 Cong., 2 Sess., 2023.

[234] *Ibid.*

[235] *Ibid.*

[236] John Sebrie Watts (1816–1876), a native of Kentucky, studied law in Indiana and served in the legislature of that state in 1846 and 1847. From 1851 to 1854 he was associate justice of the territorial court of New Mexico. Political differences caused him to fight a duel with Miguel Antonio Otero on September 4, 1859, and in 1861 he succeeded Otero as territorial delegate to Congress, serving until 1863. Five years later President Johnson appointed him chief justice of the supreme court of New Mexico, but shortly thereafter he resumed the practice of law in Santa Fe. *Biographical Directory of the American Congress, 1774–1961* (Washington, 1961), 1784. Cited hereafter as Biographical Directory (1961). For an account of the duel with Otero, see Tucson *Weekly Arizonian*, September 15, 1859, and St. Louis *Missouri Republican*, September 27, 1859.

[237] *Cong. Globe*, 37 Cong., 2 Sess., 2024.

[238] On the 17th of January, 1860, the Legislative Council of New Mexico passed a bill creating Arizona County, to consist of "all that part of the Territory of New Mexico west of a line running due north and south from the northern to the southern boundary of the county of Doña Ana, through a point one mile distant eastwardly from the . . . Overland Mail Station, to the Apache Cañon." Tubac was designated as the county seat. The House concurred on the 28th, and the act was approved by the governor on February 1. *Journal of the Legislative Council of the Territory of New Mexico . . . being the Ninth Session of the Legislative Assembly* (Santa Fe, 1860), 73; *Journal of the House of Representatives . . .* (Santa Fe, 1860), 122; and *Laws of the Territory of New Mexico . . . 1859–60* (Santa Fe, 1860), 74, 76, 80. A bill to change the seat of government of Arizona County from Tubac to Tucson was passed in the House of the Tenth Legislative Assembly on January 2, 1861, concurred in by the Council on the 4th, and approved by the governor on the 8th. *Journal of the Council . . .* (Santa Fe, 1861), 73, 77, 87; and *Laws of the Territory of New Mexico . . . 1860–61* (Santa Fe, 1861), 16. The Eleventh Legislative Assembly restored the lands of Arizona County to Doña Ana County by an act approved on January 12, 1862. *Laws of the Territory of New Mexico . . . 1861–62* (Santa Fe, 1862), 16, 18.

[239] *Cong. Globe*, 37 Cong., 2 Sess., 2024. Watts was mistaken in his reading of the 1860 census figures for New Mexico. The returns for Arizona County, as defined in note 238, showed 2,421 whites, 4,040 Indians, and 21 free colored. Doña Ana County, on the other hand, now had a white population of 6,239; the Indian and free colored inhabitants were not recorded. Since Doña Ana County no longer included the lands of the western section of the Gadsden Purchase, *i.e.*, Arizona County, the figures for Doña Ana County were not relevant in estimating the population of the proposed Territory of Arizona as defined in the bill then before the House. The truth is that in 1860 there were less than 3,000 white residents – including all the soldiers at Forts Buchanan, Breckenridge, Mojave, and Defiance – in the future Territory of Arizona. The majority of this population was Mexican. J. C. G. Kennedy (comp.), *Population of the United States in 1860 compiled from the Original Returns of the Eighth Census . . .* (Washington, 1864).

[240] *Cong. Globe*, 37 Cong., 2 Sess., 2024–25.

[241] Born in Connecticut in 1813, Gurley was a pastor in Methuen, Massachusetts, before removing to Cincinnati in 1838 to become owner and editor of the *Star and Sentinel*, later known as the *Star of the West*, which he sold in 1854. He ran unsuccessfully for Congress in 1856 but was elected to the House of Representatives in 1858 and again in 1860. In the

summer of 1861 he served briefly as colonel and aide-de-camp on the staff of General John Charles Frémont. *Biographical Directory* (1961), 983. Defeated for re-election in 1862, he was appointed by President Lincoln in 1863 as the first governor of the Territory of Arizona but died before taking office. See page 87 and note 298.

242 *Cong. Globe,* 37 Cong., 2 Sess., 2025.

243 *Ibid.,* 2026.

244 James Pollack to Charles D. Poston, May 2, 1862, *ibid.*

245 *Ibid.,* 2026–27.

246 *Ibid.,* 2027.

247 *Ibid.,* 2028.

248 There can be no doubt that the man in the gallery was Poston.

249 *Ibid.*

250 *Ibid.,* 2029.

251 *Ibid.,* 2030.

252 Bancroft (*Arizona and New Mexico,* 509) was doubtless in error in stating that the measure was approved by a small majority.

253 *Cong. Globe,* 37 Cong., 2 Sess., 2570.

254 For the role of the territorial governor in this capacity, see William M. Neill, "The Territorial Governor as Indian Superintendent in the Trans-Mississippi West," *Mississippi Valley Historical Review,* XLIII (September 1956), 213–37.

255 Bancroft (*Arizona and New Mexico,* 508) intimates that Tucson was named as the capital in the bill which Ashley introduced and the House passed. Tucson actually was not mentioned until it appeared in the Senate amendment.

256 Trumbull had a long political career. Born of a distinguished family in Connecticut in 1813, he served in the Illinois legislature before becoming chief justice of the supreme court in that state. In 1854 he was elected to the House of Representatives, but before his term began he won a seat in the Senate. Lincoln frequently sought his advice. See Roy P. Basler (ed.), *The Collected Works of Abraham Lincoln* (9 vols., Rutgers University Press, 1953–55), IV, 45–46. Trumbull died in Chicago in 1896. See Horace White, *The Life of Lyman Trumbull* (Boston, 1913) and *DAB,* XIX, 19–20. Further data will be found in Trumbull Papers, Library of Congress.

257 *Cong. Globe,* 37 Cong., 2 Sess., 2571.

258 *Ibid.*

259 *Ibid.,* 3093.

260 *Ibid.,* 3094.

261 Benjamin Franklin Wade, born in Massachusetts in 1800, was one of the most powerful members of the antislavery faction in the Senate, where he had held a seat since 1851. After Lincoln's election he was for a time willing to conciliate the Democrats in Congress, as in the instance of agreeing to the organization of Colorado, Dakota, and Nevada without a ban on slavery. With the outbreak of hostilities, however, his stand on slavery became uncompromising and he supported relentless war against the seceded states. Incapable of understanding Lincoln, he deplored the President's cautious conservatism and was co-author of the Wade-Davis manifesto of 1864 condemning the usurpation of executive authority. He called Andrew Johnson "either a knave or a fool" and, in league with Charles Sumner and Thaddeus Stevens, waged an aggressive campaign against Lincoln's successor. Had Johnson been removed, he would have been replaced in the White House by the president of the Senate *pro tempore.* Since the Radicals had elevated Wade to this position in March of 1867, he failed to become President of the United States by the one vote which saved Johnson from impeachment. So confident was Wade of victory in the impeachment proceedings that he had begun to select a cabinet before the trial. He was defeated for re-election to the Senate in 1868, and in that year lost the vice presidential nomination to Schuyler Colfax.

Wade resumed the practice of law in Ohio, was appointed a government director of the Union Pacific and a member of the Santo Domingo Commission, and died in 1878. See H. L. Trefousse, *Benjamin Franklin Wade: Radical Republican from Ohio* (New York: Twayne, 1963); T. Harry Williams, *Lincoln and the Radicals* (U. of Wisconsin Press, 1941); and Vincent G. Tegeder, "Lincoln and the Territorial Patronage: The Ascendancy of the Radicals in the West," *Mississippi Valley Historical Review,* XXXV (June 1948), 77–90. The Wade Papers are in the Library of Congress.

262 *Cong. Globe,* 37 Cong., 2 Sess., 3094. Jurisdiction over territorial affairs was transferred to the Department of the Interior in 1873.

263 *Ibid.*

264 *Ibid.,* 3094–95.

265 *Ibid.,* 3095.

266 *Cong. Globe,* 37 Cong., 3 Sess., 1101–1102.

267 *Ibid.,* 1125.

268 *Ibid.,* 1126.

269 *Ibid.,* 1126–27.

270 *Ibid.,* 1128.

271 *Ibid.*

272 *Ibid.,* Appendix, 189.

273 This journal, which covers almost fifty years (1850–1899) of Poston's life, is in the Sharlot Hall Museum, Prescott, Arizona. It was edited by Byrd H. Granger for publication in three parts in *Arizona Quarterly,* XIII (1957), 152–63, 251–61, 353–62. The entries pertinent here are in Part 2 (Autumn), 255–57. Cited hereafter as Poston's Journal.

274 Tucson *Arizona Weekly Citizen,* April 12, 1884.

275 Florence *Arizona Enterprise,* September 26, 1891.

276 *Phoenix Herald,* December 30, 1893.

277 Charles D. Poston, "Building a State in Apache Land," *Overland Monthly,* 2nd Series, XXIV (October 1894), 403–404.

278 MS in Department of Library and Archives, State of Arizona, Phoenix.

279 When Poston returned he had in hand a personal lease to work the properties of the Sonora Exploring and Mining Company. In the meantime Samuel Colt, the Connecticut armsmaker, had succeeded Heintzelman to the presidency. Years later Poston wrote erroneously in his journal that he had "resumed attention to business" in Arizona in October of 1859. Poston's Journal, 256. This entry under date of November 6, 1860, on page 18 of Record Book A, Pima County, Arizona, sets the matter straight: "As superintendent of the Sonora Exploring and Mining Company, I have this day delivered to Charles D. Poston the property named in the within lease. — ANDREW TALCOTT, Agent, S. E. & M. Co. Witness: John Walker, Palatine Robinson, Jno. L. Poston." As it was, financial complications compelled Poston to transfer his lease to Colt on February 2, 1861, as indicated on pages 219–22 of Record Book A, Pima County. The lease was also recorded in 1863 at Poston's home, Elizabethtown, Kentucky, in Deed Book 5, Records of Hardin County Court, 532–33.

280 *Supra,* 61.

281 *Phoenix Herald,* December 30, 1893.

282 The same error appears in the preface of *Journals of the First Legislative Assembly of the Territory of Arizona* (Prescott, 1865), 11.

283 "Removed my family to New York where we remained at Doctor Taylors in 38th St. the year 1862." Poston here goes on to say that he came to Washington in 1863. Poston's Journal, 256–57.

284 *Cong. Globe,* 37 Cong., 2 Sess., 2023, 2025, 2026, 2027.

[285] Heintzelman Journal, February 24, 1862.

[286] Florence *Arizona Enterprise,* September 26, 1891; *Overland Monthly,* October 1894, 403.

[287] Haycraft and Berry Account Book. Cited in Louis A. Warren, *Lincoln's Parentage and Childhood* (New York: Century, 1926), 40.

[288] The Lincoln-Haycraft correspondence consists of the following letters: (1) Haycraft to Lincoln, undated but probably written in May, 1860; (2) Lincoln to Haycraft, May 28, 1860, for which see Ida M. Tarbell, *The Life of Abraham Lincoln* (4 vols., New York, 1924), IV, 125, and Paul M. Angle and E. S. Miers (eds.), *The Living Lincoln* (Rutgers University Press, 1955), 333–34; (3) Haycraft to Lincoln, May 31, 1860; (4) Lincoln to Haycraft, June 4, 1860, for which see Tarbell's *Lincoln,* IV, 126, and *The Living Lincoln,* 341–42, and *ibid.,* 350–51, for the complications which arose from an innocent remark in this letter; (5) Lincoln to Haycraft, August 16, 1860, for which see *ibid.,* 352; (6) Haycraft to Lincoln, August 19, 1860; (7) Lincoln to Haycraft, August 23, 1860, for which see *ibid.,* 352–53; (8) Haycraft to Lincoln, October 26, 1860; (9) Haycraft to Lincoln, November 9, 1860; (10) Haycraft to Lincoln, November 13, 1860; and (11) Lincoln to Haycraft, November 13, 1860, for which see *ibid.,* 361–62 and *Collected Works of Abraham Lincoln,* IV, 139. Lincoln's letters of June 4, August 16, August 23, and November 13 are in the Huntington Library, San Marino, California. Haycraft's letters of August 19, October 26, November 9, and November 13 are in the Library of Congress.

[289] Genealogical data in the author's files. In his letter to Samuel Haycraft on June 4, 1860, Lincoln wrote: "It may not be altogether without interest to let you know that my wife is a daughter of the late Robert S. Todd of Lexington, Kentucky, and that a half sister of hers is the wife of Ben Hardin Helm, born and raised at your town." *The Living Lincoln,* 341–42. Since Lincoln apparently did not know that his wife's brother-in-law was a cousin of Mrs. Haycraft, it may be confidently assumed that Poston mentioned the relationship in his interview with the President. Poston may also have known that Samuel Haycraft's father and uncles were acquainted with the President's grandfather, Captain Abraham Lincoln, in the Revolutionary War, and that the captain and the senior Haycraft became associated through the latter's foster father, Colonel Neville. It is possible also that Lincoln and Poston knew that the wife of the senior Haycraft was, before her marriage, a good friend of the President's grandmother, Bersheba (or Bathsheba) Lincoln. See Harvey H. Smith, *Lincoln and the Lincolns* (New York, 1931), 4, 6, 31.

[290] In March, 1865, Poston presented Lincoln with a handsome inkstand fashioned from Arizona silver by Tiffany of New York. See Bert Fireman, "Lincoln's Inkstand Comes to Arizona," Phoenix *Arizona Republic,* "Arizona Days and Ways Magazine," February 14, 1960, 10–12, and Sacks, *Charles Debrille Poston,* 9. The inkstand was donated to the Library of Congress in 1937 by Robert Todd Lincoln's daughter, Mrs. Charles Isham.

[291] In 1891, for example, Poston wrote: "I have seen the Mikado of Japan, the Emperor of China, the Viceroy of India, the Khedive of Egypt, the Sultan of Turkey, the Shah of Persia, the kings along the Mediterranean, Louis Napoleon in the glories of the Second [Third] Empire, three Czars of Russia, William of Prussia, the Queen of England, the Prince of Wales, and nearly all the great men of my time, but never did I see such a man as Abraham Lincoln. He embodied the majesty of humanity." Florence *Arizona Enterprise,* September 26, 1891, and quoted in Sacks, *Charles Debrille Poston,* 9. In his "Christmas Lecture" at Phoenix in 1895 he declared: "In the constellation of patriots, heroes and statesmen who illuminated public life in that momentous era in the nation's history, Lincoln was the central figure.

> 'He climbed the ladder of fame so high,
> From the round of the top he stepped to the sky.' "

[292] The late Rufus Kay Wyllys, an able historian, did raise some question concerning its complete reliability without attempting to probe into the matter. Wyllys wrote: "There is an odd story, the truth of which is now and will probably always be uncertain, about the influence of Charles D. Poston in bringing about the passage of the bill. Poston was a somewhat eccentric character with a good deal of impish humor. Yet his own account of what happened is circumstantial enough to win attention." R. K. Wyllys, *Arizona: The History of a Frontier State* (Phoenix, 1950), 165.

293 Giving as a reason the fact that "thirty years have elapsed since the purchase of Arizona by the United States," Poston in January, 1884, called a meeting at the Palace Hotel in Tucson that resulted in the organization of the "Society of Arizona Pioneers," the name of which was changed to "Arizona Pioneers' Historical Society" by the territorial legislature in 1897. See Eleanor B. Sloan, "Seventy-Five Years of the Arizona Pioneers' Historical Society, 1884–1959," *Arizona and the West,* I (Spring 1959), 66–70, and Sacks, *Charles Debrille Poston,* 10. It is worthy of note that Poston's first publication of his story of "wire-pulling" followed that meeting by less than three months. It is possible that Poston was motivated to publicize the part he had played in Washington because, as a result of sharp differences with other organizers of the Society of Arizona Pioneers, his name had been crossed off the register and regular membership in the society denied to him. On Christmas Day, 1885, "having forgiven all my enemies," he asked to be enrolled as a honorary member, and was so elected on January 7, 1886. See *ibid.,* 11, for a reproduction of Poston's letter making this request. On the other hand, there may have been a significant connection between Poston's article and a letter which he addressed on April 3, 1884, to Clark Churchill, chairman of the Territorial Republican Committee of Arizona. In this communication Poston asked to lay his claims for nomination as territorial delegate to Congress before the Republican convention scheduled to be held three weeks later at Phoenix. Tucson *Arizona Weekly Citizen,* April 5, 1884.

294 Tucson *Arizona Weekly Citizen,* April 12, 1884; *History of Arizona Territory* (San Francisco: Wallace W. Elliott & Co., 1884), 207–10. Slight alterations in punctuation and paragraphing have been made here for purpose of clarity.

295 Florence *Arizona Enterprise,* September 26, 1891.

296 *Biographical Directory* (1961), 1356.

297 John Noble Goodwin, born in Maine in 1824, was graduated from Dartmouth College in 1844 and admitted to the bar four years later. Elected to the House of Representatives in 1860, he was defeated in 1862. On March 6, 1863, Goodwin was appointed chief justice of the Territory of Arizona by President Lincoln, and upon the death of Gurley in August he was named to the governorship. In September, 1865, Goodwin was elected delegate to Congress, winning over Poston who ran for re-election. The defeated candidate unsuccessfully contested the vote, charging fraud. See *House Misc. Doc.* 26, 39 Cong., 1 Sess., January 17, 1866, Serial 1270, and Lawrence Poston, III, "Poston *vs.* Goodwin: A Document on the Congressional Election of 1865," *Arizona and the West,* III (Winter 1961), 351–54. Goodwin was not a candidate for re-election in 1866, and did not return to Arizona. He resumed the practice of law at New York and died in California in 1887. See Eugene E. Williams, "The Territorial Governors of Arizona: John Noble Goodwin," *Arizona Historical Review,* VI (July 1935), 59–73, and Farish, *History of Arizona,* III, 47–70. Additional data may be obtained in Goodwin's biographical file, the Goodwin Papers, and the F. L. Carroll Papers, all at APHS; and in Territorial Papers: Arizona, 1864–1872, General Records of the Department of State, RG 59, National Archives.

298 Gurley died in Ohio on the 19th of August, 1863. In his journal on that date Heintzelman wrote: "When I got home I found a telegram from Dr. George Mendenhall [of Cincinnati] informing me of the death of Gov. Gurley and for me to see the President immediately about a successor." Heintzelman Journal, August 19, 1863.

299 On August 21 Heintzelman noted that Richard C. McCormick, secretary of the territory, and "Judge Allen" [Joseph P. Allyn], associate justice of the territorial supreme court, had arrived in Washington that morning and, with Secretary of the Navy Gideon Welles, had gone to see the President, who "transferred Judge Goodwin of Maine from Judgeship to Governor and appointed a man from the West he has wanted to make Judge in his place." *Ibid.,* August 21, 1863. On that same day McCormick, Hiram W. Read, and Secretary W. F. M. Arny of the Territory of New Mexico addressed a letter to the President, urging that Goodwin be appointed to fill the vacancy caused by Gurley's death. McCormick signed himself "Secy & Act. Governor of Arizona." Read, a Baptist minister, was appointed postmaster of Tucson, but served instead in Prescott. See John and Lillian Theobald, *Arizona Territory: Post Offices and Postmasters,* 115, 120, 134. Turner and Goodwin were, of course, given interim appointments since the Senate was not in session in August, 1863. The

Senate confirmed the appointments within a few days after referral of both nominations on January 7, 1864. Senate Records, 38 Congress, 1 Session, No. 43 and No. 44.

300 *Ibid.*, 38 Congress, Special Session, No. 44.

301 Appointment Records for Surveyor-General, Arizona, Records of Department of Interior.

302 Appointment Records during Administration of President Lincoln, Records of Department of State.

303 *Supra*, pt. 1, 6 *et seq*. When Mowry learned that Congress had passed a law organizing Arizona, he wrote with more than a hint of bitterness: "It is somewhat gratifying to me to know that gentlemen who, four years since, denied the necessity of this measure, and opposed it by vote and influence most virulently on political grounds, have seen the error of their ways. By reproducing my arguments and authorities, and even my words *verbatim et literatim*, they have paid a tribute to truth the more valuable that it comes from an unexpected source. As I had then and have now an ambition for Arizona far beyond private or personal views, I thank these gentlemen heartily, and make them welcome to 'all the thunder' and all the political honors they have stolen from me." Sylvester Mowry, *Arizona and Sonora: The Geography, History, and Resources of the Silver Region of North America* (3rd ed., New York: Harper, 1864), vii.

304 Tucson *Arizona Daily Star*, March 6, 1880; Tucson *Arizona Weekly Star*, March 11, 1880.

305 Phoenix *Arizona Republican*, February 16, 1892. Poston was in error when he stated that Heintzelman and Wrightson were the only people in Washington (other than himself, of course) who had been in Arizona. In the debate on the Arizona bill the two Senators from California, Milton S. Latham and James A. McDougall, declared that they had been there. "I have been through the Territory twice," Latham said on June 5, 1862, and on July 3 McDougall remarked: "I have travelled all over that country, and I understand its necessities." *Cong. Globe*, 37 Cong., 2 Sess., 2571, 3094.

306 *Phoenix Herald*, December 30, 1893. Poston had made a similar statement as early as 1884: "It is more than twenty years now since I went to Washington with my own money and my own influence and procured the organization of the Territorial government." Tucson *Arizona Weekly Citizen*, April 5, 1884.

307 Samuel Peter Heintzelman had a long and notable career in the Army. Born in Manheim, Lancaster County, Pennsylvania, on September 30, 1805, he was admitted to West Point upon the recommendation of James Buchanan, then a Congressman, and in 1826 was graduated seventeenth in a class of forty-one and commissioned a second lieutenant of infantry. In 1835 he was promoted to captain and served in this rank on quartermaster duty in Florida during the Seminole War. Ordered to Buffalo, New York, in 1843, he was married the next year to Margaret Stewart of Albany. For gallant and meritorious service at Huamantla he was brevetted major during the Mexican War, and during the gold rush he was sent to California where late in 1850 he established the post which became Fort Yuma. There he waged a successful campaign against the Yuma Indians and championed steam navigation on the Colorado River. As early as 1852 he felt confident that this river would provide the best route to the lower Utah settlements. In July, 1855, he was commissioned major of the 1st U.S. Infantry and for two years thereafter served as superintendent of Western recruiting. From November of 1859 to April of 1860 he was in command of operations in south Texas against the Mexican bandit Cortina, the "Red Robber of the Rio Grande," and then was stationed in New York harbor as general superintendent of recruiting. Upon the outbreak of the Civil War he was ordered to the capital as acting inspector of the Department of Washington, was commissioned colonel of the 17th U.S. Infantry on May 14, 1861, and three days later was made brigadier general of volunteers and given command of a brigade at Alexandria, Virginia. Commanding the third division of McDowell's army at Bull Run, he was severely wounded in the right arm; but, refusing to dismount, he insisted on having his mangled arm treated while he remained in the saddle. During the Peninsula campaign he commanded the III Corps of McClellan's army in the siege of Yorktown and at Williamsburg, becoming major general of volunteers on May 5, 1862. On the 31st of that month he was brevetted brigadier general, U.S.A., for gallantry at Fair Oaks. After the second Battle of Bull Run, in which his corps formed the right wing of Pope's army, he was put in command of the defences of Washington and served here until

October, 1863. In March, 1865, he was brevetted major general, U.S.A., for gallant and meritorious service in the Battle of Williamsburg. After Appomattox he resumed command of his regiment, the 17th U.S. Infantry, serving in New York harbor and in Texas until retirement on February 22, 1869. By special act of Congress on April 29 of that year he was placed on the retired list in the rank of major general. Heintzelman was described as "a man of an intense nature, of vehement actions, guided by sound judgment and a cultivated taste." Critics accused him of lacking initiative. See Cullum, *Biographical Register of . . . Graduates of the U.S. Military Academy,* I, 372–74; *DAB,* IV, 505–06; and A. K. Hostetter, "Major General Samuel Peter Heintzelman," Lancaster Historical Society *Papers,* XVII (1912), 57–81. See also Arthur Woodward (ed.), *Journal of Lt. Thomas W. Sweeny, 1849–1853* (Los Angeles: Westernlore Press, 1956); New York *Times,* July 14, 1863; Frank J. Branhall, *The Military Souvenir* (New York, 1864); *Sketches of Men of Mark* (New York, 1871), 753–60; Washington *Evening Star,* May 1, 1880; and Charles D. Poston, "In Memoriam," Tucson *Arizona Daily Star,* May 9, 1880. Much additional information may be obtained in Heintzelman Journal and Papers, Library of Congress.

308 *Supra,* pt. 1, 9 and note 22. Heintzelman served as president until succeeded by Samuel Colt in the spring of 1859.

309 Heintzelman Journal, December 21, 1862.

310 *Ibid.,* January, 1863, *passim.* The general did not know that on January 16 President Lincoln wrote on an envelope containing recommendations for Charles S. Heintzelman: "When the time comes I should like to make this appointment, if not pressed too hardly in other directions." *Collected Works of Abraham Lincoln,* VI, 60. The young man entered West Point on July 1, 1863, and was graduated in June of 1867.

311 *Ibid.,* February 3, 1863.

312 *Ibid.,* February 8, 1863.

313 *Ibid.,* February 10, 1863.

314 *Ibid.,* February 14, 1863.

315 *Ibid.,* February 15, 1863.

316 *Ibid.,* February 16, 1863.

317 *Ibid.,* February 17, 1863. Edward E. Cross, editor of the Tubac *Weekly Arizonian* in 1859, was now colonel of "the Fighting Fifth" (5th New Hampshire Volunteers); R. W. H. Jarvis and Solon H. Lathrop were officials of the Sonora Exploring and Mining Company; Puleston was a speculator in mining properties.

318 *Ibid.,* February 18, 1863.

319 *Ibid.,* February 20, 1863.

320 *Ibid.,* February 21, 1863. In Heintzelman's office on the 21st Senator Wade, Poston, Wrightson, Colonel Edward E. Cross, R. W. H. Jarvis, and Solon H. Lathrop "signed a paper recommending Mr. Gurley for Governor of Arizona." They then went together to see the President, who received them favorably. *Ibid.,* February 22, 1863. The letter which they wrote is filed under Gurley's name in Appointment Records during Administration of President Lincoln, Records of Department of State. Among other letters of recommendation in the file is one from the future Vice President, Representative Schuyler Colfax of Indiana, who, after authorizing Gurley to inform Lincoln of his approval, quipped: ". . . when you get to Arizona if you can learn [*sic*] these Spaniards and Indians the true Republican faith, you will delight

Yours truly
SCHUYLER COLFAX"

321 The parchment on which the organic act is inscribed was signed by the President, by Solomon Foot of Vermont, president of the Senate *pro tempore,* and by Galusha A. Grow of Pennsylvania, the Speaker of the House. It is preserved in a bound volume of statutes in the General Records of the United States Government, RG 11, National Archives. Facsimiles were prepared by the Arizona Historical Foundation for distribution during the centennial year of 1963.

[322]The gubernatorial party, late in starting and headed by Gurley's successor, John N. Goodwin, left Fort Leavenworth on the Missouri River on September 25, 1863, reached Santa Fe on November 14, and two weeks later arrived at Albuquerque. Leaving Fort Wingate, New Mexico, with a military escort on the 20th of December and travelling by Whipple's route along the thirty-fifth parallel, they crossed the eastern boundary of the new territory seven days later. On the morning of December 29, 1863, they arrived at Navajo Springs, and that afternoon the Territory of Arizona was formally proclaimed. Secretary Richard C. McCormick made a speech and read Governor Goodwin's proclamation; the postmaster, Rev. Hiram W. Read, read a Spanish translation. The flag was then hoisted, and Read offered a prayer. In a letter that day to Carleton in Santa Fe, McCormick reported: "We . . . have fairly started the wheels of our government. The official oaths were taken this afternoon with some little ceremony, and the Governor has issued his proclamation. . . . The weather clear and frosty, the grass excellent. . . ." Letters Received, Department of New Mexico, Records of Army Commands. McCormick's remark on the weather destroys the tradition that the formalities at Navajo Springs were conducted in a snowstorm. The party continued westward to the San Francisco Mountains and thence south to the new military post in Chino Valley, Fort Whipple, where the seat of government was established. When the officials arrived on January 22, 1864, they were greeted by an anvil salute of eighteen shots. In May, 1864, Fort Whipple was removed to the site of Prescott, named by McCormick after the noted historian of the Mexican conquest, William Hickling Prescott, who died in 1859. Prescott served as the territorial capital until 1867, and again from 1877 to 1889, when it was definitively established at Phoenix.

[323]See L. B. Schmidt, "Manifest Opportunity and the Gadsden Purchase," *Arizona and the West,* III (Autumn 1961), 264, note 54.

[324]B. Sacks, *"Sylvester Mowry . . .",* note 169.

[325]Poston died in obscurity in an adobe hovel at Phoenix on June 24, 1902, at the age of seventy-seven. See Sacks, *Charles Debrille Poston,* for details on his latter years.

APPENDIX A

In the 1850s a large number of documents were sent to Congress urging the organization of a new territory to be separated from New Mexico and to be known as Arizona. These documents were principally in the form of memorials or petitions which originated in the proposed territory and in various states. There were also resolutions from the legislatures of New Mexico and Tennessee. Once presented to Congress, they generally were referred to the House or Senate Committee on Territories. In some instances these petitions inspired the drafting of territorial bills; in others they simply were ignored.

Documents reproduced here in whole or in part but with many of the signatures omitted are the following:

(1) Memorial in Spanish drafted by W. C. Jones in 1856 and signed by residents of the Rio Grande Valley. The original of the translation of this document is in the handwriting of Sylvester Mowry.

(2) Memorial prepared at the instance of the convention held in Tucson on August 29, 1856. Among the more than 260 signers there were more Anglo-American names than in the "Jones Memorial," but in both documents there was a great preponderance of Mexican names.

(3) The 1857 "Kippen Memorial," so-called for brevity because George Kippen's name heads one of the lists of signers, originated in the western section of the Gadsden Purchase. There were some 500 signers. A copy of this memorial, without the signatures, appears in Mowry's 1857 *Memoir*.

(4) The 1857 "Bradley Memorial," so-called because M. E. Bradley's name heads the list of some one thousand petitioners. The signatories, the majority of whom were Mexicans and many of whom signed with a cross, were principally from Mesilla and nearby communities along the Rio Grande. Both 1857 memorials were brought to the attention of Congress by Arizona's delegate, Lieutenant Mowry.

(5) Petition signed by eighty-one farmers, merchants, and mechanics, residing in the city and county of St. Louis, Missouri, urging Congress to organize Arizona. The signers, who requested federal

grants of land and arms, were prepared themselves to emigrate to the proposed territory. *The manuscript document has been transcribed in order to make more legible the quaint spelling of the untutored man who prepared the petition.*

(6) Petition from citizens of New York, memorializing Congress to organize Arizona in order to encourage settlement and to secure a mail route through the proposed territory. Promoters of the Overland Mail distributed a large number of the printed forms to various parts of the country for signing by local residents.

(7) Printed report of Senate Committee on Territories in 1858, rejecting the petition of Giles S. Isham for a large grant of land to establish a colony of farmers and mechanics in the proposed Territory of Arizona.

(8) Resolutions of the Territorial Legislature of New Mexico, presented to the United States Senate on February 27, 1860. This document has been transcribed from a copy in the handwriting of Mowry which was certified by New Mexico's Delegate Otero. This was not the first time that New Mexico was willing to surrender a large part of her lands to create the Territory of Arizona.

APPENDIX A(1)

Al Senado y Camara de Representantes de los Estados Unidos de America en Congreso ~~asamblado~~ reunido

Sus memorialistos ciudadanos de la Mesilla y vecindad en el Territorio adquirido por tratado con la Republica de Mexico en el mes de ~~Septiembre~~ Diciembre de 1853, piden respetuosamente la organisacion de un Territorio à ser llamado el Territorio de "Arizona" que se lindará como sigue: Empezando en el centro del canal principal del Rio Colorado del occidente, veinte millas abajo de la boca del rio Gila; de alli, siguiendo dicho canal principal del ~~principal~~ Rio Colorado hasta la punta en donde el paralelo de 34° 20' N. cruza dicho rio; de alli, oriente, por dicho linea de 34° 20' hasta el centro del canal principal del Rio Pecos; de alli, siguiendo el canal principal de dicho rio Pecos hasta los limites del Estado de Texas; de allí, poniente por dichos limites hasta el centro del canal principal del rio Bravo del Norte ó rio Grande; de alli, siguiendo dicho canal principal del rio Grande por abajo hasta la punta en donde los limites norte de la Republica de Mexico toca el mismo rio; de allí, poniente, siguiendo dichos limites ó linderos de dicha Republica hasta el lugar de empezar.

Sus memorialistos piden la organisacion de este Territorio porque—

1º No tienen del Gobierno la proteccion q: les corresponden, sino una administracion de las leyes limitada y inconveniente.—

2º Viven demasiado remotos del Gobierno Territorial de Nuevo Mexico en Santa Fé de ser bajo de su jurisdiccion inmediata é de tener provecho de el.

3º Son geograficalmente desunidos de Neuvo Mexico por desiertos esteriles, sierras asperas, y jornadas desolados y inhabitables, los cuales son infectados por indios barbaros y salvages.

4º Ni ahora y no pueden nunca consumarse con el pueblo de Nuevo Mexico como un mismo pueblo y gobierno: q. han sido siempre separados y tendran siempre el mismo deseo. -

5º Tendran ahora un solo representante y no pueden conseguir mas de uno, aunque viven en un condado mediendo ocho cientos millas de largo y cienti noventa de ancho, con una poblacion q. exceda mas q. cualquiera otra condado de Neuvo Mexico.

6º No tienen una organisacion suficiente y no tendran nunca jamas mientras q. quedan anexados à Nuevo Mexico.

7º Que las poblaciones del poniente como Tucson y otras, no han tenido un oficial ni un precinto – tampoco no se ha estendido ningun ley de los Estados Unidos ó del Territorio allí. – Sus derechos no han sido protegidos y no les han admitido el privelegio de votar por el solo representante q. tienen proporcionado por la legislatura del Territorio.

8º Que los intereses del pueblo de Nuevo Mexico son tan distintos de los nuestros, q. somos tratado con desprecio ó maldecidos con una legislacion parcial.

9º Que tenemos un pais estendido, rico en minas, en recursos agricultural y pastoral, con una poblacion activa y industriosa, creciendose ahora rapidamente por emigrantes inteligentos de los Estados del poniente y ser de la Union Americana y de los Estados del norte de Mexico; tambien se han colocado muchos mineros en este condado de California y Mexico.

Se puede computar nuestra poblacion como sigue:-

Las Cruces, Brazito y Doña Ana	5000
Mesilla y los Ranchos	10000
Minas de Los Organos	200
Santo Tomas y ranchos	1000
Rio Bonita	100
Los Amoles y ranchos	1000
Santa Barbara y ranchos	500
Valverde, San Antonio y ranchos	1000
Luis Lopez y ranchos	500
Tucson y ranchos	1000
Calavasas, Ajo y Tubac	500
Ciudad de Colorado (boca del rio Gila)	100
Haciendo agregado	21.800

ciudadanos viviendo en confusion y anarquia y sin la proteccion q. las leyes deben dar á la vida, la libertad y la propiedad.

Por tanto, piden la organisacion legal q. les corresponden, por justicia, derecho, ley— y bajo el compacto de un tratado solemna.

Respetuosamente &c.

N. Claude Jones
Remigio Saenz
Jesus ... Zabrita
Luis Garcia
Ernest Angorstein

Rafael Ruelas
Rafael Elountritto
Santiago Arguello
Mateo Guerrera
Pedro Peres
Ygnacio Gonzales
Valentin Bernal
Candelario Trujillo

[TRANSLATION]

To the Senate and House of Representatives, of the United States in Congress assembled —

Your memorialists, citizens of La Messilla and vicinity, in the Territory acquired by treaty with the Republic of Mexico in the month of December 1853, respectfully pray for the organization of a Territory, to be called Arizona with the following boundaries —

Beginning in the centre of the principal channel of the Rio Colorado of the West, twenty miles below the mouth of the Gila, from thence following said principal channel of the Colorado, to the point at which the parallell of 34° 20′ N. crosses said River, from thence East with said line of 34° 20′ N. to the centre of the principal channel of the Rio Pecos, from thence following the principal channel of said Rio Pecos, to the boundary of the State of Texas, from thence West with said boundary, to the centre of the main channel of the Rio Bravo del Norte, or Rio Grande from thence following said Main channel of the Rio Grande, downward, to the point at which the Northern boundary of the Republic of Mexico strikes the same River, from thence, West, following said limits or boundarys of said Republic to the place of beginning.

Your Memorialists pray for the organization of this Territory, because —

1st They have not from the Government the protection which belongs to them, only a limited and inconvenient administration of the Laws.

2nd They live very remote, from the Territorial Government of New Mexico in Santa Fé being outside of, (or below) its immediate jurisdiction, without having its protection.

3rd They are geographically disunited from New Mexico, by sterile deserts, difficult (or rough) mountains, and desolate jornadas, and uninhabitable — which are infested, by barbarous and savage Indians.

4th They are now entirely unable to assemble with the people of New Mexico as the same people and government, that they have always been separated, and they always wish to be.

5th They have but one Representative and are able to obtain but one, notwithstanding they live in a country about eight hundred miles long and one hundred and nineteen broad, with a population greater than that of any other county of New Mexico.

6th They have no sufficcint organization — and have never had since they were annexed to New Mexico.

7th That the population of the West, viz Tucson — and other places, have had no officers, nor precincts, neither has the laws of the United States or the Territory extended there. Their rights have not been protected, nor have they been permitted the privilege of voting, for the only representative that they have had apportionately, in the Legislature of New Mexico.

8th That the interests of the people of New Mexico are very distinct from ours, and that we are treated, with contempt or cursed with a partial legislation.

9th That we have an extended country rich in minerals, in agricultural and pastoral resources, with an active and industrious population, now rapidly increasing, by intelligent emigrants, from the Western States, from those of the American Union, and from the Northern States of Mexico, likewise we have collected in this country many miners from California and Mexico.

We are able to compute our population, as follows—

Los Cruces, Brazita and Doña Ana	5,000
Messilla and its Ranches	10.000
The Organ Mines	200
Santo Tomas and its Ranches	1,000
Bonita River	100
Los Amoles and its Ranches	1,000
Santa Barbara and its Ranches	500
Valverde, San Antonio and its Ranches	1,000
Luis Lopez and its Ranches	500
Tucson and its Ranches	1,000
Calavasas, Ajo and Tubac	500
Colorado City, at the Mouth of the Gila	100
Total	21.500 [20,900]

citizens living in confusion and anarchy and without the protection that the laws ought to give to life, liberty and property.

Therefore they pray the organization, that belongs to them in justice, right and law, and under the compact of a solemn treaty.

Respectfully....

[Here were written the names of 57 persons, the first being that of W. Claude Jones.]

I certify that the above is a correct translation of the original petition herewith appended, and that it is signed by the principal citizens of the Rio Grande valley.

Sylvester Mowry
Delegate

APPENDIX A(2)

To the Senate and House of Representatives of the United States of America
in Congress Assembled
Your Memorialists citizens of the Territory acquired by the Treaty with
the Republic of Mexico on the 31st day of December 1853 respectfully
pray for the organization of a new Territory to be called the Terri-
=tory of Arizona. To be bounded as follows Beginning at a point on
the Colorado river where the new line between the United States and
Mexico intersects the same; thence up the main channel of the Colorado
river to the boundary line of the State of California; thence along
said boundary line to its intersection with parallel of 34 deg 20'
north latitude; thence east along said parallel to its intersection
with the Rio Grande; thence down the middle of the main channel
of the Rio Grande to its intersection with the northern boundary
of Mexico; thence westwardly along said ~~northern~~ boundary line
of Mexico to the place of beginning
Your Memorialists respectfully present the following considerations
which induce them to ask for this organization
First That since the Treaty of 1853 they have resided in this Territory
a period of nearly three years without having exercised the rights of
freemen under the constitution and laws of the United States
Second That they have neither Magistrates laws nor courts under
the Government of the United States.
Third That they are isolated — cut off among savage tribes
with no legal organization — no vote — no Representation — and
without any of the privileges of citizenship
Fourth That although nominally within the county of Dona Ana
in the Territory of New Mexico they have never had the benefit of
laws or civil officers nor have they any protection for life liberty
or property.
Fifth, That the vast extent of Territory within the limits of New
Mexico, and the natural barriers between the Eastern and western
portions of the same does, and will forever, cause adverse interests
and prevent a harmonious administration of either a Territorial or
State Government

They therefore, respectfully pray that Congress will take under consideration the grievances of your memorialists, and extend to them the protection of a separate Territorial Government. Also take measures for the speedy settlement of land titles — for the survey of the public lands — for the protection of mining interests — for the establishing of Post Routes — and the subjugation of the hostile Indian tribes that infest their Territory.

They further pray that you will admit to a seat in your Honorable Body the delegate elect from this Territory, granting to him all the privileges of delegates from other Territories. And your petitioners will ever pray &c

[illegible]
[illegible]
Herman Ehrenberg
[illegible]
Ignacio Ortiz
[illegible] McLain
Rodolfo Spence
Pedro Ramires
[illegible]
W. H. Bonner
[illegible]
[illegible]
Guillermo Telles
Dolores + Herran
Fra.co Salar
Fra.co Ybello
Julian Soles
[illegible] Castro
Ramon Castro
Dolores Castro
Fran.co [illegible]
Juan J. Grehalba
Fra.co Grehalba
[illegible]
Guadalupe [illegible]

[illegible] Aldrich
[illegible]
W. [illegible]
Juan Elias
F. R. Rogers
F. A. Ronstadt
Henry Burch
[illegible]
[illegible]
Wm. [illegible]
Mariano Cruz
[illegible]
Jose Gallego
Marcelino [illegible]
Juan Jose Lopes
Thos. J. Davis
Anastacia Telles
Mariano Acedo
J. D. Simons
Teodoro Ramirez
Samuel [illegible]
J. [illegible]
James Duncan
Jesus [illegible]
Wm. M. Rowlett

APPENDIX A(3)

To the Senate and House of Representatives in Congress Assembled

The undersigned, your humble petitioners, citizens of the United States, and residents of the Territory known as the Gadsen Purchase, respectfully represent:

That since the annexation of their Territory to the United States, they have been totally unprotected from Indian-depredations and civil crimes.

That the protection of the Mexican Government has been withdrawn, and that it has not been replaced by any visible protection from the United States.

That the annexation of the Purchase to New Mexico, carried with it no protection for life or property.

That the present force of United State's troops, four companies of dragoons, reduced by desertion and death to about one-half, is entirely inadequate to protect us against the depredations of the Apaches.

That many of your petitioners have expended their time and means in opening and prospecting rich mines of Copper and Silver, and have been driven from them by the Indians—losing their all—and also many valuable lives.

That the Territory is immensely rich in minerals, especially Silver and Copper; and, as your petitioners most firmly believe, the development of these mines will make a change in the currency of the world, only equalled by that caused by the gold mines of California.

That a great part of the Territory, between the Rio Grande and Tucson, is susceptible of cultivation and will support a large agricultural population.

That this portion of the Territory is in the hands of the Apaches, and useless, unless redeemed from their grasp and protected to the farmer.

That the highways of the Territory are stained with the blood of citizens of the United States, shed by Indians and by public marauders, who commit their crimes in open day, knowing there is no law to restrain and no magistrte to arrest them.

That this Territory under a separate organization, would attract a large population and become immediatsly developed; and, that its isolation — its large Indian population — its proximity to a semi-civilized Mexican province, and its peculiar and wonderful resources demand protection from the Government more emphatically than any other territory yet recognized.

That our soil has been stained with the blood of American citizens, shed by Mexican hands, in an armed invasion of our Territory near Scnoita, and that there is no civil magistrate or officer here to even protest against such an outrage.

That throughout their whole Territory from the Rio Grande to the Rio Colorado, six hundred miles, there is no Court of Record, and no redress except that inefficiently administered in a Justices Court, for civil injuries or crimes.

That the population of the Territory is much greater than was that of Kansas or Nebraska, or Washington Territory, at the time of their organization, and that it is steadily increasing and will, under the influence of the Road and Mail Bills of tho last Congress, be greatly augmented.

That there are no post routes or mail facilities throughout the Territory, and that finally we are cut off from all the comforts of civilization—and that we claim, as a right, that protection which the United States should everywhere extend to her humblest citizen. Wherefore your petitioners humbly pray that the Gadsden Purchase may be separated from New Mexico and erected into a separate Territory under the name of Arizona with such boundaries as may seem proper to your honorable bodies, and that such other legislation may be made as shall be best calculated to place us on the same footing as our more fortunate brethren of Kansas, Nebraska, Minneeota, Oregon and Washington, that we may be enabled to build up a prosperous and thriving State, and to nourish on this extreme frontier a healthy national sentiment. And we, as in duty bound, will ever pray.

Geo Kippen
Wm. H. Martin
John W Kilbride
John Williams
James Jones
Francis Butler
William White
Joseph Holton

B H Dearmitt
Eugene Wakefield
Benjamin Steward

Granville H Oury
J. H. Carothers
Alfred Friar
Hiram Stevens
S. L. Swaney
Willis N. Bonner
Rafael Sainz
A. La M'Kinza
John Long
Thomas Abbott
Charles Schuchard
Nelson Van Alstine
Herman Ehrenberg
Mariano Cruz
Francisco Granillo
Charles Burr
John Berry
John Kerwan
John Bregmaier
George W. Fuller
Mordecai Adams
George W. Clark
W McNees
William Graham
Philip Morris
Dolores Rodriguez
[illegible]
W. H. Turner

Joseph Lancaster
Mason Bland
Jose Espinosa
Pedro Reyes
Stephen Reynolds
Hilario Ygarra
Ignacio Buelna
Stephen Johnson
J. M. Stewart
H. Cline
Peter Alvarez
William Ziegler
John Hanlon
Jno. Anderson
Wm. Smith.
Jno. P. Baker
J. Silbereisen
John C. Spining
Antonio Ruiz
Ramon Bustamente
Creole Bustamente
Emil Fritz
J. J. Jones
M. C. Tuttle
Wm. B. Simpson
John McNulty
Louis Blacksmith
J. A. Stewart
P. K. Travis
Guillermo Rubio
John Hamblin

APPENDIX A(4)

To the Senate & House of representatives
in Congress assembled,
The undersigned your petitioners, Citizens
of the united States, and Residents of the Coun-
-try known as the Gadsden purchase and
southern portion of new mexico. Respectfully
pray for a seperation from new mexico, and
the orgainization of a new Territory to be called
"The Territory of Arizona", with the following
boundaries, to wit:
Commencing at a point on the Colorado
River west where the boundary line between
the united States and mexico intersects the Same
thence up the Main chanel of said river
to its intersection with the parallell of thirty four
degrees twenty minutes north Latitude, thence
East along said paralell to the boundary
line of the State of Texas thence along the
several boundary lines of Texas & mexico
to the place of beginning,
Your petitioners would beg leave to recite
the following reasons which Compel them
to ask for this seperation,
1st That they are Geographically seperated from
new mexico by intervening mountains and
deserts. as, also, in a social point of view
being american in their feeling, and pro-
-gressive in their Character,
2nd That the Territorial Legislature of new mexico
has refused to pass an apportionment Bill
thereby denying us the representation to which
we are entitled or to extend the Laws

of Said Territory over large portions of the above described Territory, leaving us in a State of anarchy with out any of the privileges of citizenship,

3rd That a large portion of the aforesaid Territory has been since its aggregation to New Mexico totally unprotected from Indian depredations & civil crimes.

4th That the protection of the Mexican Government has been withdrawn, and it has not been re-placed by any visible protection from the United States,

5th That so long as they continue within the Juris-sdiction of New Mexico their interests will ever be neglected, crime will go unpunished and their lives & property will remain unprotected,

6th That the Territory is immensely rich in minerals especially silver and copper, and your petitioners firmly believe that the development of these mines will make a change in the currency of the world, only equaled by that caused by the gold mines of California;

7th That a great part of the Territory is susceptable of cultivation and will support a large aggricultural population,

8th That throughout their whole Territory, which contains a population of Fifteen Thousand souls, they have no court, and consequently no redress for civil injuries or crimes

Where-fore your petitioners humbly pray that the above described country be erected into a seperate Territory with the name and boundaries above said. & that such

other Legislation may be made as shall
be best calculated to place us on the same
footing as our more fortunate Brethren
of other Territories, that we may be enabled
to build up a prosperous and thriving
state, and to nourish on this extreme
frontier a healthy national sentiment. And
we as in duty bound will ever Pray &c.

[illegible] Cooke	M. E. Bradley
[illegible]	Samuel G. Bean
Alex Geo Lachlan	W. Claude Jones
R. Campbell	S. J. Hawley
Jose Ma Chaves	Thomas McDermott
Joseph Coquard	Robert Haner
Joshua S. Slade	George Buehl
Jas. H. B. Thompson	Wm. W. Blake
[illegible]	Charles Dinn
Frank Morton	Silverio [illegible]
Wm. J. Musick	Rafael Garcia
Juan Jose Lopez	[illegible]
José Alert	Chas. Morgan
Pedro Telles	Juan Marolane
Calletano Dominguez	Wm. E. Glasscock
Pedro Aldaete	J. H. Harper
Antto Gonzales	Pedro Contreras
Jose Ma Telles	Gregorio Lujan
Daniel Fritze	Antº Jeanez
Pablo Alvarado	Julian Villanueva
José Ma Tames	Cenobio Villanueva
[illegible]	Rafael Bermudes
	N. B. Appel.

APPENDIX A(5)

[St Louus Missoura Feb 13th 1858
To the Honerable Senate and House of Representatives in Congress assembed —

Wee the undersined Americans and Residents of the citty & county of Saint Louus and State of Missoura Being Farmers and Merchants and Mechanicks and Being Desirous of Emigrateing and settleing near the pacific occian at or near the Mouth of the River Gila on colorado or along either of those streams here above named and as wee know the undertaking is a hazurdous one on act of the large bands of Indians whoo Rome over that part of the country prey your honerable Boddys to pass a law to grant to each head of a fameley six hundred and forty acres of the publick lands now Belonging to the united states and furthe to each sigle Mann over the age of twenty one years of age one hundred and sixty acres on these conditions that the locate and settle on the land with in two years from the paseage of this act and further that you will allso grant to us arms of the united states and and escort of cavelry to protect uss on oure way to said terrytors and that you pass a law for a terytoral covernment where By we May have a Delagate to Represent uss in the congress of the united states so as to make kowen oure wants from year to year all whitch wee humbley pray your honerabl bodys will Grant oure petiton]

APPENDIX A(6)

To the Senate and House of Representatives, in Congress assembled:

The undersigned your humble petitioners, citizens of the State of New York feeling deeply interested in the successful establishment of the great Overland Mail Route to California and our Western Possessions,—and having full confidence in the ability and good faith of the Contractors for the carriage of this mail,—respectfully represent:

That upon good and sufficient evidence it appears an established fact, that throughout the entire length of the Gadsden Purchase—six hundred miles—from the Rio Grande to the Colorado of the West, there is no ostensible or real protection to life or property;—

That throughout this vast extent of country, there is no Court of Record, and no redress for civil injuries, nor punishment for crimes;—

That the Territory of New Mexico can exercise no influence for good over the Gadsden Purchase;—

That the great Overland Mail will traverse the Gadsden Purchase throughout its ent. length;—

That in view of the proper fulfillment of the mail contract, it is a matter of absolute necessity that both civil and military protection should be guaranteed to the Contractors and to the People of the new Territory; civil protection in Courts of Law, that contracts may be enforced and rights protected; military, that the mail stations and stages may be protected from Indian attacks:

Wherefore, your Petitioners most respectfully join in the prayer of the People of the Gadsden Purchase, "That the Gadsden Purchase may be separated from New Mexico and erected into a distinct Territory under the name of Arizona, with such boundaries as may seem proper to your honorable bodies"—to the end that emigration and settlement of this remote frontier may be encouraged, a national and healthy American sentiment diffused, and a secure and speedy route opened to California and the Pacific; and as in duty bound we will ever pray.

Darius Peck
A. P. Cooke
Henry J. Baringer
Isaac E. Houke
A. Scott
R. W. Evans
George Barker
Josiah Jeffers
Stephen A. DuBois
Henry B. Barnard
Robt A. Barnard
Geo. Purton
Chas Waterman
John G. Apsey
H. Hogeboom
James McCardhore
John H. Best
Fayette M. Butler
William Bryant
Henry Walden
D. C. Neefus
William G. Dyer
A. Rossman
Joseph Hardwick
Geo. B. Fairfield
Charles Paul
R. J. King
Peter Quivan
Wm R. Osborn
G. H. Osborn

APPENDIX A(7)

35TH CONGRESS, } 1st Session. } SENATE. { REP. COM. { No. 283.

IN THE SENATE OF THE UNITED STATES.

MAY 27, 1858.—Ordered to be printed.

Mr. GREEN submitted the following

REPORT.

The Committee on Territories, to whom was referred the memorial of Giles S. Isham, praying a grant of land in the proposed Territory of Arizona for the purpose of establishing a colony of industrious farmers, mechanics, and artizans, have considered the same, and make the following report:

The memorialist makes the *modest* request of land amounting to twelve miles square, equal to four entire townships, with the addition of Sharp's rifles, munitions, howitzers, and other warlike implements, for the settlement of *one hundred* inhabitants on said land within three years from the making of the grant. The committee do not know who Giles S. Isham is, nor whether he is responsible for what he undertakes to perform. It is certain that the proposition presented imposes no *obligation* on Mr. Giles S. Isham to cause the one hundred inhabitants to settle on the lands asked for, and it seems to be a mere matter of speculation on his part to profit by the proposed bill, if it should pass, but in no case to incur any responsibility.

Under these circumstances the committee do not believe Mr. Isham entitled to any special consideration on the part of Congress.

But beyond all this, the committee cannot subscribe to the dangerous doctrine that Congress can inaugurate any policy merely for the purpose of protecting the interests of farmers or mechanics. They are honorable citizens, and entitled to the full measure of consideration conceded to others; but it would be a flagrant wrong to make discriminations between any classes of our citizens, whether they be farmers or mechanics.

The committee cannot, and will not, make any distinction between them, but leave all to stand upon their merits, with the full assurance that each shall receive the reward due upon a proper consideration of the powers and the duties of the government.

The territory of the Union belongs to *all the States*, and Congress ought not to make any disposition of it which would be either *partial* or *unconstitutional*.

The prayer of the memorialist is believed to be both *wrong* and impolititic itself, and beyond the appropriate scope of congressional power, and it is therefore reported against.

APPENDIX A(8)

Memorial to the Congress of the United States, touching the organization of the Territory of Arizona.

Whereas — The people of the Southern and Western portion of the Territory of New Mexico - being within the limits of the proposed Territory of Arizona. have been for the last three years. asking of Congress - a separate Territorial organization; and whereas the peculiar situation of that people which, owing to the want of protection, legal and military and the utter inadequacy - of the Government of New Mexico to administer to their necessities - from geographical barriers that the country itself imposes - and whereas the great majority of the people of New Mexico - sympathize with these in their endeavors to procure that

that consideration and protection from the Congress of the United States that they as american citizens are so justly entitled to. Therefore

Be it Resolved. By the Senate and House of Representatives of the Territory of New Mexico in legislature assembled. That the Congress of the United States, be and they are hereby memorialized in behalf of the citizens of Arizona. and that we join them in their endeavors to obtain the Territorial organization of Arizona.

Resolved. That the Congress of the United States, in granting to Arizona a Territorial organization, will be doing an act of justice, which the peculiar necessities of that people demand.

(Signed.) Levi J. Keithly
Speaker of the House of Representatives

(Signed). Jose G. Gallegos
Presidente de Consejo

APPENDIX B

When the provisional government of the Territory of Arizona was established in April of 1860, a pamphlet was issued containing the proceedings at Tucson, the constitution which was agreed upon, the schedule, and the inaugural address of the governor, Dr. Lewis S. Owings. This rare pamphlet, which was the first imprint published in Arizona, was produced on the press of the *Weekly Arizonian,* which had been purchased by Sylvester Mowry in July, 1859 and removed from Tubac to Tucson.

There is some discrepancy between the two lists of delegates which are given. A few of the names which appear in the first list are omitted from the second, and conversely. Among the delegates listed was the brother of Charles D. Poston, John Lee Poston, who was murdered at the Heintzelman Mine in 1861.

In March of 1861, after Baylor's Confederate military government was established, Governor Owings wrote to W. B. Ochiltree, delegate from Texas, requesting that the constitution of the provisional government of Arizona be legalized by the Confederacy. Ochiltree presented Owings' communication and a copy of the pamphlet to the Confederate Congress on April 29, 1861. Both exhibits were referred to the Committee on Territories, but no action was taken.

The title page of the original pamphlet has been reproduced in facsimile, but the text has been copied in new and larger type, with different pagination. The original spelling and punctuation have been retained although some names and other words are misspelled.

THE

CONSTITUTION AND SCHEDULE

—OF—

THE PROVISIONAL GOVERNMENT

—OF—

THE TERRITORY OF ARIZONA,

AND THE PROCEEDINGS OF THE CONVENTION

HELD AT TUCSON.

TUCSON:

J. HOWARD WELLS, PUBLISHER.

1860.

Published by order of the Constitutional Convention — assembled at Tucson,
Arizona Territory, April 2, 1860.

CONSTITUTIONAL CONVENTION

The delegates elected to form a Provisional Constitution for Arizona, as per previous call, assembled in Tucson on Monday, the 2d day of April, 1860.

At 10 o'clock A. M., the Convention was called to order by J. Howard Wells of Tucson, who moved its temporary organization and the election of S. W. Cozzens, Esq., of Mesilla, as Chairman *pro tem.*, and G. H. Oury, Esq., as Secretary.

These gentlemen having been unanimously elected,

The Chairman declared the Convention convened, and in a few brief but pertinent remarks, stated the object for which the delegates had assembled.

On motion of Judge E. McGowan of Mesilla, a committee of five was appointed upon credentials.

The Chair appointed Messrs. McGowan of Mesilla, Wordsworth of Sonoita, Lucas of Mesilla, Wells of Tucson, and Neal of Gila City, as such committee.

On motion of J. D. Alden, Esq., of Tubac, the Committee on Credentials were also authorized to report upon a permanent organization.

On motion, a recess of half an hour was taken by the Convention, to allow the committee time to report.

The Convention met pursuant to adjournment, when the committee, through its chairman, submitted the following report:

Your committee having examined the credentials presented, beg leave to report the following persons entitled to seats as delegates in this Convention:

MESILLA — James A. Lucas, Ygnacio Orrantia, Raphael Ruelas, S. W. Cozzens, Edward McGowan, L. S. Owens, S. G. Bean, T. J. Bull.

SANTA RITA DEL COBRE — Leonada Liqueras, T. J. Thibault.

LAS CRUCES — Frank DeRuyther, Samuel B. Ford.

DONA ANA — Pablo Melendres, Pedro Aguirre.

LA MESA — T. J. Miller, G. W. Putnam.

SANTA TOMAS — Ramon Sanchez.

PICACHO — Jose MaChavis.

AMOLES — Jose MaGarcia.

TUCSON — Wm. S. Oury, Col. Palatine Robinson, John Capron, J. Howard Wells.

ARIVACA — Rees Smith.

TUBAC — J. Dean Alden, R. M. Doss.

SONOITA — W. C. Wordsworth.

GILA CITY — B. F. Neal, Thos. J. Mastin.

We also beg leave to report, as permanent officers of this Convention – James A. Lucas, Esq., of Mesilla, as President; and Granville H. Oury, Esq., as Secretary.

S. W. Cozzens having retired, James A. Lucas was conducted to the chair, and addressed the Convention as follows:

Gentlemen of the Convention: For the honor you have cenferred, in electing me to preside over the deliberations of your honorable body, I feel deeply sensible and grateful. It is with no ordinary emotion I return to you my heartfelt thanks. There are others among you who, by age and experience in parliamentary matters, are far more able and worthy to fill the honorable position bestowed on me. My efforts, gentlemen, will be used to preside over your deliberations with impartiality and fairness; and to that end I ask your earnest co-operation and assistance.

We have assembled, gentlemen, on this occasion, to organize a Provisional Government for Arizona. The neglect of the General Government to heed our prayers and petitions – its refusal to grant us a Territorial organization, notwithstanding our application renewed year after year – the slight hopes of any favorable action from the present Congress of the United States in our behalf, compels us to look to ourselves, in our own defense. If Congress will do nothing for us, it becomes us, as freemen and American citizens, to act for ourselves. We would be menial to remain longer dormant in our present exposed and defenseless condition, without law or protection – and such a course would be suicidal to our best interests.

Our citizens cry aloud for protection. The varied interests of our Territory are paralyzed, through the insecurity to person and property existing at the present time. Crime stalks abroad in our midst, while our country is overrun by tribes of barbarous savages, who despoil our citizens of their hard-earned avails, murdering or carrying into captivity those who are weak and unprotected. This state of affairs should not longer exist. It is our duty to organize for ourselves a Government affording some protection for the future. It is useless to look to New Mexico! – a Government from which we have received only scorn and neglect – they have been regardless of our interests and necessities. For years we have been deprived of every right and privilege which, as American citizens we are entitled to; and it behooves us now – dissevered as we are from New Mexico, neglected by the Congress of the United States – to organize for ourselves a Government under which our lives will be protected, our property secured and the future growth and prosperity of the country realized. Let us go forward to the work like men; and, with econmy, prudence and wisdom, our efforts will be crowned with prosperity and happiness.

Hoping that peace and harmony may prevail over the deliberations of this Convention, I again offer you my sincere and heartfelt thanks for the confidence shown by electing me your presiding officer.

Capt. John Donaldson presented his credentials as a delegate from Calabasas, which were received, and on motion he was accepted as a delegate from said Precinct.

On motion of Judge B. F. Neal of Gila City, the respective delegates were required to take the oath to support the Constitution of the United States, which was unanimously adopted.

On motion that the proceedings of this Convention should be governed by the rules and regulations as laid down in Jefferson's Manual, for governing the House of Representatives, same was adopted.

The oath was then administered by J. Howard Wells, Esq., Justice of the Peace, to the presiding officers and members.

On motion, adjourned till 2 o'clock P. M.

Convention met pursuant to adjournment. When,

On motion of S. W. Cozzens, a committee of seven was appointed to draft a Constitution for the Provisional Government of Arizona.

The Chair appointed the following named gentlemen as such committee: B. F. Neal, S. W. Cozzens, Edward McGowan, Wm. S. Oury, Ygnacio Orrantia, T. J. Miller and W. C. Wordsworth.

On motion, a recess of one hour was taken, to allow the committee time to report.

Convention met pursuant to adjournment, and was called to order by the President.

Judge B. F. Neal, Chairman of the Committee on the Formation of a Constitution for Arizona, submitted the following report:

To the Hon. James A. Lucas, President of the Convention: Your committee, to whom was referred the Constitution for the Provisional Government of the Territory of Arizona, have had the same under consideration, and respectfully beg leave to submit the accompaning Constitution for your deliberation and adoption:

It was moved and seconded that the report of the committee be accepted, and that the Convention proceed to vote upon the Constitution *ad seriatim.*

On motion, T. M. Turner Esq. of Tubac, was appointed as Assistant Secretary.

G. W. Putnam, proxy for Juan Romero, La Mesa, having appeared, was duly sworn in, and took his seat.

The Constitution was now taken up, section by section. The Preamble having been read, a motion was made that it be adopted.

After considerable debate, the ayes and noes were called on the adoption of the Preamble, and resulted — ayes, 25; noes, 2. Messrs. Alden, Wordsworth and Doss were excused from voting as their names were called.

The Preamble having been adopted, on motion the first section of the Constitution was taken up. On being read,

A motion was made that the Convention do now adjourn till Tuesday morning, at 9 o'clock, which was adopted.

Second Day's Proceedings

MORNING SESSION.

The Convention met pursuant to adjournment, at 9 o'clock A. M.

The roll of delegates having been called, and a quorum being present, the Convention was declared duly opened for business.

The minutes of the first days proceeding having been read, on motion they were declared adopted.

S. W. Cozzens submitted the following motion, which was adopted:

That the vote on the adoption of the Preamble be re-considered, and that the Preamble and Constitution be re-committed to the original committee.

On motion, the Convention took a recess for a quarter of an hour.

Convention met pursuant to adjournment, and was called to order by the President.

B. F. Neal, Chairman of the Committee on Preamble and Constitution, reported the Constitution with sundry amendments.

The report of the committee was accepted, and the Convention proceeded to vote on the adoption of the same, section by section.

The question being on the adoption of the Preamble as amended, the ayes and noes were called.

Rees Smith, on motion, was excused; on a reconsideration of the vote, it was refused him. After a few remarks, in which he defined his position, he voted in the affirmative.

Messrs. Alden, Donaldson and Wordsworth, explained their votes as their names were called.

The vote having been completed, resulted as follow: ayes, 29; noes, 1.

Whereupon the Preamble was declared adopted.

The Constitution having been voted upon, section by section, and sundry amendments incorporated, on motion it was engrossed for a third reading, and finally passed.

On motion, the rules were suspended and the Constitution read by its title.

The question now being on the adoption of the Constitution, the ayes and noes were called, which resulted as follow: ayes, 28; noes, 1. Capt. John Donaldson voting in the negative.

On motion of Mr. Rees Smith, the Convention agreed to go into an election of Governor, under the Constitution.

Dr. L. S. Owings of Mesilla, was nominated for the office of Governor. No other nomination being made, the Convention proceeded to ballot, which resulted as follow: Dr. L. S. Owings, 26; 2, not voting; 3, absent.

After the enthusiasm had subsided, on the announcement of the vote, the Governor elect, in a few brief remarks, returned his warmest thanks to the gentlemen of the Convention, for the distinguished honor conferred on him, and promised at an early day to give his views at length on the policy which should govern him in the discharge of his duties.

A motion was made that the Convention do now adjourn till 7 o'clock P. M., which was adopted.

EVENING SESSION.

Convention met at 7 o'clock, pursuant to adjournment, and was called to order by the President.

On motion of S. W. Cozzens, it was resolved to appoint a Committee on County Lines and Boundaries. The Chair appointed Messrs. Mastin, Capron, Miller, Doss and McGowan, as such Committee.

On motion, the Chair appointed Messrs. Alden, Wells and Oury, a Committee on Enrolled Bills.

J. Howard Wells asked leave, being unavoidably detained from the session of the Convention in the afternoon, now to record his vote in favor of the Constitution as adopted; also, to record his vote for Dr. L. S. Owings for Governor. Leave was unanimously granted.

On motion, the Committe on Enrolled Bills was empowered to employ a clerk.

On motion, the Convention adjourned till Wednesday morning, at 11 o'clock.

Third Day's Proceedings

MORNING SESSION.

Convention met pursuant to adjournment — roll called. On motion the reading of Tuesday's proceedings was dispensed with.

The reports of committees were then called for.

Judge Neal, Chairman of the Committee on the Constitution and Schedule, reported progress, and asked further time for the completion of the Schedule. Granted.

Mr. Martin from the Committee on County Lines and Boundaries, submitted a report.

[The substance of the report, in an amended form, was afterward incorporated in the Schedule, and is therefore omitted here]

The Sergeant-at-Arms being absent, the President appointed F. G. Ake to fill the office *pro tem.*

On motion, adjourned till 2 o'clock P. M.

AFTERNOON SESSION.

Convention met, pursuant to adjournment, at 2 o'clock P. M.

Mr. Cozzens stated that Capt. R. S. Ewell, U. S. A., was present, and moved that he be invited to a seat within the bar of the House. Carried.

Capt. J. Dean Alden from the Committee on Enrollment, reported that they had secured the services of Mr. N. King, who had kindly copied the Constitution in a shape suitable for enrollment. The report was accepted, and on motion, a vote of thanks was tendered Mr. King, and he was invited to a seat within the bar of the House.

Mr. Secretary Oury, Chairman of the Committee on Printing, submitted the following report:

TUESDAY, April 3, 1860.

To the Hon James A. Lucas, President of the Convention:

The committee, to whom was referred the printing of the Constitution and the proceedings of this Convention, have had the same under consideration; and, after consultation with the proprietor of THE ARIZONIAN, find that two hundred and fifty copies printed in English and one hundred and twenty-five copies in Spanish, will cost $275; and that five hundred copies alone in English, will cost $225 — which appears to your committee too extravagant, and consequently they have made no arrangement for the performance of the service. All of which is respectfully submitted.

G. H. OURY, Chairman.

On motion, the report was accepted and the committee discharged from further consideration of the subject.

On motion, the whole subject was referred to a committee consisting of Messrs. Owings and DeRuyther.

B. F. Neal from the Standing Committee, reported a Schedule to accompany the Constitution, which was accepted, and the Convention proceeded to consider the same, section by section.

On motion of Capt. J. Dean Alden, the section entitled "Counties," was first considered.

The Secretary having read the section,

Capt. Alden moved to amend by inserting the name of "Ewell," to the county comprising the territory between the Chirrichua Mountains and the longitudinal line proposed as the western boundary of the county, in place of "Santa Rita," as called in the report.

The amendment was adopted by an unanimous vote.

The Convention then proceeded to consider the Schedule, commencing at section 1.

At the request of the Mexican delegates, Mr. T. J. Miller was appointed to interpret to them the subject matter of each section, as considered.

Pending the consideration of the Schedule, the Convention adjourned till 7 o'clock P. M.

EVENING SESSION.

Convention met at 7 o'clock, pursuant to adjournment.

The consideration of the Schedule was continued.

The whole Schedule having been voted upon, section by section, and sundry amendments incorporated, on motion it was engrossed for a third reading, and finally passed.

On motion, the rules were suspended, and the Schedule read by its title. The question now being on the adoption of the Schedule, the ayes and noes were called, when it resulted as follow: Number of votes cast, 27; ayes, 26; noes, 1.

On motion, the Schedule was committed to the Committee of Enrollment, for the purpose of being enrolled.

On motion, adjourned till Thursday morning at 9 o'clock.

Fourth Day's Proceedings

MORNING SESSION.

The Convention met, pursuant to adjournment Thursday, morning at 9 o'clock. Roll called, and a quorum being present, the Convention proceeded to business.

The minutes of second and third days' proceedings were read, and after several slight amendments, were approved.

Judge McGowan submitted the following resolutions, which were adopted:

Resolved, That we heartily approve of the pure, wise, and patriotic administration of our venerable President JAMES BUCHANAN, fully believing that his only aim in carrying out his Government, has been for the good of the whole country. And if some of the judicious measures of the administration have failed to become effective, it has been caused by the opposition of factious demagogues, whose only desire has been for their own aggrandisement and political preferment, and not for the public welfare.

Resolved, That the course pursued by our Delegate to Congress – the Hon. SYLVESTER MOWRY, and his indefatigable efforts to obtain for Arizona a Territorial organization, deserves the especial trust and confidence of the people of this Territory, and that a vote of thanks be tendered to him by the people, through their Delegates elect to this Convention, for the creditable manner in which he has discharged the obligations of his position, with the request that the same shall be continued, in our behalf.

Resolved, That in Capt. R. S. Ewell, of Fort Buchanan, the people of Arizona have found a devoted friend, and the Government a distinguished officer – one who is ever ready to pursue and bring to justice the savage robber and destroyer of human life, or to rescue the helpless captive. He has the heartfelt thanks of the people of Arizona, and we trust that Government will not be tardy in bestowing upon a meritorious soldier some evidence of its approbation, commensurate with his efficient services.

Resolved, That the Commanding and other Officers, stationed at the several Military Posts in Arizona, have faithfully discharged their duties, and have performed all that the limited means within their power would permit, for the suppression of the Indian forays, so frequent and destructive to the lives and interests of the settlers of the Territory.

Resolved, That the thanks of this Convention are due and hereby tendered to the Hon. J. A. Lucas, for the very able, impartial, and dignified manner, he has discharged the duties of President of this Convention.

Resolved, That the thanks of this Convention are also tendered to G. H. Oury and T. M. Turner, Esqs., for the efficient manner they have discharged the duties of Secretaries to the Convention.

Resolved, That the thanks of this Convention, are due to Wm. H. Burke, Esq. Serjeant-at-Arms, and Jerry Robinson, Esq., Doorkeeper, for the very efficient manner they have discharged the duties of their offices.

A motion to adjourn was negatived.

On motion, the Convention took a recess for five minutes.

Convention met pursuant to adjournment.

Mr. Cozzens submitted the following resolution, which was adopted:

Be it resolved, By the delegates of the people of Arizona, in Convention assembled, that we earnestly and particularly protest against the removal of any of the United States troops now stationed in Arizona, or the breaking up of any United States military post now established in said Territory; and particularly do we protest against the removal of Fort Fillmore upon the Rio Grande, and Fort Buchanan on the head of the Sonoita, as the citizens of those portions of the Territory are entirely without protection, and exposed to the depredations of hostile tribes of Indians who infest that section of country.

On motion of Judge Neal, a committee of three was appointed to wait upon the Governor elect, and inform him that the Convention was now ready to administer to him the oath of office.

The Committee consisted of Messrs. Neal, McGowan and Donaldson.

On motion, the name of Mr. Frank DeRuther was added to the committee.

The committee appeared with Dr. L. S. Owings, the Governor elect, who was conducted within the bar of the House, when the oath of office, as prescribed by the Schedule, was duly administered by J. Howard Wells, Esq., Justice of the Peace.

The Governor then delivered the following –

INAUGURAL ADDRESS

Mr. President and Gentlemen of the Convention:

Having taken the oath prescribed by the Constitution, I deem it necessary, before entering upon the duties devolving on me, as the Executive officer of the Provisional Government, just created, to present to this Convention, and to my fellow citizens at large, some of the views that I entertain and the policy which shall govern my actions in endeavoring to carry into effect the administration of the new Territorial Government. Previous to this however, I cannot refrain from tendering to you my heartfelt thanks, for the honor you have so generously conferred upon me, in selecting me as the chief Executive of the Provisional Government – the marks of approbation, which I have received at your hands is very flattering to my feelings indeed, and I cannot at this moment, find words, in the vocabulary of my language, strong enough to convey to you my sincere gratitude; if, however, a faithful discharge of the duties of the office pertaining to the Gubernatorial chair, will be any recompense for the honor you have with one spirit so unanimously and generously conferred on me, I pledge my sacred honor it shall be done to the strict letter of that Constitution under which we are acting, and with a proper respect to the laws of the United States. In carrying out these measures, however, should I unfortunately err, and to do so is human – you must attribute these errors to the head and not to the heart.

There were probably many reasons why I should not have accepted the office of Governor, but there is one very cogent one which has mainly prompted me in so doing, and that is, my just conviction, that every individual, however exalted or humble his position in life may be, when called upon by his fellow citizens, to serve them in a public capacity, he should cheerfully accede to their wishes, even should the sacrifice of private interests be great.

I am truly embarrassed in the fear, that my abilities may not be equal to the onerous duties imposed upon me, but with your co-operation and that of my fellow citizens, and under the influence and direction of Divine Providence, I trust I may be enabled to form, even in this chaotic region, a government calculated to insure protection, cause the Territory to prosper and render the people happy.

In the organization of a government, like the one we have just established, there are numerous difficulties to contend with, and many serious obstacles to surmount before we can mature things for the best interests of the Territory and meet the approbation of all of our fellow citizens – I shall, however, trusting in your sound judgment and wise counsel, enter upon the discharge of the duties of office, with a degree of confidence.

I harbor no doubts, as to the feasibility of the project for establishing a Provisional Government, nor do I believe in adopting a Coustitution to guide us in administering the laws of said government, that we in any way infringe upon or conflict with that sacred instrument, the Constitution of the United States.

It is well known to you, gentlemen, that we have as yet little or no statistical information, by which we can arrive at any data, in regard to the fiscal affairs of the Provisional Government – no direct tax can be levied upon the people – and the Mesilla valley and the country immediately surrounding it, are the only places that have heretofore paid merchants and pedlars licenses, etc. These licenses from all sources, amounted in the aggregate, yearly, to between eight and nine thousand dollars; this snm was payable into the treasury of New Mexico, under our present organization it will be paid into the treasury of our Provisional Government, and it will go far in helping to liquidate the expenses of the officers, printing, etc., of the new government. So soon as the County elections are held, and Probate Judges, and Sheriffs are duly installed, in the several Counties in the Territory, we shall probably be able to arrive at a correct conclusion, as what sum can be raised annually, to defray the expenses of the government. From all the information I can gather from those who are best acquainted with the facts, by pursuing a prudent and an economical course – the revenues which will accrue to the Government, under the old system, the licenses imposed by the statutes of New Mexico, and which would have been assessed in the western portion of the Territory, had the new County been organized – will be amply sufficient to meet all the wants of the Government.

The main cause, for the non-collection of licenses by the officers of the Territory of New Mexico, in the western portion of the Territory of Arizona, can be attributed to the fact, that this portion of Arizona, is far removed from Santa Fe,(Tucson being over 600 miles, and Arizona and Gila cities 900 miles from the capital of New Mexico) the location of a government, which failed to afford us any protection, or to enact the necessary laws to enable us at least to have some show of a form of government, under which we, civilized as we claim to be, could peaceably exist. The County of Dona Ana comprised the whole of the Gadsden purchase, and two towns on the east side of the Rio Grande – Las Cruces and Dona Ana, containing a population of four thousand – and the entire county containg an estimated population of 11,000 souls – and my opinion is, gentlemen, when the census of the Territory shall have been taken, it will far exceed that number. This same county, covering an area of country from the extreme east to the western boundary, of 900 miles, and in breadth, from 200 to 300 miles, and in population 11,000, was allowed *one* Senator and *one* Representative in the legislative council, which convened yearly at Santa Fe – a representation probably, not equal to the smallest county in the New Mexican Territory Why, gentlemen, the number of inhabitants to day in the Mesilla valley, far outnumber those of the ancient and far-famed City of Santa Fe. Arizona, to her honor be it said, does not avail herself of this New Mexican *liberality* by sending any one to Santa Fe to represent her; but we have sent an honorable gentleman (Mr. Mowry) to Washington to represent our necessities, and if possible, to procure for us a Territorial Government at the hands of Congress; we still have hopes, in the justness of our cause, that our Representative may yet succeed in getting an organization even before the adjournment of the present Congress, "a consummation most devotely to be wished for," by the people of this neglected country. Until that important epoch in our htstory arrives,let us, Mr. President and gentlemen of the Convention, adopt for our guidance the motto of the English Kings: *"Dieu et mon droit"* – God and and my right.

I am reminded, by a friend, that a rumor was rife some time last winter, that the New Mexican Legislature had passed a law creating a new county somewhere in the western section of the Territory. The metes and bounds of this new county no one in Arizona has ever been made acquainted with; nor is it requisite that they should be, for the people did not ask this favor at the hands of the Legislaturo then sitting at Santa Fe, and consequently never intended to organize any more counties of their creating. It is not my province, gentlemen, neither is it your desire I know, to detract from the New Mexican people any honor that properly belongs to them – far from it. At the same time, while I am willing to "render unto Caesar the things which are Caesar's," I must do justice to the people of our own Territory. The people of New Mexico have no feelings in common with the people of Arizona, and *vice versa* – our habits, tastes and pursuits are different; and while we desire to be upon friendly terms with them socially in our Territorial matters, for the future, all we ask – in order to cement the bond of friendship – *is to be let alone;* for we have the presumption to think that we have arrived at that stage of the proceedings in our Territorial affairs, which forces us to attempt, at least, to manage for ourselves.

So soon as the Territorial Legislature shall meet, I will embrace the opportunity of calling its attention to the propriety of a geological survey of the Territory. The principal object should be to ascertain and make known, abroad, the immense wealth of our Territory in minerals, and in agricultural and grazing resources, with a view to their full development. These objects are eminently practicable, and at a very triffling expense this information can be obtained. The publication of such a report, showing as it no doubt would, the inexhaustible mineral wealth of the Territory, its fine grazing properties, and its beautiful valleys adapted for agricultural purposes, capable of furnishing, to a large number of artesans and laborers, employment in our silver, gold and copper mines, and homes for hundreds of sturdy emigrants and their families; such a report I am confident, gentlemen, made by one thoroughly acquainted with the sciences of geology and mineralogy – would soon rapidly increase our population, and would add to the immensely cumulative testimony why Congress should speedily give us a Territorial Government.

It is well known to you gentlemen, that the Gadsden purchase, which comprises the vast majority of the Territory of Arizona, was at the time of the transfer by Mexico, to the United States, inhabited chiefly by wild and savage tribes of Indians – the roving, thieving and murdering Apaches – who existed mainly by forays into Sonora to steal horses and cattle. Some time since a treaty was made by some of the United States military officers, and others attached to the Indian Agency, and the chiefs of these savage tribes, who agreed in their stipulations that no further depredations should be committed by them upon the residents of Arizona – the officers, on the part of the United States agreeing to furnish the various tribes, farming implements, seeds for planting, "*manta*" to cover their nakedness, and trinkets and baubles, such as the Indian delights to display on his person. On the part of the Government officers these treaty stipulations were sacredly kept, the Indians receiving all that was promised them. But did they, gentlemen, perform their part of the contract? Far from it. It is true, for a few months after the treaty was made, we heard nothing of Apache depredations within our borders – except occasionally a horse, a mule, or a beef having been stolen, or their having made a requisition upon the Overland Mail stations for flour, corn, etc., which for the sake of peace, in every instance their demands were complied with, and their petty thefts overlooked. But recently, emboldened by success, the instincts of their savage nature have predominated; they have driven off our stock, murdered our citizens in cold blood, and forced our women and children into captivity.

Gentlemen, if we expect to live in Arizona and prosper, we must teach the savages a salutary lesson – one that will be lasting and effective – no more presents and worthless treaties. They have commenced the strife and wish for war. War, be it then – war to the knife, and the knife to the hilt.

By virtue of the office of Governor, I am Commander-in-chief of the citizen soldiery of the Territory. I shall therefore pursue that course of policy best calculated to give protection to life and property, and as speedily as surrounding circumstances will permit, appoint the most efficient officers, and organize the militia of the Territory. Believing, from past experience, however that volunteers will be the most effective for frontier service, I shall, as soon as arrangements can be made for their equipment and supplies, order out several Ranging Companies, and detail them into service until the Indians are thoroughly chastised and our Indian border troubles are quieted.

There are other subjects that I might touch upon at this time, but believing it more appropriate for some future day, I shall not longer occupy the time of the Convention by extending my remarks. In conclusion Mr. President and gentlemen of the Convention, allow me again to return you my thanks for the distinguished honor you have conferred on me, in selecting me as your chief Executive officer, and for the courteous attention and politeness you have displayed toward me, during my poor effort at speech making.

At the conclusion of his remarks His Excellency announced the appointment of James A. Lucas as Secretary of the Territory.

On motion of Judge McGowan, it was resolved, that when this Convention adjourns, it shall adjourn to meet at 4 o'clock P. M.

No further business being presented, on motion, adjourned.

AFTERNOON SESSION.

Convention met at 4 o'clock, pursuant to adjournment.

Mr. Miller submitted the following resolution, which was adopted:

Resolved, That the Governor be required to send a copy of the Constitution to the President of the United States, to the heads of Departments, to the members of the Committee on Territories of the two Houses, and also to the Governors of the different States and Territories; and if deemed expedient, the Governor shall have power to send a special messenger to the President. *Provided,* that the same shall be done without expense to the Government.

Governor Owings, Chairman of the Committee on Printing, reported that the proprietor of THE ARIZONIAN would print the copies of the Constitution and Proceedings required by the Convention, at the following rates: For 250 copies in English and 150 copies in Spanish, $250.

The report was accepted, and on motion the committee was authorized to contract for the same at the rates agreed upon.

On motion of J. Howard Wells, a vote of thanks was tendered to Senor Augustine Ainsa, who had kindly offered to translate the Constitution into Spanisih, for publication, free of charge.

The Committee on Enrolled Constitution made a verbal report – that they had attended to their duty, and reported the Constitution and Schedule on the table, ready for signatures. The report of the committee was accepted, and the members of the Convention proceeded to sign the paper.

Capt. John Donaldson presented the following protest, which, by vote of the House, was ordered to be spread on the minutes:

I wish to enter my protest against the Constitution and Schedule, and beg leave that the same be entered upon the record of this Convention.

JNO. DONALDSON.

The signing of the Constitution having been completed,

On motion, Convention adjourned till 7 o'clock P. M.

EVENING SESSION.

Convention met at 7 o'clock, pursuant to adjournment.

Mr. Cozzens moved the adoption of the following resolution:

Resolved, That Mr. Wordsworth be requested to furnish a copy of his remarks, on the adoption of the Provisional Constitution, for publication with the proceedings.

Capt. J. Dean Alden moved the adoption of the following resolution, which was unanimously passed:

Resolved, That the thanks of the members of this Convention be, and are hereby tendered to the Hon. Benj. F. Neal, for the able assistance he has rendered the Convention by his advice, and the laborious duties he has personally performed.

Gov. L. S. Owings presented the following letter, written to the Convention by Samuel G. Bean, which was ordered to be spread on the minutes:

MESILLA, March 28, 1860.

To the Delegates of the General Convention, to be held at Tucson, for the purpose of forming a Povisional Government for Arizona, on the first Monday in April, 1860:

GENTLEMEN: Having the honor to be a delegate from this place, regret very much my inability to attend on so important an occasion. I have chosen my friend James A. Lucas to represent my views, and he is hereby fully authorized to act for me in the Convention. The project of forming a Provisional Government for Arizona I have only to say, meets my hearty concurrence; and though absent, I am with you, heart and hand.

I will stand to the Constitution you may adopt, and support it through "a sea of troubles." My most ardent desire is to see the consummation of this work, in my conception so nobly begun; and I assure you I have not "weakened," and that there is no back out in me on the subject.

I am, very respectfully, your obedient servant,

SAMUEL G. BEAN.

After the reading of the letter, His Excellencv announced the appointment of military officials.

Judge McGowan moved the adoption of the following resolution:

Resolved, That Messrs. Wordsworth and Doss be earnestly requested to accept the positions to which they have been nominated by the Governor.

Mr. Donaldson asked to have it stated on the minutes that he declined voting.

The motion was carried by acclamation.

The following resolution, submitted by Judge McGowan, was adopteed:

Resolved, That the Treasurer be directed to pay for the printing authorized by the Convention, out of the first moneys which shall come into the Treasury.

The object for which the Convention was called having been accomplished, and no further business being brought before the body, the Convention adjourned *sine die.*

JAMES A. LUCAS, President.

GRANVILLE H. OURY,
T. M. TURNER, } Secretaries.

PROVISIONAL CONSTITUTION

We, the people of Arizona, in order to form a government, establish justice, insure domestic tranquility and provide for the common defense, do ordain and establish this Constitution: *Provided,* that the same shall remain in force until Congress shall organize a Territorial Government, and no longer.

ARTICLE I.

SECTION 1. That there is, shall be, and hereby is created for Arizona, a Provisional Government for all that part of the Territory of the United States included within the following limits, to wit: Beginning on the Colorado, at the parallel of north latitude thirty-three degrees forty minutes; thence with said parallel to the eastern boundary of New Mexico; thence with said boundary until it intersects the line of Texas; thence with said line to the Rio Grande, and so on to the line of Mexico on said river, as fixed by the treaty of eighteen hundred and fifty-four; thence with the boundary line established by said treaty between the United States and Mexico, to the Colorado; thence up the Colorado to the place of beginning. Which said Government shall be divided into three separate and distinct departments, viz.: Legislative, Executive and Judicial.

SEC. 2. The legislative power shall be vested in a Senate and House of Representatives.

SEC. 3. The Senate shall consist of nine members. The House of Representatives shall consist of eighteen members — each of which members shall hold their term of office for one year.

SEC. 4. The first Legislature of Arizona shall be convened by the Governor, at such time and place as this Convention shall decide — which said Convention shall also make an apportionment giving to each portion of the Territory representation in the ratio of its population, as nearly as may be — Indians excepted.

SEC. 5. All members of the Senate and House of Representatives shall be *bona fide* citizens of the county or District they may represent.

SEC. 6. An election for members of the Senate and House of Representatives shall be ordered by the Governor at least thirty days before the first day of the first session of the said Legislature; and those persons having the highest number of votes in their respective districts, for said offices, shall be by the Governor declared duly elected as members of the Senate and House of Representatives for the term of one year; and the persons, so declared duly elccted, shall meet as hereinbefore prescribed by the Governor.

SEC. 7. The time, place and manner of holding and conducting all elections and apportioning the representation in the several counties or districts, to the

Senate and House of Representatives, shall in future be prescribed by law, as well as the time of convening the Legislature. *Provided,* that no session shall continue longer than thirty days. *Provided further,* that the Governor, in case of necessity, shall have power to call an extra session.

SEC. 8. Every white male person who shall have attained the age of twenty-one years, and who shall be a citizen of the United States and shall have resided in the Territory of Arizona three months next preceding an election, and the last thirty days within the county, city or town, in which he offers to vote, (Indians excepted,) shall be deemed a qualified elector; and every person who shall have resided six months in said Territory, shall be eligible to any office in the gift of the people. *Provided,* that no soldier, seaman or mariner, in the army or navy of the United States, shall be entitled to vote at any election created by this Constitution.

SEC. 9. The legislative power shall extend to all rightful subjects of legislation consistent with the provisions of the Constitution of the United States, and not inconsistent with the provisions of this Constitution.

SEC. 10. Immediately after the adjournment of this Convention, the Governor of the Provisional Government of the Territory of Arizona shall issue his Proclamation, directing and requiring elections to be holden in all the counties of this Territory, on the first Monday in May, A. D. 1860, for all county officers created by this constitution, to be elected by the people, which said elections shall be conducted by law.

ARTICLE II.

SEC. 1. The Executive authority of this Territory shall be vested in a Governor, who shall be styled the Governor of the Provisional Government of Arizona.

SEC. 2. The first Governor of this Territory shall be elected by this Convention, and hold his office for one year; and all subsequent elections for Governor shall be by the people, in such manner and at such times as the Legislature shall prescribe.

SEC. 3. The Governor shall be a resident of this Territory; shall approve all laws passed by the Legislature, before they shall go into effect; shall be Commander-in-Chief of the Militia of the Territory; may grant pardons for offenses against the laws of the Territory; shall commission all officers who shall be appointed or elected to office under the laws of the Territory, and shall see that the laws of the Provisional Government are duly executed.

SEC. 4. In case of the death, absence or inability, of the Governor to act, the Lieutenant Governor shall be Governor *ex officio,* during such absence or inability; or in case of death, for the unexpired term; he shall preside over the Senate, but shall not vote on any question unless the Senate be equally divided, and shall receive during the session of the Senate the same pay, including mileage, which is allowed members of the Senate. And in the further event of the death or inability of the Lieutenant Governor, the duties of the Governor shall devolve on the Secretary of the Territory.

SEC. 5. The Governor shall have power, by and with the advice and consent of the Senate, to appoint a Lieutenant Governor, a Secretary of the Territory, a Controller, a Treasurer and a Marshal, three District Judges and an Attorney General.

Sec. 6. The Secretary shall attest all of the official acts of the Governor; and shall also keep a correct record of all the laws, resolutions, etc., passed by the Legislature — together with a copy of the proceedings of the Legislative Assembly — on file in his office; he shall also have the care and custody of the seal of the Territory.

Sec. 7. The Controller shall audit all the accounts of the Territory, and shall draw warrants upon the Treasury for all moneys to pay the necessary expenditure for the Provisional Government and for the salaries of the Territorial officers; he shall keep a correct and true record of all accounts audited by him and the orders drawn by him on the Territorial Treasury. His books shall be open to inspection at all times, and he shall give a bond, payable to the people of the Provisional Government of Arizona, in such sum as may hereafter be provided by law, conditioned for the faithful discharge of the duties of his office.

Sec. 8. The Treasurer shall receive all fines that may be imposed by the courts of the Territory, receive all licenses and other revenues accruing to the Territory; shall pay all orders that may be drawn upon him by the Controller, by virtue of his office; shall keep a set of books in which these accounts shall be entered, which books shall be open for the inspection of the public at all times; shall make a balance sheet showing the exact state of the finances of the Territory quarterly, which balance sheet shall be submitted to the Governor for his inspection, and shall be by him published in some newspaper in the Territory; shall give a bond to the people of the Territory of Arizona, with four sureties, in such sum as shall hereinafter be established by law, conditioned for the faithful discharge of the duties of his office; and shall receive, as salary, two per cent on all the moneys received by him, and no other compensation.

Sec. 9. The Marshal shall have jurisdiction in all counties or districts in the Territory; shall serve all processes that may be placed in his hands emanating from the Supreme Court; shall receive the same fees now allowed United States Marshal for services in New Mexico, and shall give a bond, with proper sureties, to the people of Arizona, in such sum as shall hereafter be established by law, conditioned for the faithful discharge of his duties.

Sec. 10. All bonds given by Territorial officers shall be approved by the Governor, until otherwise ordered by law.

ARTICLE III.

Sec. 1. The Judicial power of this Government shall be vested in a Supreme Court, three District Courts, Probate Courts and Alcaldes or Justices of the Peace; and the Legislature may, from time to time, create municipal and other inferior courts, as the wants of the people may require.

Sec. 2. The three District Judges shall constitute the Supreme Court, which shall hold one session each year, at the seat of Government of the Territory.

Sec. 3. The three District Judges shall be appoitned by the Governor, for the term of two years; one of their number shall be appointed by the said Governor, Chief Justice of the Territory, whose duty it shall be to preside at all sessions of the Supreme Court. The powers and duties which are prescribed to govern the Supreme and District Courts, by the laws of New Mexico, are hereby declared to govern the Supreme and District Courts of this Territory, until altered or amended by the Legislature of this Territory.

Sec. 4. The said District Judges shall receive, as compensation for their services, such sum as shall hereafter be established by law.

Sec. 5. The District Judges shall hold two terms of court every year, in each county in their district, which terms shall continue in session until the business before the court be disposed of, until otherwise provided by law.

Sec. 6. The Governor shall appoint an Attorney General for the Territory, whose duty it shall be to prosecute all criminal offenses arising under the laws of the Territory, in the District and Supreme Courts, and shall receive such salary as shall hereafter be established by law, and the same fees allowed the Attorney General by the laws of New Mexico, and whose term of office shall be coequal with that of the Judges of the District Courts.

Sec. 7. Special terms may be called by either of the three District Judges when, in their opinion, the ends of Justice will be subserved.

Sec. 8. The county offices, including Probate Judges, Justices of the Peace, Sheriffs, Constables, etc., as now provided for by the laws of New Mexico, together with their fees of office shall, and the same are hereby declared to govern the elections, proceedures, etc., of the said county offices in this Territory — except that the Probate Judges of the different counties shall receive the fees formerly allowed said Judges by the laws of New Mexico, instead of a salary, as now provided.

Sec. 9. All the general laws, both Civil and Criminal Codes of practice, and all laws applicable to this Territory not inconsistent with the Constitution now in force in the Territory of New Mexico, be, and the same are hereby declared to be in full force and effect in this, the Territory of Arizona. *Provided,* the Legislature shall have no power to levy any direct tax upon the people.

SCHEDULE

Section 1. Members of the Legislature and all officers, before they enter upon the duties of their offices, shall take the following oath or affirmation:

I, A—— B——, do solemnly swear (or affirm) that I will faithfully discharge and perform all the duties incumbent on me, as ———————— of the Territory of Arizona, according to the best of my skill and ability, agreeably to the Constitution and laws of the United States and of this Territory.

Sec. 2. The first session of the Legislature of the Provisional Government of the Territory of Arizona shall be holden on the first Monday in March, A. D. 1861, at Tucson; and thereafter, annually, at such time and place as may be designated by law. The members of the Legislature shall each receive five dollars per day during the time they may be in session, and fifteen cents a mile in going to and from the Seat of Government.

JUDICIAL DEPARTMENT

Section 1. All Judges of the Supreme and District Courts shall, by virtue of their offices, be conservators of the peace throughout the Territory. The style of all writs and processes shall be, "The Provisional Government of the Territory of Arizona." All prosecutions shall be carried on in the name and by the authority of the Provisional Government of Arizona.

JUDICIAL DISTRICTS

Section 1. The Judicial Districts of the Territory of Arizona shall be divided as follow, viz.: The following named counties shall comprise the First Judicial District – Dona Ana and La Mesilla. The county of Ewell shall compose the Second Judicial District. The county of Castle Dome shall constitute the Third Judicial District.

Sec. 2. The District Courts of the First Judicial District shall be holden on the first Mondays of June and December, in the county of Dona Ana; in the county of La Mesilla, on the second Mondays of July and December. The District Court of the Second Judicial District shall be holden on the first Mondays of March and September. The District Court of the Third Judicial District shall be holden on the third Mondays of May and October.

Sec. 3. The Supreme and District Judges shall receive each a salary of fifteen hundred dollars per annum, payable quarterly, and fifteen cents per mile to and from attending on the Court, until otherwise provided by the law.

Sec. 4. Each Dictrict Judge shall have power to appoint, for his Judicial District, a clerk who shall be *ex officio* clerk of the Probate Court of the county in which the District Court is held. He shall be a resident of the district or county for which he has been appointed, and shall receive the same fees and emoluments as are now allowed by law to the clerk of the Supreme Courts of the Territory of New Mexico. He shall give a bond in the sum of one thousand dollars, to be approved by the District Judge, for the faithful performance of his duties.

Sec. 5. That no inconvenience may arise from a change of Government, it is declared that all processes which shall be issued in the name of the Territory of New Mexico, prior to the organization of a Provisional Government under this Constitution, shall be as valid as if issued in the name of the Provisional Government of Arizona.

Sec. 6. The validity of all bonds and recognizances, executed in conformity with the laws of New Mexico, shall not be impaired by the change of government; but may be sued for and recovered in the name of the Provisional Government of the Territory of Arizona; and all criminal prosecutions or penal actions, which shall have arisen prior to the organization of a Provisional Government under this Constitution, in any of the courts of the Territory of New Mexico, shall be prosecuted to judgment and execution in the name of the Provisional Government of the Territory of Arizona. All suits at law and equity which may be pending in any of the courts of New Mexico, prior to the organization of this Government under this Constitution, shall be transferred to the proper court of this Territory, which shall have jurisdiction of the subject matter thereof.

OFFICERS

Section 1. The Attorney General shall receive a salary of one thousand dollars per annum and such fees as are established by law, payable quarterly.

Sec. 2. The Governor shall have power to appoint, for each Judicial District, a suitable person to act as District Attorney; he shall be a resident of the district for which he has been appointed, and shall be clothed with the same powers and receive the same compensation for his services, the same fees and emoluments of office, as are now allowed by law to Circuit Attorneys in the Territory of New Mexico.

Sec. 3. The Secretary of State shall receive, as a compensation for his services, as follow, to wit.: Two dollars for every certificate and seal, and such other fees as may be established by law.

Sec. 4. The Treasurer of the Provisional Government of the Territory of Arizona, in addition to the fees now allowed by the Constitution shall receive two and one-half per cent. for all moneys by him disbursed, and shall, previous to entering upon the duties of his office, enter into bonds in the sum of ten thousand dollars, for the faithful performance of his duties.

Sec. 5. It shall be the duty of the Treasurer, as soon as qualified, to demand and receive all moneys and revenues now collected and in the hands of the several officers, which have been collected under the laws of New Mexico, from the people residing within the limits of the Territory of Arizona.

Sec. 6. The Controller shall receive, as compensation for his services, a salary of five hundred dollars per annum, payable quarterly. The duties of the Controller shall be the same (where not otherwise provided for) as the duties prescribed by the laws of New Mexico for Auditor.

CENSUS

Section 1. The Sheriff of each county shall take an enumeration of the inhabitants of the Territory of Arizona, to wit: In the first column, the number of qualified electors; in the second column, all the white males over the age of eighteen years and under forty-five years; in the third column, all the white males under the age of eighteen years; in the fourth column, all the white males over the age of forty-five years; in the fifth column, all the white females; in the sixth column, all the slaves; in the seventh column, all the free white population. That the several Sheriffs shall receive three cents for each white inhabitant, slave or free person of color, enumerated by them. That the said several Sheriffs shall make the returns of the Census of said Territory to the Secretary of State, at least thirty days previous to the first setting of the Legislature of said Territory.

COUNTIES

Section 1. The county of Dona Ana shall comprise all that portion of Territory lying east of the Rio Grande.

Sec. 2. The county of La Mesilla is hereby established with the following boundaries, viz.: The Rio Grande on the east, the Chericahui mountains on the west.

Sec. 3. The county of Ewell comprises all that section of Territory lying between the Chericahui mountains on the east, and the longitudinal line which crosses what is known as the Little Desert, near the the center thereof, on the west.

Sec. 4. The county of Castle Dome comprises all that portion of the Territory lying west of the western boundary of Ewell county.

Sec. 5. It is understood that the above specified boundary-lines of counties above defined, traverse the entire Territory from north to south, crossing the St. Louis and San Francisco Overland Mail route at the points above specified.

Provided, that the Rio Grande shall be the permanent boundary between Dona Ana and La Mesilla counties.

SEC. 7. The Governor of the Provisional Government of Arizona shall appoint, in each precinct of each county, a suitable person to superintend the first election for county officers, to be holden on the first Monday of May next. Said Superintendent shall appoint two Judges and two Clerks, who shall conduct said elections according to law, and make due return thereof to the Secretary of State; and elections shall hereafter be holden and conducted as now provided by law.

MODE OF AMENDING CONSTITUTION

SECTION 1. The Legislature, whenever two-thirds of each House shall deem it necessary, may propose amendments to this Constitution; which proposed amendments shall be duly published in some newspaper, at least sixty days before the election for Representatives, for the consideration of the people; and it shall be the duty of the several election officers, at the next election which shall be thus holden, to open a poll for, and make a return to the Secretary of State, of all those who have voted on such proposed amendments; and if thereupon it shall appear that a majority of all the citizens of this Territory voting for Representatives, have voted in favor of such proposed amendments, and two-thirds of each House of the next Legislature shall, after such election, vote for the same amendment by ayes and noes, they shall be valid to all intents and purposes, as parts of this Constitution.

OFFENSES AGAINST THE PROVISIONAL GOVERNMENT

SECTION 1. That if any person who is a citizen or transient person within the Territory, shall levy war or conspire to levy war against the same, or shall in any way give aid in resisting the officers in executing the laws adopted under the Constitution of the Provisional Government of Arizona, either upon confession in open court or by the testimony of two or more witnesses, such person shall be adjudged guilty of treason, and shall be punished by fine and imprisonment, at the discretion of the court before whom the offender may be arraigned.

SEC. 2. The Schedule adopted on the 5th day of April shall be attached to the Constitution, and form part and parcel of the same.

WHEREAS, For the better protection of life and property against Indians or otherwise; and WHEREAS, in the absence of any legislative action, it is deemed necessary to organize an efficient militia system for the present protection of our citizens, and until the Legislature shall have more fully organized the militia of the Territory; therefore, be it

Resolved, By this Convention assembled:

First, That every free white male inhabitant over eighteen and under forty-five years of age, who is not disabled by bodily infirmity, shall constitute the militia of this Territory, and perform the duties as hereinafter stated. Provided, that no person exempt from bearing arms under the laws of the United States, shall be compelled to serve.

Second, The militia of this Territory shall be divided into two divisions, as hereinafter provided. The said divisions shall be commanded by one Major-General, whose staff shall consist of one Adjutant General with the rank of Colonel, one Quartermaster with the rank of Captain, and two aids with the rank of 1st Lieutenant.

Third, That the counties of Dona Ana and La Mesilla shall comprise the First Division, to be called the Eastern Division. The counties of Ewell and Castle Dome shall comprise the second division, to be called the Western Division. Each of said divisions shall be divided into two regiments, each composed of two companies, or as many as can be enrolled in the service. Each regiment shall be commanded by one Colonel, one Lieutenant-Colonel and one Major. The staff shall consist of a Quartermaster, Paymaster, and Adjutant with the rank of Lieutenant, and one Surgeon; and shall also have attached to it a Sergeant-Major, one Quartermaster's Sergeant, and one drum and fife Major. Each company shall consist of one Captain, a 1st and 2d Lieutenant, four Sergeants, four Corporals, two musicians, and not less than thirty-two nor more than sixty-four privates. The Governor shall appoint all field officers; the Colonels shall appoint their respective staff officers; each company to elect its own officers. The laws and regulations regulating the militia of the Territory of New Mexico, so far as they may be applicable to this Territory and not inconsistent with the provisions above named and the laws of the United States, shall govern the militia of the Provisional Government of the Territory of Arizona, until otherwise altered or amended by the Legislature of the Territory.

VOLUNTEERS.

The laws regulating the calling out of Volunteers, now in force in the Territory of New Mexico, are declared to be in force in this Territory.

Done in Convention, by the Deputies of the people of the Territory of Arizona, at Tucson, on the 5th day of April, in the year of our Lord one thousand eight hundred and sixty.

In testimony whereof we have hereunto subscribed our names.

JAES A. LUCAS, President,.

G. H. Oury,
T. M. Turner, } Secretaries.

DELEGATES:

Epifanio Aguirre,
J. Dean Alden,
Sam'l G. Bean,
Thos. J. Bull,
Jose MaChavez,
J. G. Capron,
R. M. Doss,
Sam'l B. Ford,
Jose MaGarcia,
Edw. McGowan,
Pablo Melendrez, 2d.,
Theodore J. Miller,
Thos. J. Mastin,
Benj. F. Neal,
Ygnacio Orrantia,
L. S. Owings,
Wm. S. Oury,
J. L. Poston,
W. C. Wordsworth.
Estaban Ochao,
Juan Romero,
Raphael Ruelas,
Palatine Robinson,
Samuel W. Cozzens,
Ramon Sanches,
Phillipe Fiquera,
J. J. Thibault,
J. Howard Wells,

Executive department
City of Mesilla Arizona
Hon W B Ochiltree. March the 12th 1861

Dear Sir I have taken the Liberty of forwarding to you a copy of the Constitution of the Provisional government of Arizona and request of you that you have the Same Legalized by your Congress with an amendment to the Second Section of the Second Article in order to place the appointment of the governor in the hands of the President. Should your Congress adopt this Constitution for us you will at ounce recognise us as your Territory which I hope you will do and that without delay. please to press this matter on Congress at an early day

Yours as ever
L S Owings

I would not Live in any other government than that of the South yes my native South

APPENDIX C

Arizona bills introduced in the federal Congress are listed in note 60 on pages 48 and 49. Three of these proposed only to establish a new judicial district within New Mexico, while all the others were designed to create a separate territory. A bill to organize Arizona also was presented to the Confederate Congress, and enacted into law.

The various bills for the most part are too long to copy in their entirety. For this reason only sample pages of some of the bills are here reproduced, except in the instance of the successful H. R. 357:

(1) First page of Senator Rusk's manuscript bill of March 18, 1856, to establish a separate judicial district to be known as the "district of Gila" (S. 176). A surveyor's office, as well as a land office, was to be opened at Mesilla. In the amended version of this bill the boundaries were enlarged *(Fig. 2)*, and the name of the district changed to Arizona. The names of the counties into which the district was to be divided were changed by amendment from East Gila and West Gila to Washington and Jefferson, respectively.

(2) Initial page of first bill to organize Arizona (S.8). Democratic Senator Gwin who introduced this bill named three of the four proposed counties after Democratic Presidents Jefferson, Jackson, and Buchanan. The fourth county, part of the former Doña Ana County of New Mexico, was to be called Washington. The bill subsequently was amended, and in one revision, the northern boundary of the proposed territory was changed from 34° to 33° 40′, north latitude.

(3) Endorsement on later printed version of S. 8 *(see above)*, showing dates of amendment and the final disposition of the bill.

(4) First page of Senator Green's bill to organize the "Territory of Arizuma" (S. 365), which inspired acrimonious debate on the slavery question. A similar bill had been introduced in December, 1859 by Senator Jefferson Davis, the future chief executive of the Confederacy. The language of the bill was based in large part on H. R. 836, which had been introduced in the previous Congress by Representative Alex-

ander H. Stephens of Georgia, but the name of the proposed territory was changed deliberately to *Arizuma*.

(5) First page of printed version of Confederate bill to organize the Territory of Arizona, with manuscript revisions. This bill with some further amendment was approved by President Jefferson Davis on January 18, 1862, and proclaimed into law on February 14. According to its terms, slavery was to be protected in the territory and the boundaries were the same as those in Gwin's federal bill of December, 1857. *(Fig. 5.)* Legislative sessions were to be held in Mesilla, which was designated as the seat of government. The governor also was required to assume the duties of "Commissioner of Indian Affairs," for which service he was to receive additional compensation. In departure from the practice in New Mexico, the act specified that the legislative proceedings of the Confederate Territory of Arizona were to be conducted only in English.

(6) Final working copy of H. R. 357 as amended and passed in the Senate. This shows manuscript notations and deletions made by the Committee on Territories, which agreed to remove all amendments previously passed in the Senate, including the one which located the capital at Tucson.

APPENDIX C(1)

34 Cong)
1 Sess)

S. 176
In the Senate of the U.S.
March 18. 1856.

agreeably to notice Mr Rusk asked & obtained leave to bring in the following bill; which was read twice, referred to the Committee on Territories & ordered to be printed.

~~An act~~ A Bill to establish a separate judicial District south of the Gila, and to create the Office of Surveyor General therein, to provide for the adjudication of certain land claims, to grant Donations to actual settlers, to survey certain lands, and for other purposes.

Sec: 1.

Be it enacted by the Senate and House of Representatives of the United States of America in Congress assembled, That all that Territory of the United States included within the following boundaries, beginning on the Rio Grande at the point where the dividing parallel of latitude of 31° 47 m between the United States and Mexico touches that River, thence up the middle of the same to the 33d parallel N.L, thence a north westerly direction to the junction of the upper forks of the Gila, ~~as designated by a red line which has this date been drawn upon the map of A.B. Gray, and which~~ is filed ~~with the~~

APPENDIX C(2)

35 Cong
1 Sess

S. 8.

In the Senate of the U.S.
Decr 17. 1857.

Agreeably to notice Mr Gwin asked & obtained leave to bring in the following bill; which was read twice, referred to the Comm: on Territories & ordered to be printed.

A Bill

~~An Act~~ to organize the Territory of Arizona, and to create the Office of Surveyor General therein; to provide for the examination of ~~certain~~ private land claims, to grant donations to actual settlers, to survey the public and private lands, and for other purposes.

Be it enacted by the Senate and the House of Representatives of the United States of America in Congress assembled, That all that part of the Territory of the United States included within the following limits (except such ~~such~~ portions thereof as ~~are~~ may here-inafter be expressly exempted from the operations of this act:) To Wit: Beginning on the Colorado at the 34th parallel of North latitude, thence with said parallel to the eastern boundary of New Mexico, thence South with said Boundary until it intersects the line of Texas, and thence with said line to the Rio Grande and so on to the line of Mexico of on said River as ~~established~~ fixed by the treaty of 1854, thence with

APPENDIX C(3)

35 CONGRESS, 1st Session. } S. 8.

A BILL

To organize the Territory of Arizona, and to create the office of surveyor general therein; to provide for the examination of private land claims; to grant donations to actual settlers; to survey the public and private lands, and for other purposes.

1857—December 17.—Read twice, referred to the Committee on Territories, and ordered to be printed.

1858 April 8. Reported with an amendment. (See amdt)

" June 14. Considered in C.W. Agr. to & made the Special Order for Tuesday 14th day of Decr 1858.

" Decr 13. Recommitted to the Comee on Territories.

1859 Feby 8. Reported without amendt and adversely.

Docketed.

Page—1.

No:—2

No:—1. 2d Session.

Mr Gwin

No papers.

APPENDIX C(4)

~~Same boundaries as Senate bill~~

~~35TH CONGRESS, 2D SESSION.~~ ~~H. R. 836.~~

~~[No Report.]~~

36TH CONGRESS, 1ST SESSION.

S. 365

IN THE SENATE OF THE UNITED STATES.

April 3. 1860

Mr. Green from the Committee on Territories ~~submitted a~~ reported ~~accompanied by~~ the following bill; which was read and passed to a second reading:

A BILL

To provide a temporary government for the Territory of ~~Arizona~~ Arizuma and to create the office of surveyor general therein.

Be it enacted by the Senate and House of Representatives of the United States of America in Congress assembled, That all that portion of the territory of the United States included within the following limits, to wit: commencing at a point where the boundary line of New Mexico intersects the Colorado river of the west; thence northwardly with said river to a point where it intersects the parallel of thirty-three degrees and forty minutes north latitude; thence due east with said parallel to the boundary of Texas; thence with said boundary of Texas to the Rio Grande; thence down said river, and so on with the boundary between Mexico and the United States,

APPENDIX C(5)

IN CONGRESS, November 22, 1861.—Read first and second times, and referred to Committee on Territories. December 11, reported back favorably, made special order for 1 o'clock Saturday, December 14, 1861, placed on Calendar, and 100 copies ordered to be printed.

[By Mr. CAMPBELL.]

A BILL *to be Entitled An Act,*

To organize the Territory of Arizona, ~~and to create the office of Surveyor General therein.~~

Section One

~~Be it enacted by~~ *The Congress of the Confederate States of America, do enact,* That all that part of the present Territory of New Mexico, included within the following limits, to-wit: Beginning on the Colorado river at the parallel of North latitude 30- ~~thirty~~-four degrees, thence with said parallel to the eastern boundary of New Mexico; thence South with said boundary until it intersects the line of Texas; and thence with said line to the Rio Grande, and so on to the line of Mexico, on said river, as fixed by the treaty of eighteen hundred and fifty-four; thence with the boundary line established by said treaty between the late United States and Mexico to the Colorado river, thence up the Colorado to the place of beginning, be, and the same is hereby, created into a temporary government, by the name of the Territory of Arizona; and nothing in this act shall be so construed as to inhibit the Government of the Confederate States from dividing said Territory into two or more territories,

APPENDIX C(6)

37TH CONGRESS,
2D SESSION.

H. R. 357.

IN THE SENATE OF THE UNITED STATES.

MAY 9, 1862.

Read twice, and referred to the Committee on Territories.

MAY 15, 1862.

Reported by Mr. WADE with amendments, viz: Insert the words printed in *italics*.

AN ACT

To provide a temporary government for the Territory of Arizona.

Be it enacted by the Senate and House of Representatives of the United States of America in Congress assembled, That all that part of the present Territory of New Mexico situate west of a line running due south from the point where the southwest corner of the Territory of Colorado joins the northern boundary of the Territory of New Mexico to the southern boundary line of said Territory of New Mexico be, and the same is hereby, erected into a temporary government, by the name of the Territory of Arizona: *Provided,* That nothing contained in the provisions of this act shall be construed to prohibit the Congress of the United States from dividing said Territory, or changing its boundaries, in such manner and at such time as it may deem proper: *Provided, further,* That said government shall be maintained and con-

2

tinued until such time as the people residing in said Territory shall, with the consent of Congress, form a State government, republican in form, as prescribed in the Constitution of the United States, and apply for and obtain admission into the Union as a State, on an equal footing with the original States.

SEC. 2. *And be it further enacted,* That the government hereby authorized shall consist of an executive, legislative, and judicial power. The executive power shall be vested in a governor, ~~*who, in addition to his other duties, shall be ex officio superintendent of Indian affairs, but shall receive no additional salary therefor.*~~ The legislative power shall consist of a council of nine members and a house of representatives of eighteen The judicial power shall be vested in a supreme court, to consist of three judges, and such inferior courts as the legislative council may by law prescribe; there shall also be a secretary, a marshal, a district attorney, and a surveyor general for said Territory, who, together with the governor and judges of the supreme court, shall be appointed by the President, by and with the advice and consent of the Senate, and the term of office for each, the manner of their appointment, and the powers, duties, and the compensation of the governor, legislative assembly, judges of the supreme court, secretary, marshal, district attorney, and surveyor general aforesaid, with their clerks, draughtsman, deputies, and sergeant-at-arms, shall be such as are conferred upon the same officers by the

Made to reconsider agreed Reconsidered & Not agreed

agreed

Made to reconsider amendments

act organizing the territorial government of New Mexico, which subordinate officers shall be appointed in the same manner, and not exceed in number those created by said act; and acts amendatory thereto, together with all legislative enactments of the Territory of New Mexico not inconsistent with the provisions of this act, are hereby extended to and continued in force in the said Territory of Arizona, until repealed or amended by future legislation: *Provided*, That no salary shall be due or paid the officers created by this act until they have entered upon the duties of their respective offices within the said Territory. *And, until otherwise provided, the seat of government of said Territory shall be at Tucson: And provided, further, That no one session of the legislative assembly shall exceed forty days in duration.*

Sec. 3. *And be it further enacted*, That there shall neither be slavery nor involuntary servitude in the said Territory, otherwise than in the punishment of crimes, whereof the parties shall have been duly convicted; and all acts and parts of acts, either of Congress or of the Territory of New Mexico, establishing, regulating, or in any way recognizing the relation of master and slave in said Territory, are hereby repealed.

Passed the House of Representatives May 8, 1862.

Attest:

EM. ETHERIDGE, *Clerk*.

37TH CONGRESS, 2D SESSION. } **H. R. 357.**

AN ACT

To provide a temporary government for the Territory of Arizona.

1862—MAY 9.—Read twice, and referred to the Committee on Territories.

MAY 15.—Reported with amendments.

June 5. Doolittle to consider
agreed CW, —
amended, reported to
Senate & amendments
Concurred in — qu.
Shall the amendments be
engrossed & bill read a
third time —
July 3. Resumed in Senate
Trumbull to p.p. to 1st
monday of December, next.
yeas 25 Nays 13 -
agreed —
1863 Feb 19. Unfinished
" Feb. 20 Resumed, Wade to reconsider
amendments — reconsidered &
Not agreed —
" Read 3d time and
Passed

Passed without
amendment

APPENDIX D

Interesting speculations may be made concerning recommendations to the President for appointments to territorial office. The Civil War did not abate the vigorous efforts of office-seekers; moreover, Lincoln himself considered the distribution of patronage an important responsibility of the chief executive.

The following exhibits from the National Archives reveal the intensity of interest in Arizona as its organization was being accomplished:

(1) Recommendation of "Lame Duck" Representative John A. Gurley, the favorite choice for governor of the new Territory. Of the six who recommended him on February 21st, the day after the Arizona bill was passed, four, including Major General Heintzelman, were in some way connected with the Cincinnati companies which had opened silver mines in southern Arizona.

(2) Letter to President Lincoln signed by three Senators, recommending six men for various offices. Of these only Gurley was nominated.

(3) Undated recommendation of Gurley for governor, signed by members of the 37th Congress and others.

(4) Letter of Samuel Haycraft, Clerk of Hardin County, Kentucky, recommending his son-in-law for governor of Arizona. It is not probable that this recommendation was given serious consideration by the President.

(5) Endorsement of Poston for governor by members of the Kentucky Legislature, doubtless given at Haycraft's request.

(6) In later years Poston indicated that his selection for the office of Superintendent of Indian Affairs was an afterthought, reflecting the omission of his name from immediate consideration at the famous "oyster supper" in February of 1863. After the proposed distribution of offices, he had turned to the assembled guests to ask: "Gentlemen, what is to become of me?" Three of the five men who added their signatures in behalf of Poston had endorsed Gurley three days earlier.

(7) After signing the Organic Act on February 24, 1863, Lincoln delayed sending to the Senate his earliest selections for office in the new Territory until the first week of March. Poston's nomination was dated five days after Gurley's. Both men were confirmed quickly by the Senate.

(8) Letter written by Chief Justice John N. Goodwin, Secretary McCormick, and Associate Justice Joseph P. Allyn, requesting the President to consult with them concerning a successor to Governor Gurley who lay dying in Cincinnati.

(9) Letter by McCormick, who signed as "Secy & Act. [ing] Governor of Arizona", Rev. Hiram W. Read, and W. F. M. Arny of New Mexico, recommending Goodwin to succeed Gurley, who had died two days before. Read had been appointed postmaster for Tucson, but served only at Prescott, and together with Arny, accompanied the governor's party. The two men had been commissioned as special agents of the Treasury Department to convey a large amount of currency across the Plains to New Mexico.

APPENDIX D(1)

Washington City Feb 21. 1863

The undersigned Citizens and former Residents of Arizona being intimately acquainted with Hon John A. Gurley of Ohio, respectfully recommend him as a fit and proper person for Governor of said Territory, eminently qualified by his knowledge of the country and its wants to give general satisfaction and insure prosperity.

S. P. Heintzelman

[illegible] Jarvis

Charles D. Poston

W. Wrightson

S. H. Lathrop

Edward E. Cross
Col. 5th N.H.

I cordially join in the above recommendation of Hon John A. Gurley for Governor of Arizona.

John S. Watts

APPENDIX D(2)

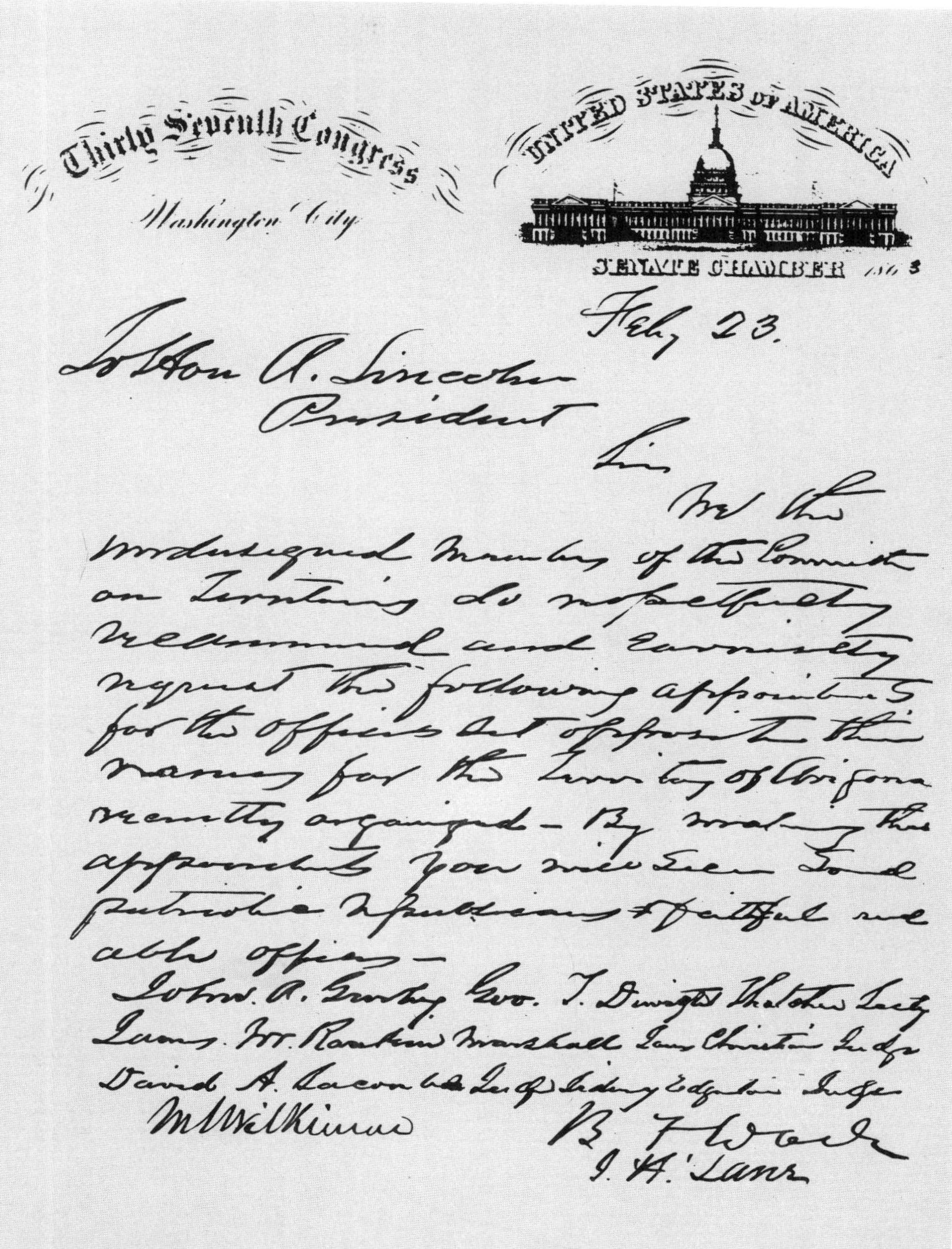

Thirty Seventh Congress
Washington City

United States of America
Senate Chamber 1863

Feby 23.

To Hon A. Lincoln
President

Sir

We the undersigned members of the Committee on Territories do respectfully recommend and earnestly request the following appointments for the offices set opposite their names for the territory of Arizona recently organized – By making these appointments you will secure good patriotic republicans & faithful and able officers –

John A. Gurley Gov. J. Dwight Thatcher Secty
Same. Wm Rankin Marshall Same Christie Judge
David A. Bacon [illegible] Sidney Edgerton Judge

M Wilkinson

B F Wade
J. H. Lane

APPENDIX D(3)

To His Excellency
The President of the United States.

We recommend for Governor of Arizona the Hon John A. Gurley of Ohio.

B. F. Wade

J. M. Ashley
Saml T. Worcester
S. Edgerton
R. A. Hamilton
H. G. Blake
John Hutchins
McCutten
S. Shellabarger
V. B. Horton
C. A. Trimble
A. G. Riddle

APPENDIX D(4)

Elizabeth Town Hardin County Ky
February 27. 1863

His Excellency
Abraham Lincoln
Prest U S

On yesterday I received a letter from Col Charles D. Poston my son in law informing me that the Bill to Organize the Territory of Arizona had passed both houses of Congress and then only awaited your Signature of Approval to become a law Which approval I suppose has by this time been made — He also informed me that he with others interested in the Territory had just had the pleasure of an interview with yourself —

Not knowing whether you have fixed upon any one as Governor of that Territory — I would Chearfully with delicacy of feeling on account of relationship name for that Office Col. Charles D Poston himself He is a very intelligent man of fine business Capacity has been longer in Arizona — and knows more about it and about its wants, the habits and peculiarities of the Natives than any other White American living, I do not know that he desires the office for in his letter he did not give me the slightest intimation, that he wanted or aspired to that Office, But it strikes me forcibly that he would be well adapted to the Office understanding & speaking to some extent the Mexican or Spanish language — He was really the Pioneer & explorer of that Territory, and is deeply interested in the protection of the Territory having considerably interests in Silver Mines —

I throw out these hints for your consideration

Very respectfully yours

Saml Haycraft

APPENDIX D(5)

His Excellency
Abraham Lincoln
Prest U. S. We members of the Kentucky Legislature would respectfully recommend Coml Charley D. Poston as a suitable person to fill the office of Governor of the Territory of Arizona.

March 2nd 1863

B. R. Young
John Draffen
J. H. Bausclean
J. H. Harney
Nat Wolfe
Rich A Buckner
Thos. Z. Morrow
James M. Jones
C. J. Bowman
A. A. Curtis
J. C. Sayers
J. R. Bailey
Geo. Poindexter
Richard Neel
John S. McFarland
D. E. Downing
E. Gabbert
J. B. Cochran

I have not the pleasure of knowing Col Poston but on the statements made above I concur cheerfully in the above recommendation

J. H. Bell
J. Hawthorn
W. L. Rankin
J. Davis

APPENDIX D(6)

Washington City Feb. 24, 1863

We recommend Charles D. Poston for Superintendent of Indian Affairs in Arizona, as particularly qualified for the office by his long residence and position in the country and personal acquaintance and influence with the chiefs and head men of the Indian tribes and knowledge of their manners, customs and wants.

S. P. Heintzelman
Major Genl.

John S. Watts Delegate from New Mexico

John A. Gurley

W. Wrightson

I cordially endorse the above and hope Mr. Poston may receive the appointment as an acknowledgement for his long and faithful services in the territory

B. F. Wade

APPENDIX D(7)

To the Senate of the United States.

I nominate John A. Gurley, of Ohio, to be Governor of the Territory of Arizona.

Abraham Lincoln

Washington,
7th March, 1863.

Washington, D. C.,
March 12, 1863.

To the Senate
of the United States:

I nominate

Charles D. Poston, of Arizona T. to be Superintendent of Indian Affairs in the Territory of Arizona.

Abraham Lincoln

APPENDIX D(8)

To President Lincoln

The undersigned officers of the Territory of Arizona learning with great sorrow that Gov John A Gurley lies dangerously ill at his residence in Ohio beg leave respectfully to ask that in the event, which we should deplore, it becomes necessary to appoint his successor, that we may have an opportunity to be heard. In connection with Gov Gurley we have endeavored to make ourselves familliar with the wants and the interests of this unexplored portions of our country and we feel that in the event alluded to, it, is important that some person thus familliar should be appointed. There are difficulties and dangers in the organisation of Arizona that do not usually fall to the lot of those intrusted with Territorial organizations which render it imperative that a wise selection should be made

New York Aug 11 1863

Joseph P. Allyn Judge

John N. Goodwin Ch J

R C McCormick Secretary

APPENDIX D(9)

Washington Aug. 21. 1863.

To President Lincoln

The undersigned officers of and persons interested in the Territory of Arizona, would respectfully ask the appointment of the Hon John N. Goodwin of Maine, to the Governorship of that Territory made vacant by the death of the Hon John A. Gurley.

We believe that Mr Goodwin is in every way qualified for the position, and what is of the first importance to the interests of the Territory, he will, if appointed, <u>go forward at once</u> – Moreover we know that his selection will be very agreeable to the officers of the Territory, and that he is already familiar with its character and wants.

We are with great respect.

R. C. McCormick
Secy & Act. Governor of Arizona.

W. F. M. Arny.   H. W. Read
Secty, Territory New Mexico

APPENDIX E

On December 29, 1863 Secretary Richard C. McCormick in a letter to General James H. Carleton gave an account of the ceremonies held at Navajo Springs to proclaim the establishment of the territorial government within the borders of Arizona. Two days earlier the gubernatorial party had crossed the eastern boundary and entered the new Territory. (*See note* 322). Two copies of Governor Goodwin's proclamation, one in English and one in Spanish, were enclosed in McCormick's letter.

(1 & 2) These documents were printed in Santa Fé in expectation of holding the formalities at Fort Whipple on Christmas day, but because of delays of one kind or another, certain revisions had to be made when ultimately it was determined to proclaim the government at Navajo Springs. The manuscript changes in the English proclamation appear to be in McCormick's handwriting. The translation into Spanish was prepared by Rev. Hiram W. Read, a member of the party, who at an earlier period had served in New Mexico as Baptist missionary and army chaplain. In all probability it was he who made the longhand revisions on the Spanish document. McCormick's letter clearly shows that the corrected proclamations, which subsequently were distributed in Arizona, also were printed in Santa Fé.

(3) The "curious document pertaining to the political history of Arizona" which McCormick acknowledged in this letter has not been identified. There is little question that his notebook, which is mentioned here but has not been found, would have provided information of great value to Arizona historians concerning events of this period. Col. James L. Collins was publisher of the *Santa Fe Gazette* and for some years the Superintendent of Indian Affairs for New Mexico.

APPENDIX E(1)

PROCLAMATION.

TO THE PEOPLE OF ARIZONA:

I, JOHN N. GOODWIN, having been appointed by the President of the United States, and duly qualified, as Governor of the TERRITORY OF ARIZONA, do hereby announce that by virtue of the powers with which I am invested by an Act of the Congress of the United States, providing a temporary government for the Territory, I shall this day proceed to organize said government. The provisions of the Act, and all laws and enactments established thereby, will be enforced by the proper Territorial officers from and after this date.

A preliminary census will forthwith be taken, and thereafter the Judicial Districts will be formed, and an election of members of the Legislative Assembly, and the other officers, provided by the Act, be ordered.

I invoke the aid and co-operation of all citizens of the Territory in my efforts to establish a government whereby the security of life and property will be maintained throughout its limits, and its varied resources be rapidly and successfully developed.

The seat of government will for the present be at or near Fort Whipple.

JOHN N. GOODWIN.

By the Governor:

RICHARD C. M'CORMICK,

Secretary of the Territory.

Navajo Springs ~~FORT WHIPPLE~~, ARIZONA,

December 29, 1863.

APPENDIX E(2)

PROCLAMACION.

AL PUEBLO DE ARIZONA:

Yó, JOHN N. GOODWIN, habiendo sido nombrado por el Presidente de los Estados Unidos, y debidiamente calificado como Gobernador del TERRITORIO DE ARIZONA, por esta anuncio que por virtud de los poderes con que estoy investido por un Acto del Congreso de los Estados Unidos, proveyendo un gobierno temporario para dicho Territorio, yo procederé este dia á organizar dicho gobierno. Las provisiones del Acto y todas las leyes y órdenes establecidas por el mismo serán enforzadas por los propios oficiales territoriales desde y despues de esta fecha.

Un censo preliminar será inmediatamente tomado, y despues, los distritos judiciales serán formados, y una eleccion será ordenada para los miembros de la Asamblea Legislativa y los otros oficiales que provee el acto.

Invoco la ayuda y co-operacion de todos los ciudadanos del Territorio en mis esfuerzos para establecer un gobierno por el cual la seguridad de vida y propiedad será mantenida por todos sus limites, y sus varios recursos serán rapida y prosperamente desarrollados.

El asiento de gubierno sera por el presente en ó cerca Fuerte Whipple

JOHN N. GOODWIN.

Por el Gobernador:

RICHARD C. M'CORMICK,

Secretario del Territorio.

Ojo de Navajo

~~FUERTE WHIPPLE~~, ARIZONA,

Diciembre 29th de 1863

APPENDIX E(3)

Navajo Springs, Arizona —
Dec. 29. 1863 —

Brigadier General James H. Carleton
Commanding Department of
New Mexico —

General

I have the honor to acknowledge the receipt of your favor covering a curious document pertaining to the political history of Arizona, for which I am much obliged.

We reached here this morning and have fairly started the wheels of our government. The official oaths were taken this afternoon with some little ceremony, and the Governor has issued his proclamation — I enclose a copy, and have requested Col. Collins, to print 50 in English and 50 in Spanish, as corrected, and send to you. When received if you will take a dozen to send to Tucson and elsewhere in the Territory as you may see fit, and forward the balance to me at Fort Whipple, I shall be much obliged.

We remain in excellent health. The weather clear and frosty. The grass excellent and no loss of stock to this time.

When at Albuquerque and Ft Wingate I received copies of the records of the weather kept by the surgeons. If you will send me the same for the period of our sojourn in Santa Fe, (Nov. 14th to 26th inclusive) you will enable me to add to the value of my note book.

I am General,

Yr obt svt,

R C McCormick.

APPENDIX F

In this group are reproduced pictures of Representatives Stephens and Grow, and Delegate Otero, each of whom reported bills to organize Arizona, and of Wheeler and Trumbull, the respective leaders of the opposition in the House and Senate in the crucial deliberations of 1862 and 1863. A photograph of the first officials of the Territorial government is also included, as well as a separate one of Governor Goodwin.

Notes concerning the contents of the pocket on the inside cover follow this appendix.

[*Library of Congress*]

LYMAN TRUMBULL
(1813–1896)

A friend and early advisor of Lincoln, Trumbull was Republican Senator from Illinois, and in the decisive debates on the Arizona bill was the leader of the opposition in the Senate.

[*Library of Congress*]

WILLIAM A. WHEELER
(1819–1887)

Republican Representative from New York who led the opposition in the House debates on Ashley's bill (H. R. 357). Wheeler served as Vice President during the administration of President Rutherford B. Hayes.

[*Library of Congress*]

GALUSHA A. GROW
(1823–1907)

This Republican Representative from Pennsylvania was the "Father of the Homestead Act" and, as Speaker of the House, was one of the three men who signed the act which created the Territory of Arizona. The bills which he introduced in behalf of Arizona are listed in note 60.

[*Library of Congress*]

ALEXANDER H. STEPHENS
(1812–1883)

Representative from Georgia, who introduced two Arizona bills in 1859 (H. R. 836 and H. R. 876), Stephens became Vice President of the Confederacy.

[*State Records Center and Archives, Santa Fe*]

MIGUEL A. OTERO
(1829–1882)

A Democrat with pro-Southern leanings, he was the first delegate to Congress from the Territory of New Mexico, serving until 1861, when he was succeeded by John S. Watts. Otero reported two Arizona bills, one in 1858 to create a separate judicial district (H. R. 172), and the other in 1860 to organize Arizona (H. R. 192).

[*Department of Library and Archives, Phoenix*]

JOHN N. GOODWIN
(1824–1887)

A former Congressman from Maine, he was the first territorial governor actually to serve in Arizona. A "lame duck" himself, he succeeded Lincoln's original appointee, Governor John A. Gurley, another "lame duck," who died before he could proceed to the new Territory.

[*Department of Library and Archives, Phoenix*]

Photograph of first territorial officials, probably taken at Prescott in 1864. From left to right (*sitting*), they were Joseph Pratt Allyn, Associate Justice; John Noble Goodwin, Governor; and Richard C. McCormick, Secretary. From left to right (*standing*), they were Henry W. Fleury, private secretary to Governor Goodwin; Milton B. Duffield, United States Marshal, and Almon Gage, United States Attorney. Duffield like Poston did not cross the continent with the gubernatorial party.

NOTES *for* CONTENTS *of* POCKET

Of the two maps in the pocket attached to the back cover the first is an enlargement of Sylvester Mowry's map which was intended to accompany his 1857 *Memoir*. This map is the same as the one previously published under the title "MAP OF THE MINERAL REGIONS on the proposed Southern Pacific Rail Road through Gadsden purchase," in *Report of the Sonora Exploring and Mining Co. . . . December, 1856*. Mowry utilized this map in connection with his promotional *Memoir* to illustrate the proposed Territory of Arizona as he visualized it. According to his definition of the boundaries, the proposed Territory was to comprise all of New Mexico south of 34° north latitude, but the map as published does not extend to the Texas boundary (at approximately the 103rd meridian), as called for in his description. Some surviving copies of the map show the proposed boundaries outlined in water color for greater emphasis, and extended eastward to Texas. Evidently Mowry's map was the first to illustrate a proposed Territory of Arizona. Although it was intended to accompany his *Memoir*, it was not included in all the copies.

This map originally was taken from a part of A. B. Gray's map of survey of a Pacific railroad, extending from Texas to California. Gray, the former surveyor of the United States Boundary Commission, was employed by the Texas Western Railroad in 1853 to make this independent survey, which was completed shortly before the Gadsden Treaty was proclaimed into law by President Franklin Pierce on June 30, 1854. The survey was published in Cincinnati in three editions beginning with 1855. The second edition of that year, entitled *Charter of the Texas Western Railroad Company and extracts from reports of Col. A. B. Gray . . . on the survey of the route from eastern borders of Texas to California . . .* was accompanied by a map of the survey, which as might be expected, did not mention the proposed Territory of Arizona. The map also was included with the best of the editions which was entitled *Survey of a route for the Southern Pacific R.R.* (Cincinnati, 1856). The "Southern Pacific Rail Road" named in Gray's title did not apply to the present day Southern Pacific, but was the name in 1856 of the earlier

Texas Western Railroad. This railroad became a part of the Texas Pacific in 1872.

The second map in the pocket is a reproduction of Robert Payne Kelley's map, which better than any other delineates the outlines of the "Territory of Arizona" as proposed in several Arizona bills and in the constitution of the 1860 Provisional Government. (*Fig.* 7). Except for a small difference in the position of the northern line, the boundaries are identical with those described by Sylvester Mowry, Senator William M. Gwin, Lieutenant Colonel John R. Baylor, and by the Confederate Congress. (*Fig.* 5). The outlines also are not basically different from those in *Fig.* 4 ("Bradley Memorial") and in *Fig.* 6. The configuration of the "Territory of Arizona" as thus depicted is very different in appearance from that established in 1863 by the federal Congress. The territorial outlines on Kelly's map have been reinforced in the facsimile for graphic emphasis. The four Arizona counties shown are delimited, and named in accordance with the schedule of the Provisional Government. Inspite of certain errors this map represents a valuable addition to the regional cartography of that period.

Kelley, a surveyor, merchant, real estate agent, and mining entrepreneur, was one of the leaders of the movement to unite Arizona with the Confederacy. He was also the principal owner of the strongly partisan *Mesilla Times* and was related by marriage to his co-publisher and editor, Bredett C. Murray. The facsimile was prepared from an original copy of the map by courtesy of Dr. Rex W. Strickland of Texas Western College, El Paso. His map was a gift from Kelley to Murray, and was acquired from a descendant of the latter.

A reproduction of the "organic act" which created the Territory of Arizona, copied from the parchment original, also is in the pocket. Passed by the 37th Congress, it was approved by President Lincoln on February 24, 1863, a little more than eight years after the first attempts were made to separate Arizona from New Mexico and to organize it as a territory. The act was much shorter and less complex than earlier unsuccessful bills to organize. Section 3 specifically forbade not only slavery but peonage as it had been practiced in New Mexico. The location of the capital was not mentioned. The signers, in addition to the President, were Solomon Foot of Vermont, former Whig and railroad president, who presided over the Senate throughout most of the 36th Congress and all of the 37th, and Speaker Galusha A. Grow of Pennsylvania, who in 1860 had introduced several Arizona bills.

This book was manufactured in Arizona. The text was set in twelve-point Fairfield by the Tucson Typographic Service, Inc. The paper is eighty-pound Victorian Text. Lithography was by the Arizona Messenger Printing Co., Phoenix, and binding by the Arizona Library Binding Co., Phoenix.

ARIZONA HISTORICAL FOUNDATION
3800 NORTH CENTRAL AVENUE
PHOENIX, ARIZONA 85012

INDEX

Adjutant General, 16, 17, 36
Ajo, 11, 177
Alabama, 61
Alaska, 20
Albuquerque, 66, 109n322
Alcalde, 11, 36
Aldrich, Mark, 11, 36, 59, 98n194
Allyn, Joseph P., 87, 88, 106n299, (*port.*) 187
Amoles, New Mexico, 100n218
Annexation, 35, 44, 47n26, 53n146, 61
Apache Cañon (Glorieta Pass), 102n238
Apache Indians (also see Indians), 61, 95
Arivaipa Creek, 61
Arizona Citizen, 82
Arizona City, 32, 33
Arizona County, New Mexico, 72, 102n238, 102n239
Arizona, District of, 48n60(1), 155
Arizona Mining and Trading Co., 11, 12
Arizona Mounted Volunteers, 97n184
Arizona Pioneers' Historical Society, 106n293
Arizona Rangers, 60
Arizona Volunteers, 66, 71
Arizonian, 35, 36
Arizuma, 42, 43, 44, 49n60(9), 49n60(11), 155, 156
Army of New Mexico, 68
Army of Northern Virginia, 37
Arny, W. F. M., 106n299, 167
Ashley, James M. (Congressman), 25, 49n60(17), 69, (*port.*) 70, 71, 75,76, 79, 82, 83, 87, 88, 95, 101n225, 101n226, 103n255
Attorney, 10, 63
Austin, Texas, 58
Bancroft, Hubert Howe, 10, 16,36
Bartlett, John Russell, 17, 31
Bashford, Levi, 87, 88
Baylor, John R. (Lieutenant Colonel), 42, 62, 63, (*port.*) 65, 98n190, 98n200, 99n204, 99n206, 130
Beale's route,
Bell, John (Senator), 15, 97n190
Bean, Samuel G., 36
Benedict, Kirby (Judge), 33, 53n133
Benét, Stephen Vincent, 36
Benton, Thomas Hart (Senator), 46n1
Black, J. S., 53n133
Blaine, James G. (Senator), 54n179, 87
Bonner, Willis N., 11
Boundaries, 3, 4, 9, 11, 23, 36, 40, 42, 46n7, 51n99, 51n101, 51n102, 62, 63, 69, 82, 83, 101n224, 101n226, 102n238, 109n322
Bradley Memorial, 25
Bradley, M. E., 51n93, 111
Brady Collection, 8
Brady, Mathew B., 81
Brady, Peter R., 11, 48n36
Brandes, Ray, 99n200
Brazil, 33
Breckenridge, Fort (see Fort Breckenridge)
Breckinridge, John C. (Vice President) 99n200
Brevoort, Elias, 42, 54n167
Brown, Albert G., 42
Brunckow, Frederick, 19
Buchanan County, 155
Buchanan, James (President), 4, 34, 35, 42, 45, 46n7, 46n9, 99n200, 107n307, 155
Bull Run (Battle), 107n307

Burr, Mr., 52n110
Butterfield, Fargo & Spencer, 17
Butterfield Overland Mail, 52n111, (also see Overland Mail)

Caborca, 16
Calabasas (or Calavasas), 11, 117
California, 3, 4, 6, 9, 16, 20, 31, 33, 36, 40, 51n99, 57, 58, 66, 75, 77, 78, 117
California Column (see Column from California)
California Volunteers, (see Column from California), 23, 66
Campbell, Josiah A., 63
Canby, Edward R. S., (Lieutenant Colonel), 61, 66, 98n199, 100n219
Carleton, James H. (Lieutenant Colonel and General), 66, (*port.*) 67, 69, 97n184, 100n219, 101n224, 109n322, 177
Carroll, F. L., 106n297
Carson, Kit, 46n1
Castle Dome County, 36
Chandler, Zachariah (Senator), 91
Charleston, South Carolina, 40, 59
Chihuahua, 3, 73
Chino Valley, 109n322
Chiricahua Apaches, 19, 96 (also see Indians)
Chivington, John M. (Major), 66
Churchill, Clark, 106n293
Cincinnati, 9, 12, 17, 20, 61, 66, 73, 75, 90, 99n202, 102n241, 106n298, 166
Civil War, 3, 4, 20, 50n84, 80, 89, 96, 100n218, 100n219, 101n226, 107n307, 166
Cobb, Howell, 59
Cochise, 19, 96
Colfax, Schuyler, 103n261, 108n320
Collins, James L. (Colonel), 177
Colorado (Territory), 45, 54n160, 54n177, 59, 69, 71, 103n261
Colorado City, 9, 117
Colorado Ferry, 50n61
Colorado River, 10, 40, 42, 51n101, 57, 101n224, 107n307, 116
Colorado Volunteers, 66
Colt, Samuel, 20, 104n279, 108n308
Column from California (California Volunteers), 66, 67, 69, 101n224
Commissioner of Indian Affairs, 32, 52n123, 52n124, 156
Committee on Territories (House and Senate), 11, 12,14, 17, 20, 23, 42, 69, 70, 77, 78, 79, 83, 87, 111, 112, 156
Compromise of 1850, 4, 57
Confederacy (Confederate States of America, Confederates), 6, 33,36, 40, 42, 43, 53n130, 57–59, 61–63, 66, 78, 80, 98n193, 98n198, 100n219, 130, 155
Confederate Army, 33, 71, 98n190
Confederate Congress, 38, 63, 100n222, 130, 155
Confederate flag, 60, 61
Confederate Territory of Arizona, 25, 40, 42, 69, 98n190, 156
Congress (Confederate), (see Confederate Congress)
Congress (United States), 3–6, 10–12, 16, 17, 20, 32–36, 45, 47n24, 62, 67, 71, 72, 75–78, 82, 88, 89, 95, 103n261, 106n297, 107n303, 111, 155, 166
Connecticut, 87, 104n279
Cook, Nathan P., 11, 12, 16, 23, 53n146
Contzen, Frederick, 12
Contzen, Julius, 12
Conventions, 10, 11, 12, 16, 23, 32–36, 40, 58, 59, 111, 130
Correspondence, 5, 10, 17, 31, 34, 40, 46n6, 49n61, 53n140, 73, 86, 89, 100n218, 105n288.
Cox, Samuel S., 71
Crabb, Henry A., 11, 16, 38, 47n35, (also see Filibusters)
Cravens, James A., (Congressman), 71, 76
Crittenden, George B. (Lieutenant Colonel), 61
Crittenden, John J. (Senator), 12
Cross, Edward E., 34, 35, 53n140, 91, 108n317, 108n320
Cuba, 44

Custom house, 9
Czars of Russia, 105n291

Dakota Land Company, 40
Dakota Territory (Dacotah), 36, 45, 49n60(7), 54n177, 59, 71, 103n261
Darmint, B. H. (De Armitt), 50n86
Dartmouth College, 106n297
Davis, Jefferson (Senator, President of Confederacy), 33,(*port.*) 43, 49n60(9), 57, 63, 66, 69, 75, 98n190, 100n222, 155, 156
Davis, Orlando, 97n182
DeArmitt, B. H. (Darmint), 12, 50n86
Delaware, 78
Delegate, 6, 11, 12, 15–17, 31–36, 38, 40, 42, 51n102, 57, 63, 69, 71, 72, 82, 102n236, 106n293
Democratic National Convention, 40
Democrat, 35, 42, 45, 71, 72, 75–78, 80, 97n190, 103n261
Denison, Texas, 36, 41
Denver, Colorado, 40
Denver, J. W., 52n124
Department of the Interior, 48n60(1), 104n262
Department of the Pacific, 69
Department of State, 77, 78
Department of War, 17
District of Arizona, 48n60(1), 155
District of Columbia, 4
District of Gila, 48n60(1), 155
District of Paso del Norte, 97n190
Doña Ana County (Dona Ana), 10, 11, 31, 33, 35, 36, 51n99, 54n167, 99n206, 102n238, 117, 155
Donner party, 33
Doolitle, James R., (Senator), 44, 80
Doss, Richard M., 42
Douglas, James W., 42
Douglas, Stephen A., (Senator), 4, 11, 12, (*port.*) 14, 23, 31, 47n32, 48n59, 51n94, 51n103, 75, 97n190
Dragoons, 37, 98n200
Dragoon Springs, 31
Dred Sctt Decision, 44
Drum, R. C., (Lieutenant Colonel), 101n224
Du Bois, John V. (Colonel), 98n198
Duel, 34, 102n236
Duffield, Milton B., 87, 88, (*port.*) 187
Duke of Kentucky, 71
Duke of Sonora, 50n84
Dunbar, Edward E., 11, 20

East, 11, 32, 90
East Gila, 155
Ehrenberg, Herman,9, 11, 17, 19, 20, 23, 47n17
Election, 32–34, 36, 40, 45, 53n146, 57, 63, 97n190, 99n207, 100n218, 103n241, 106n297
Elias, Juan, 12
Elizabethtown, Kentucky, 9, 81,83, 86, 104n279
El Paso, Texas, 16, 31, 58, 59, 61, 62, 66, 101n224
El Paso-Fort Yuma Wagon Road, 16, 31, 48n58
Emperor of China, 105n291
Ewell County, 36
Ewell, Richard S. (Captain and General), 35, 36, (*port.*) 37, 42, 53n151, 61

Father of Arizona, 87, 89, 95
Fauntleroy, Thomas T. (Colonel), 61
Filibusters, 11, 16, 38
First Dragoons, 35
First Texas Arizona Battalion of Mounted Rifles, 97n184
Fleury, Henry W., (*port.*), 187
Florence, Arizona, 53n142, 83
Florence *Arizona Enterprise*, 82
Foot, Solomon, (Senator), 108n321
Fort Breckenridge, 61, 98n200, 102n239
Fort Buchanan, 31, 34, 35, 37, 42, 61, 98n200, 102n239
Fort Craig, 66, 98n200
Fort Defiance, 102n239
Fort Fillmore, 59, 61, 62, 97n190, 98n200, 99n205
Fort Leavenworth, 109n322
Fort Mojave, 102n239

Fort McLane, 61
Fort Stanton, 62
Fort Sumter, 45, 97n182
Fort Tejon, 6
Fort Thorn, 11, 66
Fort Union, 66
Fort Whipple, 109n322, 177
Fort Wingate, 109n322
Fort Yuma, 6, 9, 16, 17, 31, 42, 48n58, 49n61, 50n62, 61, 75, 90, 107n307
Francis, John N., 88
Franklin, Texas (El Paso), 101n224
Frazer, George M. (Captain), 60, 98n196
Frémont, John C. (General), 5, 103n241
Friar, Alfred L., 12
Frost, Daniel M., 45
Fuller, Alpheus G., 36

Gadsden, James, 16, 95
Gadsden Purchase, 3, 5, 9, 11, 15–17, 19, 20, 22, 23, 25, 31, 34, 35, 37, 45, 46n1, 47n26, 50n84, 51n93, 51n100, 53n146, 57, 58, 61, 66, 71, 82, 87, 90, 95, 100n222, 102n239, 109n323, 111, 156,
Gadsden Treaty, 6, 9, 13, 15, 20
Gage, Almon, (*port.*), 187
Galoots, 87
Gandara, Governor, 11
Garcia, Luis, 47n30
"Gila", 34
Gila, District of, 48n60(1), 155
Gila River, 3, 12, 48n45, 51n99, 51n100, 116, 117
Gilbert, Alfred W. (Colonel), 88
Glorieta Pass (Apache Cañon), 66
Goodwin, John N. 87, 88, 106n297, 109n322, 167, 183, (*port.*) 186., (*port.*) 187
Grant, Ulysses S. (General and President), 99n205, 101n225
Gray, Andrew B., 11, 32, 48n36
Grayson, John B. (Lieutenant Colonel), 61
Green, James S., (Senator), 42, 44, 49n60(7), 49n60(11), 75, 155
Greenwood, A. B., 52n123, 52n125
Grimes, James W. (Senator), 46n6, 87, 88
Grow, Galusha A., (Senator), 49n60(12), 49n60(14), 49n60(15), 54n175, 69, 101n226, 108n321, 183, (*port.*) 185
Guadalupe Hidalgo, Treaty of, 3
Guaymas, Sonora, 9, 35
Gulf of California, 9, 17, 20
Gurley, John A. (Congressman), 73, (*port.*) 74, 76, 83, 87–91, 102n241, 106n297, 106n298, 106n299, 109n322, 166
Gwin, William M. (Senator), 16, 20, (*port.*) 21, 23, 49n60(3), 50n81, 50n82, 50n84, 50n86, 75, 155, 156

Hastings, Lansford W., 33, 53n130
Hardin County, Kentucky, 9, 166
Hardin County Court, 83, 104n279
Harris, Ira, (Senator), 91
Harlan, James, (Senator), 91
Harris, Congressman, 20
Hart, Simeon, 58
Haycraft and Berry Account Book, 105n287
Haycraft-Lincoln Correspondence, 81
Haycraft, Samuel, 9, 81, 83, 86, 105n288, 105n289, 166
Haycraft, Mrs. Samuel, 86, 105n289
Hayes, Rutherford B., (President), 102n232
Heintzelman, Charles, 90, 108n310
Heintzelman Mine, 61, 73, 130
Heintzelman, Samuel P. (General), 9, 16, 17, 20, 23, 31, 32, 49n61, 75, 83, 87, 89–91, (*port.*) 94, 95, 96, 104n279, 106n299, 107n305, 107n307, 108n308, 108n310, 108n320, 166
Helm, Ben Hardin, (General), 86, 105n289
Helm family, 86
Herbert's Battalion, 97n184
Herbert, Philemon T., 50, 59, 60, 97n184
Hermosillo, Sonora, 35

Homesteads, 5
Hooper, George F., 49n61
House of Representatives, (U.S.), 12, 15, 36, 45, 48n60(1), 50n86, 69, 71–73, 76, 83, 87, 88, 101n225, 102n239, 102n241, 103n255, 103n256, 106n297, 108n321, 111, 116, 183
Houston, Sam, 58
Howard, Jacob M. (Senator), 91
Howard, Russel, 63
Hulseman, Frederick, 11, 48n37
Hunter, Sherod (Captain), 66, 67, 71

Illinois, 4, 20, 46n6, 75, 77
Indians, 5, 6, 31, 32, 35, 37, 46n7, 52n110, 63, 71–73, 75, 76, 77, 102n239, 108n320, (also see Apache, Chiricahua, Papago, Pima)
Indiana, 71, 76, 91
Inkstand, 105n290
Interior, Department of, 104n262
Iowa, 91
Irwin, Dr. B. J. D., 31, 52n111
Isham, Mrs. Charles, 105n290
Isham, Giles S., 112
Ives, Joseph C. (Lieutenant), 40

Jackass Mail, 52n116
Jackson, Alexander M., 57, 58, 63, 97n182
Jackson, Andrew (General and President), 20, 36, 155
Jackson County, 155
Jackson, Stonewall, (General), 37
Jaeger, L. J. F., 50n61
Jarvis, R. W. H., 91, 108n317, 108n320
Jefferson County, 155
Jefferson, Territory of, 40, 54n160
Jefferson, Thomas (President), 155
Johnson, Andrew (Senator and President), 44, 99n205, 103n261
Johnston, Albert Sidney (General), 98n200
Jones, Samuel J., 59, 63, 97n190
Jones, William Claude, 10, 11, 47n26, 47n30, 48n59, 53n146, 59, 60, 111, 117
Jornada del Muerto, 31, 33
Josselyn, Robert, 63, 101n222
Judicial district, 12, 13, 15, 16, 23, 25, 33, 34, 36, 48n45, 49n60(4), 51n100, 155

Kansas, 4, 42, 59, 78, 88, 97n190
Kansas-Nebraska Act, 4, 14
Kentucky, 6, 12, 17, 61, 71, 73, 78, 81–83, 86
Kelley, Robert P., 23, 51n102, 59, 100n218
Khedive of Egypt, 98n198, 105n291
Kippen, George, 50n86, 111
Kippen Memorial, 22
Kirkland, William H., 12
Knoxville, 16

La Glorieta Pass (Apache Cañon), 100n220
Lame ducks, 74, 87, 88, 166
La Mesa, New Mexico, 35
Lane, Joseph H. (Senator), 78
Lane, Henry S. (Senator), 91
Las Cruces, 33–35, 54n167, 117
Latham, Milton S., (Senator), 107n305
Lathrop, Solon H., 32, 34, 91, 108n317, 108n320
Leach, James B., 16, 31, 52n110
Legislature, 10, 12, 15, 31, 35, 36, 40, 46n7, 47n26, 51n100, 58, 63, 77, 102n236, 102n238, 103n256, 103n261
Library of Congress, 105n290
Lincoln, Abraham, (President), 6, 40, 42, 44, 45, 46n8, 54n178, 57–59, 69, 80, (*port.*) 81, 82, 87–89, 91, 97n190, 103n241, 103n256, 103n261, 105n288, 105n289, 105n291, 106n297, 106n299, 108n310, 108n320, 166, 167
Lincoln, Abraham, (Captain), 105n289
Lincoln, Bersheba (Bathsheba), 105n289
Lincoln-Haycraft correspondence, 105n288

Lincoln, Mary Todd, 45, 91
Lincoln, Robert Todd, 105n290
Lincoln, Thomas, 83
London, 96
Longstreet, James, (Major), 61
Lord, Richard S. C. ,(Lieutenant), 42, 98n200
Loring, William W., (Colonel), 61, 98n198
Louisiana, 61
Louis Napoleon, (Napoleon III), 50n84, 105n291
Lucas, James A., 10, 11, 35, 36, 40, 47n24, 59, 62
Lynde, Isaac, (Major), 61, 62, 99n205

MacWillie, M. H. (Delegate), 62, 63, 66, 99n218, 100n222
McCarty, Justus I., (Mr. McCartney), 31, 32, 51n105
McClellan, George ,(General), 107n307
McCormick, Richard C., 87, 88, 106n299, 109n322, 167, 177, (*port.*), 187
McDougall, James A., (Senator), 77, 78, 107n305
McDowell, Irvin, (Major General), 52n106, 107n307
McGowan, Edward, (Ned), 40, 42
McKee, Dr. J. Cooper, 99n205
McKibbin, Joseph C., (Congressman), 49n60(5)
Maine, 87
Martin, William H., 50n86
Maricopa Indians, 32, 40
Maury, Dabney H., (Captain), 61
Mechanics' Fair, 20
Memorials (Petitions), 6, 10, 11, 20, 23, 46n6, 47n24, 47n26, 50n86, 111, 112, 116
Mendenhall, Dr. George, 106n298
Mesilla, 9, 10, 23, 31, 33–36, 40, 45, 48n60(1), 58–62, 66, 98n190, 98n192, 98n200, 99n205, 100n218, 111, 116, 117, 155, 156
Mesilla County, 36
Mesilla Times, 58–60, 99n205, 100n218
Mesilla Valley, 23, 25, 53n146, 57, 100n218
Mexican War, 3, 98n198, 107n307
Mexico, 9, 50n84, 51n99, 73, 116, 117
Mexico City, 95
Michigan, 9, 36
Mikado of Japan, 105n291
Miles, Edward, 11
Mines, 5, 6, 9, 11, 20, 23, 31, 32, 42, 45, 57, 61, 71–73, 75, 76, 82, 89, 91, 95, 96
Minnesota, 91
Mississippi, 20, 42, 63, 75
Missouri, 42, 58, 71, 78, 97n190, 101n225
Missouri Compromise, 4
Missouri Republican, 35
Mix, C. E., 52n124
Mohave County, 25
Montana, 100n219, 101n225
Montezuma, Territory of, 101n226
Montgomery, Alabama, 58, 59
Moore, Isaiah N., (Lieutenant), 42, 98n200
Morgan, Edwin D., (Senator), 88
Morrill, Justin S., (Congressman), 12, 23, 49n2(2)
Mormons, 6, 46n13
Mowry, Roger, 6
Mowry, Sylvester, (Lieutenant), 6, (*port.*) 7, 10, 11, 16, 17, 20, 21, 23, 31–36, 40, 42, 45, 46n7, 47n30, 47n32, 48n53, 49n61, 50n64, 50n85, 50n86, 51n94, 51n102, 51n103, 52n106, 52n110, 52n123, 52n124, 52n125, 53n139, 53n140, 53n146, 54n161, 54n162, 54n163, 54n164, 54n169, 89, 90, 95, 107n303, 111, 112, 117, 130
Mowry's *Memoir,* 22, 51n101

Napoleon III (see Louis Napoleon)
National Archives, 11, 49n60(9), 49n60(18), 166
National Hotel, 91
Navajo Springs, 109n322, 177
Nebraska, 4

Nevada, 25, 45, 54n177, 59, 71, 76, 80, 103n261
Neville, Colonel, 105n289
New Mexico, 3, 4, 6, 9–12, 15, 23, 25, 31, 33–36, 42, 44, 46n7, 47n24, 47n26, 49n60(4), 50n86, 51n93, 51n99, 51n100, 51n101, 53n146, 57, 58, 60–63, 66, 69, 72, 75, 78, 82, 89, 97n181, 97n182, 97n190, 98n200, 99n203, 99n204, 100n219, 101n226, 102n238, 102n239, 111, 112, 116, 155, 156, 167, 177
Newport Barracks, Kentucky, 17
New York, 9, 20, 32, 44, 71–73, 76, 83, 87, 88, 91, 112
New York City, 104n282
Nicaragua, 42
North, 59, 97n182
North Carolina, 61
Northwest Ordinance, 3

Ochiltree, W. B., 130
Ohio, 15, 35, 69, 71, 73, 76, 77, 80, 87, 90, 101n225
Ohio Life Insurance and Trust Company, 20
Ohio River, 17
Olin, Abram B., (Congressman), 71
Omnibus Bill, 4
Oregon, 36
Orrantia, Ignacio, 36
Ortiz, Ignacio, 12, 47n24
Otero, Miguel A., (Delegate), 12, 15, 23, 35, 46n7, 49n60(4), 49n60(10), 50n86, 57, 102n236, 112, 183, (*port.*) 186
Oury, Granville H., (Delegate), 12, 32, 35, 36, (*port.*) 38, 39, 40, 42, 53n149, 54n162, 59, 63, 66, 98n190, 99n207, 100n218
Overland Mail, 5, 31, 46n6, 102n238, 112
Overland Monthly, 82
Owings, Dr. Lewis S., (Governor), 36, 40, (*port.*) 41, 54n155, 57, 58, 59, 63, 100n218, 130
Oyster supper, 87, 88, 91, 166

Pacific, Department of, 69
Pacific Islands, 9
Pacific (Ocean), 57, 66, 95, 100n219
Pah-Ute County, 25
Palace Hotel, 106n293
Paso del Norte, District of, 97n190
Patagonia Mine, 42
Patronage, 5, 20, 35, 104n261, 166, 167
Patton, Mr., 60
Pennsylvania, 72, 101n225
Petitions, (also see Memorials), 5, 16, 35, 47n30, 51n93, 58, 59, 71, 72, 111
Philadelphia, 9, 73
Phoenix, 82, 109n322, 109n325
Phoenix Herald, 82
Physician, 20, 30, 52n111
Picacho Pass, 66, 100n221
Pierce, Franklin, (President), 9, 15
Pima County, 104n279
Pima Indians (also spelled Pimo), 32, 40, 52n124
Pimeria, 47n27
Pino Alto, 100n218
Pollack, James, 103n244
Population, 5, 12, 31, 33, 34, 71, 72, 77–80, 102n239, 117
Pomeroy, Samuel C., (Senator), 87, 88
Pope, John, (General), 107n307
Poston, Charles Debrille, 6, (*port.*) 8, 10–12, 17, 19, 31, 32, 45, 47n15, 47n16, 47n19, 47n21, 50n85, 52n121, 61, 71, 73, 81–83, 87–91, 95, 96, 99n202, 103n244, 103n248, 104n273, 104n277, 104n279, 104n283, 105n289, 105n290, 105n291, 105n292, 106n293, 106n297, 107n305, 107n306, 108n307, 108n320, 109n325, 130, 166, 167
Poston, John Lee, 61, 104n279, 130
Postmaster, 12, 33, 71, 97n190, 106n299
Prescott, 99n205, 106n299, 109n322, 167
Prescott, William Hickling, 109n322
Prince of Wales, 105n291
Probate Clerk, 11, 12

Providence, Rhode Island, 6, 40
Provisional Constitution, 36
Provisional Government, 6, 36, 39, 40, 53n147, 53n149, 58, 59, 63, 100n218, 130
Puleston, Colonel, 91, 108n317
Pumpelly, Raphael, 61

Queen of England, 105n291

Radicals, 45, 77, 103n261
Railroad Record, 18, 90
Railroads, 5, 15, 17, 57
Randal, Horace, (Lieutenant), 42
Read, Rev. Hiram W., 106n299, 109n322, 167, 177
Reagan, John H., 63
Rencher, Abraham, (Governor), 57
Republic of Texas, (also see Texas), 15
Republican, 40, 45, 59, 69, 71, 73, 76, 77, 80, 88, 102n232, 104n261, 106n293, 108n320
Resolutions, 6, 17, 33, 35, 36, 59
Reynolds, R. B., (Major), 61
Rhode Island, 6
Richmond, Virginia, 63, 66
Rio Bravo del Norte (Rio Grande), 116
Rio Colorado (also see Colorado River), 116
Rio Grande, 9, 10, 23, 33–35, 51n99, 57, 59, 61, 62, 66, 67, 98n200, 107n307, 111, 116, 117
Rio Grande Valley, 34, 47n30, 58, 111
Rio Pecos, 116
Robinson, Palatine, 36, 104n279
Ronstadt, Frederick A., 12
Rowlett, W. M., 12
Ruelas, Rafael, 47n30
Rusk, Thomas Jefferson, (Senator), 10, 12, (*port.*) 13, 15, 16, 23, 48n59, 48n60(1), 51n99, 57, 155

Saenz, Remigio, 47n30
Salt Lake City, Utah, 6
San Antonio, Texas, 31, 62, 66
San Augustine Pass, 62
San Francisco, 9, 17, 31, 47n18
San Francisco *Herald,* 40
San Francisco Mountains, 109n322
Santa Cruz Valley, 18
Santa Fé, New Mexico, 6, 31, 58, 61, 66, 73, 78, 97n181, 98n200, 102n236, 109n322, 116, 177
Santa Fé Gazette, 177
Santa Rita Mines, 32
Santa Rita Mining Company, 34
Santa Rita Mountains, 18
Santa Rita Silver Mining Company, 19, 32, 61
Saulsbury, Willard, (Senator), 78
Savages, (also see Indians), 33, 77
Schuchard, Charles, 12
Secession, 40, 45, 54n178, 57–60
Secessionist, 10, 58
Secretary of the Interior, 16, 48n59
Secretary of the Navy, 106n299
Sectionalism, 3–5, 45
Secretary of War, 17
Senate, (U.S.), 10, 15, 45, 76, 78, 80, 88, 91, 103n255, 103n256, 103n261, 106n299, 116, 156, 167, 183
Shah of Persia, 105n291
Sharlot Hall Museum, 104n273
Shields, Marks, 100n221
Shipwreck, 9
Sibley, Henry Hopkins, (General), 61, 66, 67, 69
Sierra Madre Mountains, 51n99
Silver, 17
Silver mines, 9, 18, 73, 75, 76, 90, 95, 166
Silver ore, 73
Sinaloa, Mexico, 9
Slavery, 3, 4, 20, 42, 44, 45, 57, 58, 63, 71, 77, 78, 83, 103n261, 156
Sledd, Joshua S., 60
Society of Arizona Pioneers, 106n293
Sonoita Creek, 61
Sonoita Valley, 36
Sonora, Mexico, 3, 11, 35, 47n19, 50n84, 73
Sonora Exploring and Mining Company, 9, 12, 17, 18, 20, 23, 32,

34, 47n22, 50n78, 70, 75, 82, 90, 104n279, 108n317
Sonora Silver Mining Company, 18
Sopori Grant, 40
Sopori Land and Mining Company, 40
Sopori Ranch, 32, 42
South, 4, 40, 44, 45, 57, 58, 97n182, 100n219
Southern California, 53n146
Southern Commercial Convention, 16, 40
Southwest, 6, 10, 31, 32, 45, 52n122, 57, 58, 66, 95, 100n219
Star and Sentinel, 102n241
Star of the West, 102n241
State, Department of, 77, 78
Steele, William, (Colonel), 69
Stephens, Alexander H., (Senator), 49n60(6), 49n60(8), 156, 183, (*port.*) 185
Steptoe, Edward J., (Lieutenant Colonel), 6
Stevens, Thaddeus, (Senator), 103n261
Stewart, Margaret, 107n307
St. John, Silas, 31, 52n110
St. Louis, Missouri, 111
St. Louis *Missouri Republican,* 34
Strickland, Dr. Rex W., 51n102
Sumner, Charles, (Senator), 103n261
Superintendent of Indian Affairs, 6, 77, 89, 166, 177
Surveyor, 9, 16, 40, 48n45
Surveyor General, 12, 15, 50n87, 87
Surveys, 11, 32, 48n1, 51n87
Sultan of Turkey, 105n291
Swilling, Jack, 100n221

Talcott, Andrew, 104n279
Taylor, Doctor, 104n283
Tennessee, 15, 61, 111
Tennessee Legislature, 46n6
Territory of Jefferson, 40, 54n160
Territory of Montezuma, 101n226
Texas, 4, 9, 10, 12, 15, 16, 23, 31, 42, 44, 51n99, 51n101, 57, 58, 61, 62, 76, 99n204, 116, 130
Texas Revolution, 15
Texas Western Railroad, 11
Thayer, Eli, (Congressman), 49n60(13)
Third Empire (France), 105n291
Thompson, Jacob, 16, 48n59
Tiffany and Company, 105n290
Titus, Henry T., 42
Todd, J. B. S., 45
Todd, Robert S., 105n289
Toledo, Ann Arbor and Northern Railroad, 101n225
Toledo, Ohio, 101n225
Townsend, E. D., (General), 52n106
Treason, 54n169
Treasury, 31
Treaty of Guadalupe Hidalgo, 3, 12
Trumbull, Lyman, (Senator), 44, 77, 78, 80, 91, 103n256, 183, (*port.*) 184
Tubac, 12, 31, 34, 35, 61, 102n238, 117, 130
Tubac *Weekly Arizonian,* 34
Tucson, 9–12, 17, 23, 33–36, 38, 40, 45, 48n60(1), 52n110, 53n142, 59, 61, 63, 66, 69, 71, 77, 78, 98n194, 102n238, 103n255, 106n293, 106n299, 111, 116, 117, 130, 156, 167
Tucson *Arizonian,* 35
Tucson *Citizen,* 87
Turner, T. M., 35
Turner, William F., 88, 106n299
Tyler, John, (President), 102n228

Union, (also see North), 4, 6, 42, 45, 58–60, 66, 76, 95, 100n219, 100n222, 117
United States, 3, 95
U. S. Land Office, 8
U. S. Marshal, 20, 87, 98n190
U. S. Military Academy, 6
U. S. Senate, (also see Senate), 12, 20, 23, 112
Upson, Columbus, 63
Utah, 4, 6, 51n99, 76, 107n307

Van Dorn, Earl, (General), 62
Valverde, 66, 117
Vermont, 12, 108n321

Viceroy of India, 105n291
Virginia, 61, 78

Wade, Benjamin F., (Senator), 15, 49n60(18), 77, 78, (*port.*) 79, 80, 83, 87, 89, 91, 95, 103n261, 108n320
Wade-Davis Manifesto, 103n261
Wagon Road, El Paso-Ft. Yuma, 31
Wagon roads, 15, 16, 31, 48n55, 57
Wakefield, Eugene, 50n86
Walker, John, 33, 104n279
War Department, 17
Warner, Solomon, 11
Washington County, 155
Washington, District of Columbia, 6, 11, 16, 17, 20, 32, 35, 40, 42, 45, 82, 83, 87, 89–91, 104n283, 107n307, 155
Watts, John S., (Delegate), 25, 49n60(16), 69, 72, 73, 75, 83, 89, 101n226, 102n236, 102n239
Way, Phocian R., 52n116
Webster, Daniel, (Senator), 87
Weekly Arizonian, 130
Weller, John B., (Governor), 46n9
Welles, Gideon, 106n299
West Gila, 155
West, Joseph R., (General), 23, 51n96, 66
West, 78, 87
West Point (U. S. Military Academy), 6, 90, 107n307, 108n310
Wheeler, William A., (Senator), 71–73, 76, 102n232, 183, (*port.*) 184
Whigs, 76, 77, 80, 102n228
Whipple's route, 109n322
White House, 91, 103n261
Wickliffe, Charles A., (Senator), 71, 73, 83, 102n228
Wilkinson, Morton S., (Senator), 91
Willard's Hotel, 97n184
William of Prussia, 105n291
Wilmot Proviso, 83
Wisconsin, 44, 80, 87
Wordsworth, William C., 36
Wright, George, (General), 69
Wright, James M., 46n6
Wrightson, Thomas, 18, 90
Wrightson, William, 18, 19, 32, 34, 89–91, 95, 96, 107n305, 108n320
Wyllys, Dr. Rufus Kay, 105n292

Yuma, 9, 47n20
Yuma Indians, 107n307

Zoraida, 9, 47n18